The Ultimate Guide to Starting a Sole Proprietorship

Sole Proprietorship

Small Business Start-Up Kit

The Ultimate Guide to Starting a Sole Proprietorship

Sole Proprietorship

Small Business Start-Up Kit

DANIEL SITARZ, ATTORNEY-AT-LAW

Nova Publishing Company
Small Business and Consumer Legal Books
Carbondale Illinois

Editorial and research assistance by Janet Harris Sitarz, Melanie Bray and Caitlin King. Cover and interior design by Melanie Bray. Manufactured in the United States.

ISBN 978-1-892949-59-2   Book w/CD   ($29.95)
Library of Congress Catalog Card Number 99-28052

Library of Congress Cataloging-in-Publication Data
      Sitarz, Dan, 1948-
      Sole Proprietorship : small business start-up kit / Daniel Sitarz
      P. cm-(Small business made simple)
      ISBN 978-1-892949-59-2
      1. Sole Proprietorship—United States. 2. Small business-Law and Legislation-United States.
      I. Title. II. Title: Small Business Start-up kit. III. Series
      KF1355.Z9 S58 2011   346.73'0652-dc21   CIP 99-28052

Nova Publishing Company is dedicated to providing up-to-date and accurate legal information to the public. All Nova publications are periodically revised to contain the latest available legal information.

3rd Edition; 1st Printing: January, 2011
2nd Edition; 2nd Printing: April, 2007
2nd Edition; 1st Printing: December, 2005
1st Edition; 1st Printing: January, 2000

This publication is designed to provide accurate and authoritative information in regard to the subject matter covered. It is sold with the understanding that the publisher and author are not engaged in rendering legal, accounting, or other professional services. If legal advice or other expert assistance is required, the services of a competent professional person should be sought.

—From a Declaration of Principles jointly adopted by a Committee of the American Bar Association and a Committee of Publishers

DISCLAIMER

Because of possible unanticipated changes in governing statutes and case law relating to the application of any information contained in this book, the author, publisher, and any and all persons or entities involved in any way in the preparation, publication, sale, or distribution of this book disclaim all responsibility for the legal effects or consequences of any document prepared or action taken in reliance upon information contained in this book. No representations, either express or implied, are made or given regarding the legal consequences of the use of any information contained in this book. Purchasers and persons intending to use this book for the preparation of any legal documents are advised to check specifically on the current applicable laws in any jurisdiction in which they intend the documents to be effective.

Nova Publishing Green Business Policies

Nova Publishing Company takes seriously the impact of book publishing on the Earth and its resources. Nova Publishing Company is committed to protecting the environment and to the responsible use of natural resources. As a book publisher, with paper as a core part of our business, we are very concerned about the future of the world's remaining endangered forests and the environmental impacts of paper production. We are committed to implementing policies that will support the preservation of endangered forests globally and to advancing 'best practices' within the book and paper industries. Nova Publishing Company is committed to preserving ancient forests and natural resources. Our company's policy is to print all of our books on 100% recycled paper, with 100% post-consumer waste content, de-inked in a chlorine-free process. In addition, all Nova Publishing Company books are printed using soy-based inks. As a result of these environmental policies, Nova Publishing Company has saved hundreds of thousands of gallons of water, hundreds of thousands of kilowatts of electricity, thousand of pounds of pollution and carbon dioxide, and thousands of trees that would otherwise have been used in the traditional manner of publishing its books. Nova Publishing Company is very proud to be one of the first members of the Green Press Initiative, a nonprofit program dedicated to supporting publishers in their efforts to reduce their use of fiber obtained from endangered forests. (see www.greenpressinitiative.org). Nova Publishing Company is also proud to be an initial signatory on the Book Industry Treatise on Responsible Paper Use. In addition, Nova Publishing Company uses all compact fluorescent lighting; recycles all office paper products, aluminum and plastic beverage containers, and printer cartridges; uses 100% post-consumer fiber, process-chlorine-free, acid-free paper for 95% of in-house paper use; and, when possible, uses electronic equipment that is EPA Energy Star-certified. Nova's freight shipments are coordinated to minimize energy use whenever possible. Finally, all carbon emissions from Nova Publishing Company office energy use are offset by the purchase of wind-energy credits that are used to subsidize the building of wind turbines on the Rosebud Sioux Reservation in South Dakota (see www.nativeenergy.com). We strongly encourage other publishers and all partners in publishing supply chains to adopt similar policies.

Nova Publishing Company
Small Business and Consumer Legal Books and Software
1103 West College St.
Carbondale, IL 62901
Editorial: (800) 748-1175
www.novapublishing.com

Distributed by:
National Book Network
4501 Forbes Blvd., Suite 200
Lanham, MD 20706
Orders: (800) 462-6420

Table of Contents

LIST of FORMS 7
INTRODUCTION to Sole Proprietorship: Small Business Start-Up Kit 10
    Installation Instructions for Installing Forms-on-CD 11
    Instructions for Using Forms-on-CD 12
    Technical Support 16
CHAPTER 1: Deciding to Start Your Business as a Sole Proprietorship 17
    Partnership 18
    Corporation 21
    S-Corporation 25
    Limited Liability Company 26
    Sole Proprietorship 28
CHAPTER 2: Business Start-Up Checklist 31
    Sole Proprietorship Start-Up Checklist 32
CHAPTER 3: Developing a Business Plan 33
    Business Plan Worksheet 35
    Preparing Your Business Plan 43
    Preparing Your Executive Summary 44
    Executive Summary 45
    Compiling Your Business Plan 48
CHAPTER 4: Developing a Business Marketing Plan 50
    Business Marketing Worksheet 51
CHAPTER 5: Developing a Business Financial Plan 56
    Business Financial Worksheet 57
    Preparing a Profit and Loss Statement 60
        Estimated Profit and Loss Statement 62
    Preparing a Balance Sheet 64
        Current Balance Sheet 66
CHAPTER 6: Operating a Sole Proprietorship 67
    Formation of a Sole Proprietorship 68
    Sole Proprietorship Property 68
    Sole Proprietorship Liability 69
    Sole Proprietorship Books and Records 70
CHAPTER 7: Sole Proprietorship Paperwork 71
    Sole Proprietorship Paperwork Checklist 74
CHAPTER 8: Pre-Start-up Activities 75
    Pre-Start-up Worksheet 78
    Pre-Start-up Checklist 80
CHAPTER 9: Sole Proprietorship Plan 81
    Sole Proprietorship Plan Checklist 82
    Sole Proprietorship Plan 83

CHAPTER 10: Registration of Sole Proprietorship Name 85
Statement of Intention to Conduct Business Under an Assumed or Fictitious Name 87

CHAPTER 11: Employee Documents 88
General Employment Contract 91
Independent Contractor Agreement 93
Contractor/Subcontractor Agreement 95

CHAPTER 12: Business Financial Recordkeeping 97
Recordkeeping Terminology 98
The Balance Sheet 98
The Profit and Loss Statement 101
Accounting Methods 102
Accounting Systems 103
Accounting Periods 103
Recordkeeping Review 104
Accounting Software 104
Simplified Accounting System 105
Financial Recordkeeping Checklist............... 106

CHAPTER 13: Business Accounts 107
Income Accounts 109
Income Chart of Accounts 110
Expense Accounts 111
Expense Chart of Accounts 112
Asset and Liability Accounts 113
Balance Sheet Chart of Accounts 114
Sample Chart of Accounts 115
Current Assets 117
Inventory 120
    Physical Inventory Report 122
    Periodic Inventory Record 124
    Perpetual Inventory Record 126
    Cost of Goods Sold Report 128
Fixed Assets 130
    Deductible Expenses/Depreciable Property 133
    Fixed Asset Account Record 134
Tracking Business Debts 136
    Accounts Payable Record 137
    Long-Term Debt Record 139
Tracking Business Expenses 141
    Travel, Auto, Meals, and Entertainment Expenses 141
    Tracking Expenses 142
    Weekly Expense Record 143
    Monthly Expense Summary 146
    Annual Expense Summary 148
Tracking Business Income 150
    Tracking Your Cash 151
    Weekly Cash Report 151
    Monthly Cash Report Summary 154

Tracking Income 156
    Weekly Income Records 156
    Monthly Income Summary 158
    Annual Income Summary 160
Tracking Credit Sales 162
    Weekly or Monthly Credit Sales Records...162
    Credit Sales Aging Report 165
    Invoices and Statements 167
    Invoice 167
    Statement and Past Due Statement 169
    Credit Memo 172

CHAPTER 14: Business Payroll 174

Setting up Your Payroll 175
Payroll Checklist 177
Quarterly Payroll Timesheet 178
Employee Payroll Record 180
Payroll Depository Record 182
Annual Payroll Summary 184

CHAPTER 15: Taxation of Sole Proprietorships 186

Sole Proprietorship Tax Forms Checklist 187
Sole Proprietorship Monthly Tax Schedules 188
Sole Proprietorship Quarterly Tax Schedules 188
Sole Proprietorship Annual Tax Schedules 188
Sample IRS Tax Forms 190

CHAPTER 16: Additional Legal Forms 213

Instructions for Releases 213
Instructions for Receipts 218
Instructions for Rental/Sale of Personal Property 222
Instructions for Promissory Notes...230
Instructions for Sale of Business/Sale of Business Assets 236
Instructions for Contract/Modification of Contract....................................244

APPENDIX of State Business Information 248

GLOSSARY 278

INDEX 286

List of Forms (in book and on CD)

All Forms on CD are in both PDF and text format unless noted.

Forms are in Folders on CD as noted in bold text below

Business Start-up Checklist
    Sole Proprietorship Business Start-up Checklist (text and PDF form)
Developing a Business Plan
    Business Plan Worksheet (text and PDF form-not fillable)
    Executive Summary (text and PDF form)

Developing a Business Marketing Plan
   Business Marketing Worksheet (text and PDF form-not fillable)
Developing a Business Financial Plan
   Business Financial Worksheet (text and PDF form-not fillable)
   Estimated Profit and Loss Statement (PDF form-2 forms: fillable and not fillable)
   Current Balance Sheet (PDF form-2 forms: fillable and not fillable)
Sole Proprietorship Paperwork
   Sole Proprietorship Paperwork Checklist (text and PDF form)
Pre-Start-up Activities
   Pre-Start-up Worksheet (text and PDF form)
   Pre-Start-up Checklist (text and PDF form)
Sole Proprietorship Plan
   Sole Proprietorship Plan Checklist (text and PDF form)
   Sole Proprietorship Plan (text and PDF form)
Registration of Sole Proprietorship Name
   Statement of Intention to Conduct Business Under an Assumed or Fictitious Name
Employee Documents
   General Employment Contract (text and PDF form)
   Independent Contractor Agreement (text and PDF form)
   Contractor/Subcontractor Agreement (text and PDF form)
Business Financial Recordkeeping
   Financial Recordkeeping Checklist (text and PDF form)
Business Accounts
   Income Chart of Accounts (PDF form)
   Expense Chart of Accounts (PDF form)
   Balance Sheet Chart of Accounts (PDF form)
   Chart of Accounts (PDF form)
   Current Asset Account (PDF form)
   Physical Inventory Report (PDF form-2 forms: fillable and not fillable)
   Periodic Inventory Record (PDF form)
   Perpetual Inventory Record (PDF form)
   Cost of Goods Sold Report (PDF form-2 forms: fillable and not fillable)
   Fixed Asset Account (PDF form)
   Accounts Payable Record (PDF form)
   Long-Term Debt Record (PDF form)
   Weekly Expense Record (PDF form)
   Monthly Expense Summary (PDF form)
   Annual Expense Summary (PDF form)
   Weekly Cash Report (PDF form)
   Monthly Cash Report Summary (PDF form)
   Weekly Income Record (PDF form)
   Monthly Income Summary (PDF form)
   Annual Income Summary (PDF form)
   Weekly Credit Sales Record (PDF form)
   Monthly Credit Sales Record (PDF form)
   Credit Sales Aging Report (PDF form)
   Invoice (PDF form-2 forms: fillable and not fillable)
   Statement (PDF form)
   Past Due Statement (PDF form)
   Credit Memo (PDF form)

Business Payroll
Payroll Checklist (text and PDF form)
Quarterly Payroll Time Sheet (PDF form)
Employee Payroll Record (PDF form)
Payroll Depository Record (PDF form)
Annual Payroll Summary (PDF form)

Taxation of Sole Proprietorships
Sole Proprietorship Tax Forms Checklist
Sole Proprietorship Tax Schedules

IRS Forms folder
IRS Form SS-4: Application for Employer Identification Number
IRS 1040: U.S. Individual Income Tax Return
IRS Schedule C (Form 1040): Profit or Loss from Business (Sole Proprietorship)
IRS Schedule C-EZ (Form 1040): Net Profit from Business (Sole Proprietorship)
IRS 1040-ES: Estimated Tax for Individuals
IRS 1040-SS: U.S. Self Employment Tax Return
IRS Form 8109: Federal Tax Deposit Coupon
IRS Form 8829: Expenses for Business Use of Your Home
IRS Form 940: Employer's Annual Federal Unemployment (FUTA) Tax Return
IRS Form 941: Employer's Quarterly Federal Tax Return
IRS Form W-2: Wage and Tax Statement
IRS Form W-3: Transmittal of Wage and Tax Statements
IRS Form W-4: Employee's Withholding Allowance Certificate

Additional Legal Forms
General Release
Mutual Release
Specific Release
Receipt in Full
Receipt on Account
Receipt for Goods
Personal Property Rental Agreement
Bill of Sale, with Warranties
Bill of Sale, without Warranties
Bill of Sale, Subject to Debt
Promissory Note (Installment Repayment)
Promissory Note (Lump Sum Repayment)
Promissory Note (On Demand)
Release of Promissory Note
Demand and Notice of Default on Installment Promissory Note
Agreement for Sale of Business
Agreement for Sale of Business Assets
General Contract
Modification of Contract

FORMS-ON-CD (Not included in book) (All forms are PDF forms)

State-specific Sole Proprietorship Forms (see Appendix for listing)

Introduction to Sole Proprietorship: Small Business Start-Up Kit

This book is designed to assist its readers in understanding the general aspects of the law as it relates to starting your business as a Sole Proprietorship. Regardless of whether or not a lawyer is ultimately retained in certain situations, the legal information in this handbook will enable the reader to understand the framework of law in this country as it relates to Sole Proprietorship start-up. To try and make that task as easy as possible, technical legal jargon has been eliminated whenever possible and plain English used instead. When it is necessary to use a legal term which may be unfamiliar to most people, it will be shown in *italics* and defined when first used. There is a glossary of most legal terms used in the process of starting your business on the accompanying CD. Lawyers often caution people that such antiquated language is most important and that, of course, only they, the lawyers, can properly prepare and interpret legal documents using such language. Naturally, plain and easily-understood English is not only perfectly proper for use in all legal documents, but in most cases, leads to far less confusion on the part of later readers.

Chapter 1 of this book contains information regarding the advantages and disadvantages of the various types of business entities that are available to new businesses. In Chapter 2, an easy-to-use checklist is provided that will help to set up your Sole Proprietorship. The mechanics of developing and preparing a business plan and its executive summary are provided in

Chapter 3. Chapter 4 outlines the development of your business marketing objectives. The details of preparing a financial plan, estimated balance sheet, and estimated profit and loss statement are outlined in Chapter 5. The basic mechanics of operating your business as a Sole Proprietorship are explained in Chapter 6. The importance of business recordkeeping is explained in Chapter 7. Chapters 8-10 provide all of the information, instructions, and paperwork necessary for you to set up your business as a Sole Proprietorship. Chapter 11 provides various forms for use if you will have any employees in your new business. The basics of financial recordkeeping and accounting are explained in Chapter 12 & 13. Chapter 14 provides details for setting up an employee payroll. The various ways of taxation possible for your Sole Proprietorship is detailed in Chapter 15. The Appendix in the back of this book provides a comprehensive listing of the individual state business information concerning Sole Proprietorships for each of the 50 states and the District of Columbia. A glossary of business, legal and accounting terms is also provided.

☼ Toolkit Tip!

Check your state's listing in the Appendix in the back of this book to see if there are any specific state requirements for you to operate your business as a Sole Proprietorship.

Installation Instructions for Installing Forms-on-CD

Installation Instructions for PCs

1. Insert the enclosed CD in your computer.
2. The installation program will start automatically. Follow the onscreen dialogue and make your appropriate choices.
3. If the CD installation does not start automatically, click on START, then RUN, then BROWSE, and select your CD drive, and then select the file "Install.exe." Finally, click OK to run the installation program.
4. During the installation program, you will be prompted as to whether or not you wish to install the Adobe Acrobat Reader® program. This software program is necessary to view and fill in the PDF (potable document format) forms that are included on the Forms-on-CD. If you do not already have the Adobe Acrobat Reader® program installed on your hard drive, you will need to select the full installation that will install the program on your computer.

Installation Instructions for MACs®

1. Insert the enclosed CD in your computer.
2. Copy the folder "Forms for Macs" to your hard drive. All of the PDF and text-only forms are included in this folder.
3. If you do not already have the Adobe Acrobat Reader® program installed on your hard drive, you will need to download the version of this software that is appropriate for your particular MAC operating system from www.adobe.com. Note: The latest versions of the MAC operating system (OS-X) has PDF capabilities built into it.

☀️ Toolkit Tip!

MAC users may need to down-load Adobe Acrobat Reader directly from www.adobe.com.

Instructions for Using Forms-on-CD

All of the forms that are included in this book have been provided on the Forms-on-CD for your use if you have access to a computer. If you have completed the Forms-on-CD installation program, all of the forms will have been copied to your computer's hard drive. By default, these files are installed in the C:\Sole Proprietorship\Forms folder which is created by the installation program. (Note for MAC users: see instructions above). Opening the Forms folder will provide you with access to folders for each of the topics corresponding to chapters in the book. Within each chapter, the forms are provided in two separate formats:

Text forms may be opened, prepared, and printed from within your own word processing program (such as Microsoft Word®, or WordPerfect®). The text forms all have the file extension: .txt. These forms are located in the TEXT FORMS folders supplied for each chapter's forms. You will use the forms in this format if you will be making changes to any of the text on the forms.

PDF forms may be filled in on your computer screen and printed out on any printer. This particular format provides the most widely-used format for accessing computer files. Files in this format may be opened as images on your computer and printed out on any printer. The files in PDF format all have the file extension: .pdf. Although this format provides the easiest method for completing the forms, the forms in this format can not be altered (other than to fill in the information required on the blanks provided). To access the PDF forms, please see below. If you wish to alter the language in any of the forms, you will need to access the forms in their text-only versions. To access these text-only forms, please also see page 17.

To Access PDF Forms

🔆Toolkit Tip!

Use the 'PDF' forms that are provided on the CD if you wish to simply fill in and print out the form that you select.

1. You must have already installed the Adobe Acrobat Reader® program to your computer's hard drive. This program is installed automatically by the installation program. (MAC users will need to install this program via www.adobe.com).

2. On your computer's desktop, you will find a shortcut icon labeled "Acrobat Reader®" Using your mouse, left double-click on this icon. This will open the Acrobat Reader® program. When the Acrobat Reader® program is opened for the first time, you will need to accept the Licensing Agreement from Adobe in order to use this program. Click "Accept" when given the option to accept or decline the Agreement.

3. Once the Acrobat Reader® program is open on your computer, click on FILE (in the upper left-hand corner of the upper taskbar). Then click on OPEN in the drop down menu. Depending on which version of Windows or other operating system you are using, a box will open which will allow you to access files on your computer's hard drive. The files for estate planning forms are located on your computer's "C" drive, under the folder "Sole Proprietorship." In this folder, you will find a subfolder "Forms." (Note: if you installed the forms folder on a different drive, access the forms on that particular drive).

4. If you desire to work with one of the forms, you should then left double-click your mouse on the sub-folder: "Forms." A list of form topics (corresponding to the chapters in the book) will appear and you should then left double-click

your mouse on the topic of your choice. This will open two folders: one for text forms and one for PDF forms. Left double click your mouse on the PDF forms folder and a list of the PDF forms for that topic should appear. Left double-click your mouse on the form of your choice. This will open the appropriate form within the Acrobat Reader® program.

To Fill in and Use PDF Forms

1. Once you have opened the appropriate form in the Acrobat Reader® program, filling in the form is a simple process. A 'hand tool' icon will be your cursor in the Acrobat Reader® program. Move the 'hand tool' cursor to the first blank space that will need to be completed on the form. A vertical line or "I-beam" should appear at the beginning of the first space on a form that you will need to fill in. You may then begin to type the necessary information in the space provided. When you have filled in the first blank space, hit the TAB key on your keyboard. This will move the 'hand' cursor to the next space which must be filled in. Please note that some of the spaces in the forms must be completed by hand, specifically the signature blanks.

2. Move through the form, completing each required space, and hitting TAB to move to the next space to be filled in. For details on the information required for each blank on the forms, please read the instructions in this book. When you have completed all of the fill-ins, you may print out the form on your computer's printer. (Please note: hitting TAB after the last fill-in will return you to the first page of the form.)

3. When the form is complete, you may print out the completed form and you may save the completed form. If you wish to save the completed form, you should rename the form so that your hard drive will retain an unaltered original version of the form.

To Access and Complete Text Forms

For your convenience, all of the forms in this book (except certain state-specific forms and IRS forms) are also provided as text-only forms which may be altered and saved. To open and use any of the text forms:

1. First, open your preferred word processing program. Then click on FILE (in the upper left-hand corner of the upper taskbar). Then click on OPEN in the drop down menu. Depending on which version of Windows or other operating system you are using, a box will open which will allow you to access files on your computer's hard drive. The files for Sole Proprietorship forms are located on your computer's "C" drive, under the folder "Sole Proprietorship." In this folder, you will find a sub-folder: "Forms."

2. If you desire to work with one of the forms, you should then left double-click your mouse on the sub-folder: "Forms." A list of form topics (corresponding to the chapters in the book) will appear and you should then left double-click your mouse on the topic of your choice. This will open two folders: one for text forms and one for PDF forms. Left double-click your mouse on the text forms folder and a list of the text forms for that topic should appear. Left double-click your mouse on the form of your choice. This will open the appropriate form within your word processing program.

3. You may now fill in the necessary information while the text-only file is open in your word processing program. You may need to adjust margins and/or line endings of the form to fit your particular word processing program. Note that there is an asterisk (*) in every location in these forms where information will need to be included. Replace each asterisk with the necessary information. When the form is complete, you may print out the completed form and you may save the completed form. If you wish to save the completed form, you should rename the form so that your hard drive will retain an unaltered version of the original form.

> **☼ Toolkit Tip!**
>
> Text forms are the forms you should use if you will be making changes to any of the text on the forms.

Technical Support

Please also note that Nova Publishing Company cannot provide legal advice regarding the effect or use of the forms in this book or on the CD. For questions about installing the Forms-on-CD and software, you may call Nova Technical Support at 1-800-748-1175 or access the Nova Publishing Website for support at www.novapublishing.com.

For any questions relating to Adobe Acrobat Reader®, please access Adobe Technical Support at www.adobe.com/support/main.html or you may search for assistance in the HELP area of Adobe Acrobat Reader® (located in approximately the center of the top line of the program's desktop).

Note regarding legal updates: Although business law is relatively stable and the information provided in this book is based on the most current state statutes, laws regarding business start-up are subject to constant change. In the Appendix of this book, we provide internet addresses for each state's legislature and statutes. These sites may be accessed to check if any of the laws have changed since the publication of this book. In addition, the Nova Publishing website also provides legal updates for information that has changed since the publication of any Nova titles.

♀ Toolkit Tip!

Check online at *www.nova publishing. com* for any updates to the legal information in this book.

Chapter 1

Deciding to Start Your Business as a Sole Proprietorship

One of the first decisions that potential business owners must confront is how their business should be structured and operated. This crucial decision must be made even before the business has actually begun operations. The legal documents that will generally accompany the formation of a business can follow many different patterns, depending on the particular situation and the type of business to be undertaken.

Initially, the type of business entity to be used must be selected. There are many basic forms of business operating entities. The five most common forms are:

- Partnership
- Corporation
- S-corporation
- Limited liability company
- Sole proprietorship

The choice of entity for a particular business depends on many factors. Which of these forms of business organization is chosen can have a great impact on the success of the business. The structure chosen will have an effect on how easy it is to obtain financing, how taxes are paid, how accounting records are kept,

☼Toolkit Tip!

The type of business organization that you choose can have a great impact on the success of your business. Take time to read all of the advantages and disadvantages of each entity.

whether personal assets are at risk in the venture, the amount of control the "owner" has over the business, and many other aspects of the business. Keep in mind that the initial choice of business organization need not be the final choice. It is often wise to begin with the simplest form, the sole proprietorship, until the business progresses to a point where another form is clearly indicated. This allows the business to begin in the least complicated manner and allows the owner to retain total control in the important formative period of the business. As the business grows and the potential for liability and tax burdens increase, circumstances may dictate a re-examination of the business structure. The advantages and disadvantages of the five choices of business operation are detailed below.

Partnership

A partnership is a relationship existing between two or more persons who join together to carry on a trade or business. Each partner contributes money, property, labor, and/or skill to the partnership and, in return, expects to share in the profits or losses of the business. A partnership is usually based on a partnership agreement of some type, although the agreement need not be a formal document. It may even simply be an oral understanding between the partners, although this is not recommended.

A simple joint undertaking to share expenses is not considered a partnership, nor is a mere co-ownership of property that is maintained and leased or rented. To be considered a partnership for legal and tax purposes, the following factors are usually considered:

- The partners' conduct in carrying out provisions of the partnership agreement
- The relationship of the parties
- The abilities and contributions of each party to the partnership
- The control each partner has over the partnership income and the purposes for which the income is used

> **⊘ Definition:**
>
> **Partnership:**
> A partnership is a relationship existing between two or more persons who join together to carry on a trade or business.

Disadvantages

The disadvantages of the partnership form of business begin with the potential for conflict between partners. Of all forms of business organization, the partnership has spawned more disagreements than any other. This is generally traceable to the lack of a decisive initial partnership agreement that clearly outlines the rights and duties of the partners. This disadvantage can be partially overcome with a comprehensive partnership agreement. However, there is still the seemingly inherent difficulty many people have in working within the framework of a partnership, regardless of the initial agreement between the partners.

A further disadvantage to the partnership structure is that each partner is subject to unlimited personal liability for the debts of the partnership. The potential liability in a partnership is even greater than that encountered in a sole proprietorship. This is due to the fact that in a partnership the personal risk for which one may be liable is partially out of one's direct control and may be accrued due to actions on the part of another person. Each partner is liable for all of the debts of the partnership, regardless of which partner may have been responsible for their accumulation.
Related to the business risks of personal financial liability is the potential personal legal liability for the negligence of another partner. In addition, each partner may even be liable for the negligence of an employee of the partnership if such negligence takes place during the usual course of business of the partnership. Again, the attendant risks are broadened by the potential for liability based on the acts of other persons. Of course, general liability insurance can counteract this drawback to some extent to protect the personal and partnership assets of each partner.

Again, as with the sole proprietorship, the partnership lacks the advantage of continuity. A partnership is usually automatically terminated upon the death of any partner. A final accounting and a division of assets and liabilities is generally necessary in such an instance unless specific methods under which the partnership may be continued have been outlined in the partnership agreement.

Finally, certain benefits of corporate organization are not avail-

⚡ Warning!

Each partner is liable for all of the debts of the partnership, regardless of which partner may have been responsible for their accumulation.

💡 Toolkit Tip!

A partnership is usually based on a partnership agreement of some type, although the agreement need not be a formal document. It may even simply be an oral understanding between the partners, although this is not recommended.

able to a partnership. Since a partnership cannot obtain financing through public stock offerings, large infusions of capital are more difficult for a partnership to raise than for a corporation. In addition, many of the fringe benefit programs that are available to corporations (such as certain pension and profit-sharing arrangements) are not available to partnerships.

Advantages

A partnership, by virtue of combining the credit potential of the various partners, has an inherently greater opportunity for business credit than is generally available to a sole proprietorship. In addition, the assets which are placed in the name of the partnership may often be used directly as collateral for business loans. The pooling of the personal capital of the partners generally provides the partnership with an advantage over the sole proprietorship in the area of cash availability. However, as noted above, the partnership does not have as great a potential for financing as does a corporation.

As with the sole proprietorship, there may be certain tax advantages to operation of a business as a partnership, as opposed to a corporation. The profits generated by a partnership may be distributed directly to the partners without incurring any "double" tax liability, as is the case with the distribution of corporate profits in the form of dividends to the shareholders. Income from a partnership is taxed at personal income tax rates. Note, however, that depending on the individual tax situation of each partner, this aspect could prove to be a disadvantage.

For a business in which two or more people desire to share in the work and in the profits, a partnership is often the structure chosen. It is, potentially, a much simpler form of business organization than the corporate form. Less start-up costs are necessary and there is limited regulation of partnerships. However, the simplicity of this form of business can be deceiving. A sole proprietor knows that his or her actions will determine how the business will prosper, and that he or she is, ultimately, personally responsible for the success or failure of the enterprise. In a partnership, however, the duties, obligations, and commitments of each partner are often ill-defined. This lack of definition of the status of each partner can lead to serious difficulties and disagreements. In order to clarify the rights and responsibilities of each partner and to be certain of the tax status of the partnership, it is good business procedure to have a written partnership agreement. All states have adopted a version of the Uniform Partnership Act, which provides an outline of partnership law. Although state law will supply the general boundaries of partnerships and even specific partnership agreement terms if they are not addressed by a written partnership agreement, it is better for a clear understanding of the business structure if the partner's agreements are put in writing.

Corporation

A corporation is a creation of law. It is governed by the laws of the state where it was incorporated and of the state or states in which it does business. In recent years, it has become the business structure of choice for many small businesses. Corporations are, generally, a more complex form of business operation than either a sole proprietorship or partnership. Corporations are also subject to far more state regulations regarding both their formation and operation. The following discussion is provided in order to allow the potential business owner an understanding of this type of business operation.

The corporation is an artificial entity. It is created by filing Articles of Incorporation with the proper state authorities. This gives the corporation its legal existence and the right to carry on business. The Articles of Incorporation act as a public record of certain formalities of corporate existence. Adoption of corporate bylaws, or internal rules of operation, is often the first business of the corporation, after it has been given the authority to conduct business by the state. The bylaws of the corporation outline the actual mechanics of the operation and management of the corporation.

There are two basic types of corporations: C-corporations and S-corporations. These prefixes refer to the particular chapter in the U.S. Tax Codes that specify the tax consequences of either

☼ Toolkit Tip!

There are two basic types of corporations: C-corporations and S-corporations. These prefixes refer to the particular chapter in the U.S. Tax Codes that specify the tax consequences of either type of corporate organization.

21

type of corporate organization. In general, both of these two types of corporations are organized and operated in similar fashion. There are specific rules that apply to the ability to be recognized by the U.S. Internal Revenue Service as an S-corporation. In addition, there are significant differences in the tax treatment of these two types of corporations. These differences will be clarified later in this chapter under the heading "S-Corporations." The basic structure and organizational rules below apply to both types of corporations, unless noted.

⚡ Warning!

Corporations are subject to a greater level of governmental regulation than any other type of business entity.

C-Corporation

In its simplest form, the corporate organizational structure consists of the following levels:

- Shareholders: who own shares of the business but do not contribute to the direct management of the corporation, other than by electing the directors of the corporation and voting on major corporate issues

- Directors: who may be shareholders, but as directors do not own any of the business. They are responsible, jointly as members of the board of directors of the corporation, for making the major business decisions of the corporation, including appointing the officers of the corporation

- Officers: who may be shareholders and/or directors, but, as officers, do not own any of the business. Officers (generally the president, vice president, secretary, and treasurer) are responsible for day-to-day operation of the corporate business

Disadvantages

Due to the nature of the organizational structure in a corporation, a certain degree of individual control is necessarily lost by incorporation. The officers, as appointees of the board of directors, are answerable to the board for management decisions. The board of directors, on the other hand, is not entirely free from restraint, since it is responsible to the shareholders for the prudent business management of the corporation.

The technical formalities of corporation formation and operation must be strictly observed in order for a business to reap the benefits of corporate existence. For this reason, there is an additional burden and expense to the corporation of detailed recordkeeping that is seldom present in other forms of business organization. Corporate decisions are, in general, more complicated due to the various levels of control and all such decisions must be carefully documented. Corporate meetings, both at the shareholder and director levels, are more formal and more frequent. In addition, the actual formation of the corporation is more expensive than the formation of either a sole proprietorship or partnership. The initial state fees that must be paid for registration of a corporation with a state can run as high as $900.00 for a minimally capitalized corporation. Corporations are also subject to a greater level of governmental regulation than any other type of business entity. These complications have the potential to overburden a small business struggling to survive.

> ### ⚡Toolkit Tip!
> As the business grows and the potential for liability and tax burdens increase, circumstances may dictate a re-examination of the business structure.

Finally, the profits of a corporation, when distributed to the shareholders in the form of dividends, are subject to being taxed twice. The first tax comes at the corporate level. The distribution of any corporate profits to the investors in the form of dividends is not a deductible business expense for the corporation. Thus, any dividends that are distributed to shareholders have already been subject to corporate income tax. The second level of tax is imposed at the personal level. The receipt of corporate dividends is considered income to the individual shareholder and is taxed as such. This potential for higher taxes due to a corporate business structure can be moderated by many factors, however.

Advantages

One of the most important advantages to the corporate form of business structure is the potential limited liability of the founders of and investors in the corporation. The liability for corporate debts is limited, in general, to the amount of money each owner has contributed to the corporation. Unless the corporation is essentially a shell for a one-person business or unless the corporation is grossly under-capitalized or under-insured, the personal assets of the owners are not at risk if the corporation fails. The shareholders stand to lose only what they invested. This factor is very important in attracting investors as the business grows.

A corporation can have a perpetual existence. Theoretically, a corporation can last forever. This may be a great advantage if there are potential future changes in ownership of the business that are imminent. Changes that would cause a partnership to be dissolved or terminated will often not affect the corporation. This continuity can be an important factor in establishing a stable business image and a permanent relationship with others in the industry.

Unlike a partnership, in which no one may become a partner without the consent of the other partners, a shareholder of corporate stock may freely sell, trade, or give away his or her stock unless this right is formally restricted by reasonable corporate decisions. The new owner of such stock is then a new owner of the business in the proportionate share of stock obtained. This freedom offers potential investors a liquidity to shift assets that is not present in the partnership form of business. The sale of shares by the corporation is also an attractive method by which to raise needed capital. The sale of shares of a corporation, however, is subject to many governmental regulations on both the state and federal levels.

Taxation is listed both as an advantage and as a disadvantage for the corporation. Depending on many factors, the use of a corporation can increase or decrease the actual income tax paid in operating a corporate business. In addition, corporations may set aside surplus earnings (up to certain levels) without any negative tax consequences. Finally, corporations are able to offer a much greater variety of fringe benefit programs to employees and officers than any other type of business entity. Various retirement, stock option, and profit-sharing plans are only open to corporate participation.

S-Corporation

The S-corporation is a certain type of corporation that is available for specific tax purposes. It is a creation of the Internal Revenue Service. S-corporation status is not relevant to state corporation laws. Its purpose is to allow small corporations to choose to be taxed, at the Federal level, like a partnership, but to also enjoy many of the benefits of a corporation. It is, in many respects, similar to a limited liability company. The main difference lies in the rules that a company needs to meet in order to qualify as an S-corporation under Federal law.

> **♀ Toolkit Tip!**
> Unlike a standard corporation, shareholders of S-corporations can personally deduct any corporate losses.

In general, to qualify as an S-corporation under current IRS rules, a corporation must meet certain requirements:

- It must not have more than 100 shareholders

- All of the shareholders must, generally, be individuals and U.S. citizens

- It must only have one class of stock

- Shareholders must consent to S-corporation status

- An election of S-corporation status must be filed with the IRS prior to the 16th day of the 3rd month of the tax year, that the election is to take effect, or any time during the year before the tax year that the election is to take effect

- It must be a domestic U.S. corporation

The S-corporation retains all of the advantages and disadvantages of the traditional corporation except in the area of taxation. For tax purposes, S-corporation shareholders are treated similarly to partners in a partnership. The income, losses, and deductions generated by an S-corporation are "passed through" the corporate entity to the individual shareholders. Thus, there is no "double" taxation of an S-corporation. In addition, unlike a standard corporation, shareholders of S-corporations can personally deduct any corporate losses.

Limited Liability Company

The limited liability company is a hybrid type of business structure. It contains elements of both a traditional partnership and a corporation. The limited liability company form of business structure is relatively new. Only in the last few years has it become available as a form of business in all 50 states and Washington D.C. Its uniqueness is that it offers the limited personal liability of a corporation and the tax benefits of a partnership. A limited liability company consists of one or more members/owners who actively manage the business of the limited liability company. There may also be nonmember managers employed to handle the business.

Disadvantages

In as much as the Limited Liability Company form is still similar to a partnership in operation, there is still a potential for conflict among the members/owners of a limited liability company. Limited liability companies are formed according to individual state law, generally by filing formal Articles of Organization of a Limited Liability Company with the proper state authorities in the state of formation. Limited liability companies are, generally, a more complex form of business operation than either the sole proprietorship or the standard partnership. They are subject to more paperwork requirements than a simple partnership but somewhat less than a corporation. Limited liability companies are also subject to far more state regulations regarding both their formation and their operation than either a sole proprietorship or a partnership. In all states, they are also required to pay fees for beginning the company, and in some states, annual franchise fees of often hundreds of dollars are assessed for the right to operate as a limited liability company.

Similar to traditional partnerships, the limited liability company has an inherent lack of continuity. In recent years, however, an increasing number of states have allowed limited liability companies to exist for a perpetual duration, as can corporations. Even if the duration of a limited liability company is perpetual, however, there may be difficulties if the sole member of a one-member limited liability company becomes disabled or dies. These problems can be overcome to some extent by providing, in the Articles of Organization of the limited liability company, for an immediate reorganization of the limited liability company with the deceased member's heirs or estate becoming members of the company. In addition, similar to partnerships, it may be difficult to sell or transfer ownership interests in a limited liability company.

Advantages

The members/owners in such a business enjoy a limited liability, similar to that of a shareholder in a corporation. In general, the member's risk is limited to the amount of their investment in the limited liability company. Since none of the members will have personal liability and may not necessarily be required to personally perform any tasks of management, it is easier to attract investors to the limited liability company form of business than to a traditional partnership. The members will share in the potential profits and in the tax deductions of the limited liability company, but will share in fewer of the financial risks involved. Since the limited liability company is generally taxed as a partnership, the profits and losses of the company pass directly to each member and are taxed only at the individual level.

A further advantage of this type of business structure is that it offers a relatively flexible management structure. The company can be managed either by members (owners) themselves or by managers who may or may not be members. Thus, depending on needs or desires, the limited liability company can be a hands-on, owner-managed company or a relatively hands-off operation for its members/owners with hired managers actually operating the company.

A final advantage is that limited liability companies are allowed more flexibility than corporations in how profits and losses are actually allocated to the members/owners. Thus, one member/owner may be allocated 50 percent of the profits (or losses) even though that member/owner only contributed 10 percent of the capital to start the company.

> **🔆 Toolkit Tip!**
>
> The often complex details of LLC formation and operation must be strictly observed in order for its owners to retain their limited liability for LLC debts and obligations.

Sole Proprietorship

A sole proprietorship is both the simplest and the most prevalent form of business organization. An important reason for this is that it is the least regulated of all types of business structures. Technically, the sole proprietorship is the traditional unincorporated one-person business. For legal and tax purposes, the business is the owner. It has no existence outside the owner. The liabilities of the business are personal to the owner and the business ends when the owner dies. On the other hand, all of the profits are also personal to the owner and the sole owner has full control of the business.

Disadvantages

:◊: Toolkit Tip!

Information for dealing with taxation for sole proprietorships is provided in Chapter 15.

Perhaps the most important factor to consider before choosing this type of business structure is that all of the personal and business assets of the sole owner are at risk in the sole proprietorship. If the demands of the creditors of the business exceed those assets which were formally placed in the name of the business, the creditors may reach the personal assets of the owner of the sole proprietorship. Legal judgments for damages arising from the operation of the business may also be enforced against the owner's personal assets. This unlimited liability is probably the greatest drawback to this type of business form. Of course, insurance coverage of various types can lessen the dangers inherent in having one's personal assets at risk in a business. However, as liability insurance premiums continue to skyrocket, it is unlikely that a fledgling small business can afford to insure against all manner of contingencies and at the maximum coverage levels necessary to guard against all risk to personal assets.

A second major disadvantage to the sole proprietorship as a form of business structure is the potential difficulty in obtaining business loans. Often in starting a small business, there is insufficient collateral to obtain a loan and the sole owner must mortgage his or her own house or other personal assets to obtain the loan. This, of course, puts the sole proprietor's personal assets in a direct position of risk should the business fail. Banks and other lending institutions are often reluctant to loan money for initial small business start-ups due to the high risk of failure for small businesses. Without a proven track record, it is quite difficult for a small business owner to adequately present a loan proposal based on a sufficiently stable cash flow to satisfy most banks.

A further disadvantage to a sole proprietorship is the lack of continuity that is inherent in the business form. If the owner dies, the business ceases to exist. Of course, the assets and liabilities of the business will pass to the heirs of the owner, but the expertise and knowledge of how the business was successfully carried on will often die with the owner. Small sole proprietorships are seldom carried on profitably after the death of the owner.

Advantages

The most appealing advantage of the sole proprietorship as a business structure is the total control the owner has over the business. Subject only to economic considerations and certain legal restrictions, there is total freedom to operate the business however one chooses. Many people feel that this factor alone is enough to overcome the inherent disadvantages in this form of business.

> **☼ Toolkit Tip!**
>
> A sole proprietorship is the least regulated of all of the types of business entities.

Related to this is the simplicity of organization of the sole proprietorship. Other than maintenance of sufficient records for tax purposes, there are no legal requirements on how the business is operated. Of course, the prudent businessperson will keep adequate records and sufficiently organize the business for its most efficient operation. But there are no outside forces dictating how such internal decisions are made in the sole proprietorship. The sole owner makes all decisions in this type of business.

As was mentioned earlier, the sole proprietorship is the least regulated of all businesses. Normally, the only license necessary is a local business license, usually obtained by simply paying a fee to a local registration authority. In addition, it may be necessary to file an affidavit with local authorities and publish a notice in a local newspaper if the business is operated under an assumed or fictitious name. This is necessary to allow creditors to have access to the actual identity of the true owner of the business, since it is the owner who will be personally liable for the debts and obligations of the business.

> **⚡ Warning!**
>
> The final decision of which business entity to choose depends upon many factors and should be carefully studied.

Finally, it may be necessary to register with local, state, and federal tax bodies for I.D. numbers and for the purpose of collection of sales and other taxes. Other than these few simple registrations, from a legal standpoint little else is required to start up a business as a sole proprietorship.

A final and important advantage to the sole proprietorship is the various tax benefits available to an individual. The losses or profits of the sole proprietorship are considered personal to the owner. The losses are directly deductible against any other income the owner may have and the profits are taxed only once at the marginal rate of the owner. In many instances, this may have distinct advantages over the method by which partnerships are taxed or the double taxation of corporations, particularly in the early stages of the business.

Chapter 2

Business Start-Up Checklist

Following is the first of many checklists that are provided in this book in order to help you organize your preparation for starting a business. These initial checklists provides an overview of the entire process of starting a business and, in many ways, is your blueprint for your personal business start-up. It incorporates references to many other forms, worksheets, and checklists from throughout this book. Keep this checklist handy as you proceed through the process of starting your business as a Sole Proprietorship.

Toolkit Tip!

Keep this list handy as you proceed in setting up your business as a Sole Proprietorship.

Sole Proprietorship Start-Up Checklist

☐ Read through this entire book to understand the process of starting a Sole Proprietorship

☐ Install the software and forms from the Forms-on-CD

☐ Complete the Business Plan Worksheet

☐ Prepare your written Business Plan

☐ Complete the Business Marketing Worksheet

☐ Prepare your written Marketing Plan

☐ Prepare the Business Financial Worksheet

☐ Prepare your written Financial Plan

☐ Prepare your written Executive Summary

☐ Compile your final Business Plan package

☐ Complete the Pre-Start-up Worksheet

☐ Review the Pre-Start-up and Document Filing Checklists

☐ Prepare your Sole Proprietorship Plan

☐ File and publish Intention to Conduct Business Under Fictitious or Assumed Name (with state or local authorities, if required. Please see Appendix.)

☐ Prepare Employment Contracts for any employees of business

☐ Set up Business Accounting System

☐ Open Business Bank Account

☐ Set up business payroll (if you will have any employees)

☐ Set up company tax payment schedules

Chapter 3

Developing a Business Plan

One of the most important and often overlooked aspects of starting a business is the process of preparing a Business Plan. It is through preparation of a formal business plan than you begin the process of refining what your business will actually be and, more importantly, how you can make it successful from the start. To develop a useful plan, you will need to research your business idea and determine how it can be developed into a feasible and successful business. You will use your business plan for many purposes: for your own use to continually fine-tune your actual business start-up; for obtaining financing, even if it is only from family members; and for presenting your business ideas to potential shareholders, employees, investors, suppliers, and anyone else with whom you may be doing business. Your plan needs to be dynamic and detailed. If you prepare your plan with care and attention, it will help guide you through the process of starting a successful business. If you take shortcuts in researching, thinking about, and preparing your plan, your path to business success will become an everyday struggle.

> **Toolkit Tip!**
> Your business plan will consist of three separate parts: a business plan, a marketing plan, and a financial plan.

This book has divided the preparation of your business plan into three separate parts. In this chapter, you will develop your overall plan. However, in the two following chapters, you will also develop plans that will become an integral part of your final business plan. Chapter 4 concentrates on the plans to market your business service or product. Chapter 5 provides a worksheet and instructions for preparing and implementing a strategy for financing your business. Together, the three plans that you create will comprise your total Business Plan package. Finally, after completing all three sections, you will prepare an Executive Summary. The instructions for preparing the summary are at the end of this chapter. With the information you will have gathered and set down in your plan, starting a successful business will be simplified and streamlined.

Each of these three chapters has a similar format. A worksheet is presented into which you will enter information that you have gathered or researched. Crucial business decisions will need to be made, even at this early stage, in order for you to honestly assess your chances for success. After completing the worksheet, you will use the compiled information to complete a written (printed) plan. This process will take some time to do correctly, but time spent at this stage of your business start-up will save you many times the effort and headaches later in the evolution of your business. All three of the Business Plan Worksheets are included on the Forms-on-CD. You may enter your answers to the questions directly on the forms which you can open in your own word-processing program. This will allow you to quickly and easily compile the answers that you have written out into the final Business Plan. Following this first worksheet are more detailed instructions for preparing your final Business Plan.

᭡Toolkit Tip!

Take your time preparing your business plan. It will be the outline of how you will organize, market, and finance your business.

Business Plan Worksheet
Preliminary Business Concept Analysis

In one sentence, describe your business concept: _____
_____

What is your business service or product? _____
_____
_____

How long do you estimate that it will take to develop this service or product to the point of being ready for the public? _____
_____

What are the estimated costs of development of this product or service? _____
_____

Why do you think that this business concept will succeed? _____
_____
_____

Who is your target market? _____
_____

Is this market readily identifiable? _____
_____

What are the buying patterns of this market? _____
_____

Is there sufficient advance interest in this type of product or service? _____
_____

What are your expected annual sales/revenue volumes?
　　Year one:　　$ _____
　　Year two:　　$ _____
　　Year three:　$ _____
　　Year four:　　$ _____
　　Year five:　　$ _____

Company Description

What is your company's mission? _____
_____

What is the type of business entity of your company? **Sole Proprietorship**

Who will be the directors of the company? _____
_____

Who will serve as the officers of the company? (not applicable to sole proprietorships or partnerships)

    President: _____

    Vice President: _____

    Treasurer: _____

    Secretary: _____

Where will the physical location of your company be? _____
_____

Where will be the company's main place of doing business? _____

Will there be any additional locations for the company? _____
_____

What geographic areas will your company serve? _____

What are the long-term plans for the business? (Expand, go public, sell to competitor, etc.)
_____
_____

Industry Analysis

In what industry will your company operate? _____

What is the overall size of the industry? _____

What is the growth rate of the industry? _____

What are any seasonal or business cycles in the industry? _____
_____

What have been the main technological advances in the past five years? _____
_____

What are projected technological advances in the industry for the next five years? _____
_____

Do any industry standards apply to your business? _____
_____

Are there any government regulatory approvals or requirements? _____
_____

Are there any local or state licenses necessary for the service or product? ____
_____

What are the main trade or business associations in your industry? _____
_____

To which associations do you currently belong? _____
_____

Product or Service Analysis

Description of product or service: _____
_____

What is the main purpose of the product or service? _____
_____

Is it a luxury item or a necessity? _____

What are the unique features of your product or service? (Cost, design, quality, capabilities, etc.) _____
_____
_____

Sole Proprietorship: Small Business Start-Up Kit

What is the life of the product or service? _____

How does this product/service compare with the state-of-the-art for the industry?
_____

In what stage is the development of the product? (Idea, model, prototype, full production, etc.) _____

Describe the company's facilities: _____
_____

How will the product be produced or the service provided? _____
_____

Is it labor- or material-intensive to produce or supply? _____

What components or supplies are necessary to produce or supply this product?
_____

Has the service or product been the subject of any engineering or design tests?
_____

What types of quality control will be in place in the business? _____
_____

Are there any special technical considerations? _____
_____

What are the maintenance or updating requirements for the product/service? __
_____

Can the product be copyrighted, patented, or trade- or service-marked? _____
_____

Are there other products, services, or spin-offs that will be developed and marketed
in future years? _____
_____

Are there any known dangers associated with the manufacture, supply, or use of
the product/service? _____

What types of liabilities are posed by the product, service, or any other business operations?

    To employees: _____

    To customers: _____

    To suppliers: _____

    To distributors: _____

    To the public: _____

Are there any litigation threats posed by this business? _____

Are there any other problems or risks inherent in this type of business? _____
_____

What types of insurance coverage will be necessary for the business? _____
_____

What are the costs of the needed insurance coverage? _____

What steps will be taken to minimize any potential liabilities, dangers, or risks? _
_____
_____

Business Operations

Describe the type of facilities that your business will need to operate: _____
_____
_____

Estimate the cost of acquiring and maintaining the facilities for two years: _____
_____

Describe your production plan or service plan: _____
_____
_____

How will orders be filled and your product or service delivered?
_____

Will you work through any wholesalers or distributors? _____
_____

Sole Proprietorship: Small Business Start-Up Kit

Who will be the main wholesalers/distributors? _____
_____

Describe the equipment or machinery that you will need for your business: _____
_____

Who will be the main suppliers of this equipment? _____
_____

What are the estimated costs of obtaining this equipment? _____

What type of inventory will you need? _____

Who will be the main suppliers of the inventory? _____
_____

Estimate the costs of obtaining sufficient inventory for the first two years of operation: _____

Management Analysis

What will be the organizational structure of the company? (Include an organizational chart) _____
_____

Who will manage the day-to-day affairs of the company? _____

Describe the management style of the central manager: _____
_____

What are the qualifications of the main management? _____

What type of workforce will be necessary for your business? _____
_____

How many employees will be needed?
    Initially: _____
    First year: _____
    Second year: _____
    Third year: _____
    Fourth year: _____
    Fifth year: _____

What are the job descriptions of the employees? _____
_____

What job skills will the employees need? _____
_____

Are employment and hiring/firing procedures and guidelines in place? _____

What will be the hourly wages or salaries of the employees?
    Salaried: _____
    Full-time: _____
    Part-time: _____

Will any fringe benefits be provided to employees?
    Sick pay: _____
    Vacation pay: _____
    Bonuses: _____
    Health insurance or benefits: _____
    Profit-sharing or stock options: _____
    Other benefits: _____

Estimate the annual cost for employee compensation for the first two years of operations:
_____

Will you need to contract with lawyers, accountants, consultants, designers, or specialists?
_____

Who will be the outside contractors you will use? _____
_____

Estimate the annual cost of outside contractors for the first two years of operations:
_____

Is the business bookkeeping system set up and working? _____

Are business bank accounts set up? _____

Are there administrative policies set up for billings, payments, accounts, etc.? __
_____

Supporting Documentation

Do you have any professional photos of the product, equipment, or facilities? __
_____

What contracts have already been signed? _____

Does the company hold any patents, trademarks, or copyrights? _____
_____

Have the company's registration papers been filed with the state and received?
_____

Do you have any samples of advertising or marketing materials? _____

Do you have references and resumés from each of the principals in the business? _____
_____

Do you have personal financial statements from each of the principals in the business?
_____

Have you prepared a time line chart for the company's development for the first five years?
_____

Have you prepared a list of the necessary equipment, with a description, supplier, and cost of each item noted? _____

Have you prepared current and projected balance sheets and profit/loss statements? _____

Preparing Your Business Plan

Once you have completed the previous worksheet and the worksheets in the next two chapters (relating to marketing and financial plans), you will need to prepare your final Business Plan and complete the Executive Summary. The Executive Summary is, perhaps, the most important document in the entire Business Plan, for it is in this short document that you will distill your entire vision of your company. Do not attempt to prepare the Executive Summary until you have completed all of the other worksheets and plans, for they will provide you with the insight that you will need to craft an honest and enthusiastic Executive Summary for your company.

> **♀ Toolkit Tip!**
>
> You will use the three worksheets (business, marketing, and financial) to prepare your final business plan.

To prepare your Business Plan, carefully read through the answers you have prepared for the Business Plan Worksheet to obtain a complete overview of your proposed business. Your task will be to carefully put the answers to the questions on the worksheet into a narrative format. If you have taken the time to fully answer the questions, this will not be a difficult task. If you have supplied the answers to the worksheet questions on the computer file version of the worksheet, you should be able to easily cut and paste your Business Plan sections together, adding only sentence and paragraph structure and connecting information. Keep the plan to the point but try to convey both a broad outline of the industry that you will be operating in and a clear picture of how your particular company will fit into that industry and succeed. Emphasize the uniqueness of your company, product, or service, but don't intentionally avoid the potential problems that your business will face. An honest appraisal of your company's risks and potential problems at this stage of the development of your company will convey to investors and bankers that you have thoroughly and carefully investigated the potential for your company to succeed.

For each subsection of the Business Plan Worksheet, use the answers to the questions to prepare your written plan. You may rearrange the answers within each section if you feel that it will present a clearer picture to those who will be reading your Business Plan. Try, however, to keep the information for each section in its own discreet portion of the Business Plan. You will use this same technique to prepare the written Marketing and Financial Plans in the following two chapters. Once you have prepared your written Business, Marketing, and Financial Plans, you are ready to prepare your Executive Summary.

Preparing Your Executive Summary

It is in the Executive Summary that you will need to convey your vision of the company and its potential for success. It is with this document that you will convince investors, suppliers, bankers, and others to take the risks necessary to back your dreams and help you to make them a reality. The Executive Summary portion of your Business Plan should be about one to three pages long. It should be concise, straightforward, and clearly written. Don't use any terms or technical jargon that the average person cannot understand. You may go into more detail in the body of the Business Plan itself, but keep the Executive Summary short and to the point. This document will be a distillation of the key points in your entire Business Plan. It is in the Executive Summary that you will need to infuse your potential backers with your enthusiasm and commitment to success. However, you will need to remain honest and forthright in the picture that you paint of your business and its competition. Use the following outline as a guide to assist you in preparing your Executive Summary. You will, of course, be using the information that you have included in your written Business, Marketing, and Financial Plans to prepare the Executive Summary. After completing your Executive Summary, there are some brief instructions to assist you in compiling your entire Business Plan package.

Executive Summary

Business Plan for _____

Executive Summary

In the year _____ , _____ was begun as a _____
in the State of _____ .

The purpose of the company is to: _____
_____

Our mission statement is as follows: This company is dedicated to providing the
highest quality _____ to a target market of _____ .

Our long-term goals are to: _____
_____
_____

Industry Analysis

The industry in which this company will operate is: _____
_____

The annual gross sales of the _____ industry are approximately
$ _____ .

Continue with a brief explanation of how your company will fit into this industry:
_____
_____
_____

Product or Service Analysis

The product/service that this company will provide is:_____

It is unique in its field because: _____

Continue with a brief explanation of product/service: _____
_____
_____
_____

Business Operations

Prepare a brief explanation of how the business will operate to obtain and deliver the product/service to the market. Include short explanations of strategies you will use to beat the competition: _____
_____
_____

Management of the Company

The company will be managed by: _____
_____

Include a brief summary of the management structure and the qualifications of the key management personnel and how their expertise will be the key to the success of the company: _____
_____
_____
_____

Market Strategy

The target market for this product/service is: _____

Prepare a brief analysis of your market research and marketing plans and why your product/service is better than any competitors: _____
_____
_____
_____

Financial Plans

In this section, briefly review the data on your Current Balance Sheet and Estimated Profit and Loss Statements and describe both the annual revenue projections and the company's immediate and long-term needs for financing: _____
_____
_____
_____

Compiling Your Business Plan

1. Prepare a Title page filling in the necessary information:

> Business Plan of (name of company),
> Begun in the State of (name of state)
> as a (type of entity) on (date of company organization)
> Address:
> Phone:
> Fax:
> Internet:
> E-mail:
> Date:
> Prepared by (name of preparer)

2. Include a Table of Contents listing the following items that you have:

-   Executive Summary
-   Business Plan
    Business Concept and Objectives
    Industry Analysis
    Product/Service Analysis
    Business Operations
    Management Analysis
-   Marketing Plan
    Target Market Analysis
    Competitive Analysis
    Sales and Pricing Analysis
    Marketing Strategy
        Advertising and Promotion
        Publicity and Public Relations
-   Financial Plan
    Financial Analysis
    Estimated Profit/Loss Statement
    Current Balance Sheet
-   Appendix
    Photos of Product/Service/Facilities
    Contracts
    Incorporation Documents
    Bank Account Statements
    Personal Financial Statements of Principals

Proposed List of Equipment/Supplies/Inventory
Proposed Time Line for Corporate Growth

3. Neatly print out the necessary Business/Marketing/Financial Plans.

4. Compile all of the parts of your Plan and print multiple copies.

5. Assemble all of the parts into a neat and professional folder or notebook.

Congratulations! Your completed Business Plan will serve as an essential guide to understanding your business and will allow potential backers, investors, bankers, and others to quickly see the reality behind your business goals.

Chapter 4

Developing a Business Marketing Plan

An integral part of the process of starting a business is preparing a Marketing Plan. Whether the business will provide a service or sell a product, it will need customers in some form. Who those customers are, how they will be identified and located, and how they will be attracted to the business are crucial to the success of any small business. Unfortunately, it is also one part of a business start-up that is given less than its due in terms of time and effort spent to fully investigate the possibilities. In this chapter, a Business Marketing Worksheet is provided to assist you in thinking about your business in terms of who the customers may be and how to reach them. In many ways, looking honestly at who your customers may be and how to attract them may be the most crucial part of starting your business, for if your understanding of this issue is ill-defined or unclear, your business will have a difficult time succeeding.

In order to create your written Marketing Plan, simply follow the same process that you used in creating your Business Plan in Chapter 3. Take the answers that you have supplied on the following worksheet and edit them into a narrative for each of the four sections of the worksheet: Target Market Analysis; Competitive Analysis: Sales and Pricing Analysis; and Marketing Strategy.

Business Marketing Worksheet
Target Market Analysis

What is the target market for your product or service? _____

What types of market research have you conducted to understand your market?
_____
_____

What is the geographic market area you will serve? _____

Describe a typical customer:
    Sex: _____
    Marital status: _____
    Age: _____
    Income: _____
    Geographic location: _____
    Education: _____
    Employment: _____

Estimate the number of potential people in the market in your area of service: __
_____

What is the growth potential for this market? _____

How will you satisfy the customers' needs with your product/service? _____
_____

Will your product/service make your customers' life more comfortable? _____

Will your product/service save your customers' time or money or stress? _____

Competitive Analysis

Who are your main competitors? _____
_____

Are there competitors in the same geographic area as your proposed business?
_____

Are the competitors successful and what is their market share? _____

How long have they been in business? _____

Describe your research into your competitors' business operations: _____
_____

Are there any foreseeable new competitors? _____

What are the strengths and/or weaknesses of your competitor's product/service?
_____

Why is your product/service different or better than that of your competitors? ___
_____
_____

What is the main way that you will compete with your competitors (price, quality, technology, advertising, etc.)? _____
_____

How will your customers know that your product/service is available? _____
_____

What is the main message that you want your potential customers to receive? _
_____

Why is your product/service unique? _____
_____

How will you be able to expand your customer base over time? _____
_____

Sales and Pricing Analysis

What are your competitors' prices for similar products/services? _____

Are your prices higher or lower, and why? _____

Will you offer any discounts for quantity or other factors? _____

Will you accept checks for payment? _____

Will you accept credit cards for payment? _____

Will you have a sales force? Describe: _____

What skills or education will the sales force need? _____

Will there be sales quotas? _____

Will the sales force be paid by salary, wages, or commission? _____

Are there any geographic areas or limitations on your sales or distribution? _____
_____

Will you sell through distributors or wholesalers? Describe: _____

Will there be dealer margins or wholesale discounts? _____

Do you have any plans to monitor customer feedback? Describe: _____
_____

Do you have warranty, guarantee, and customer return policies? Describe: _____
_____

Will any customer service be provided? Describe: _____
_____

What is your expected sales volume for the first five years?
Year one: _____
Year two: _____
Year three: _____
Year four: _____
Year five: _____

Marketing Strategy

What is your annual projected marketing budget? _____

Have your company's logo, letterhead, and business cards already been designed? _____

Sole Proprietorship: Small Business Start-Up Kit

Do you have a company slogan or descriptive phrase? _____

Has packaging for your product/service been designed? _____

Has signage for your facility been designed? _____

Describe your advertising plans:

    Signs: _____
    Brochures: _____
    Catalogs: _____
    Yellow Pages: _____
    Magazines: _____
    Trade journals: _____
    Radio: _____
    Television: _____
    Newspapers: _____
    Internet: _____
    Trade shows: _____
    Videos: _____
    Billboards: _____
    Newsletters: _____

Have advertisements already been designed? _____

Have you prepared a media kit for publicity? _____

Describe your plans to receive free publicity in the media via news releases or new product/service releases:

    Radio: _____
    Television: _____
    Newspapers: _____
    Magazines: _____
    Internet: _____

Have you requested inclusion in any directories, catalogs, or other marketing vehicles for your industry? _____

Describe any planned direct mail campaigns: _____

Describe any planned telemarketing campaigns: _____

Describe any internet-based marketing plans:_____

_____

    E-mail account: _____
    Website: _____
    Blog: _____

Will there be any special or seasonal promotions of your product/service? _____

_____

How will your customers actually receive the product/service? _____

_____

Chapter 5

Developing a Business Financial Plan

The third crucial part of your initial Business Plan entails how your business will obtain enough money to actually survive until it is successful. The failure of many small businesses relates directly to underestimating the amount of money needed to start and continue the business. Most business owners can, with relative ease, estimate the amount of money needed to start a business. The problem comes with arriving at a clear estimate of how much money will be necessary to keep the business operating until it is able to realistically support itself. If you can honestly determine how much is actually necessary to allow the business time to thrive before you can take out profits or pay, the next challenge is to figure out where to get that amount of money. To assist you, a Business Financial Worksheet follows. Following the worksheet are instructions on preparing both a Estimated Profit and Loss Statement and a Current Balance Sheet. Both of these financial forms will help you put some real numbers into your plans. When you have completed the Worksheet and your two financial forms, use the same technique that you used in Chapters 3 and 4 to convert your answers to a narrative. After your written Financial Plan is completed, you will need to return to the instructions at the end of Chapter 3, complete your Executive Summary, and compile your completed parts into your entire final Business Plan package.

⦿ Toolkit Tip!

Your business financial plan will be used to attract investors, approach bankers or other sources of financing. Most importantly, it will allow you to understand the financial needs of your business.

Business Financial Worksheet

Describe the current financial status of your company: _____

_____

Income and Expenses

Estimate the annual expenses for the first year in the following categories:

Advertising expenses: _____
Auto expenses: _____
Cleaning and maintenance expenses: _____
Charitable contributions: _____
Dues and publications: _____
Office equipment expenses: _____
Freight and shipping expenses: _____
Business insurance expenses: _____
Business interest expenses: _____
Legal and accounting expenses: _____
Business meals and lodging: _____
Miscellaneous expenses: _____
Postage expenses: _____
Office rent/mortgage expenses: _____
Repair expenses: _____
Office supplies: _____
Sales taxes: _____
Federal unemployment taxes: _____
State unemployment taxes: _____
Telephone/internet expenses: _____
Utility expenses: _____
Wages and commissions: _____

Estimate the first year's annual income from the following sources:
Sales income: _____
Service income: _____
Miscellaneous income: _____

Sole Proprietorship: Small Business Start-Up Kit

Estimate the amount of inventory necessary for the first year: _____
_____

Estimate the amount of inventory that will be sold during the first year: _____
_____

Estimate the Cost of Goods Sold for the first year: _____

Using the above information, complete the Estimated Profit and Loss Statement as explained later.

Assets and Liabilities

What forms of credit have already been used by the business? _____

How much cash is available to the business? _____

What are the sources of the cash? _____

What types of bank accounts are in place for the business and what are the balances?
_____
_____

What types of assets are currently owned by the business?
    Current assets: _____
    Inventory: _____
        Cash in bank: _____
        Cash on hand: _____
    Accounts receivable: _____
    Fixed and depreciable: _____
    Autos/trucks: _____
        Buildings: _____
        Equipment: _____
        Amount of depreciation taken on any of above: _____
    Fixed non-depreciable: _____
        Land: _____
    Miscellaneous: _____
        Stocks/bonds: _____

What types of debts does the business currently have?

    Current liabilities: _____

        Taxes due: _____

        Accounts payable: _____

        Short-term loans/notes payable: _____

        Payroll accrued: _____

        Miscellaneous: _____

    Long-term liabilities: _____

        Mortgage: _____

        Other loans/notes payable: _____

Financial Needs

Based on the estimated profits and losses of the business, how much credit will be necessary for the business?

    Initially: _____

    First year: _____

    Second year: _____

    Third year: _____

    Fourth year: _____

    Fifth year: _____

Estimate the cash flow for the business for the first five years:

    First year: _____

    Second year: _____

    Third year: _____

    Fourth year: _____

    Fifth year: _____

From what sources are the necessary funds expected to be raised?

    Cash on hand: _____

    Personal funds: _____

    Family: _____

    Friends: _____

    Conventional bank financing: _____

    Finance companies: _____

    Equipment manufacturers: _____

    Leasing companies: _____

    Venture capital: _____

    U.S. Small Business Administration: _____

    Equity financing _____

(Check with current Securities and Exchange rules on sales of shares)

Preparing a Profit and Loss Statement

A Profit and Loss Statement is the key financial statement for presenting how your business is performing over a period of time. The Profit and Loss Statement illuminates both the amounts of money that your business has spent on expenses and the amounts of money that your business has taken in over a specific period of time. Along with the Balance Sheet, which is discussed later in this chapter, the Profit and Loss Statement should become an integral part of both your short- and long-range business planning.

This section will explain how to prepare an Estimated Profit and Loss Statement for use in your Business Plan. The Estimated Profit and Loss Statement can serve a valuable business planning service by allowing you to project estimated changes in your business over various time periods and examine what the results may be. Projections of various business plans can be examined in detail and decisions can then be made on the basis of clear pictures of future scenarios. Your estimates of your business profits and losses can take into account industry changes, economic factors, and personal business decisions. Your estimates are primarily for internal business planning purposes, although it may be useful to use an Estimated Profit and Loss Statement to convey your future Business Plans to others. As a trial exercise, you should prepare an Estimated Profit and Loss Statement using your best estimates before you even begin business. You may wish to prepare such pre-business statements for monthly, quarterly, and annual time periods. You may also desire to prepare Estimated Profit and Loss Statements for the first several years of your business's existence.

The Estimated Profit and Loss Statement differs from other types of Profit and Loss Statements in that the figures that you will use are projections based on expected business income and expenses for a time period in the future. The value of this type of financial planning tool is to allow you to see how various scenarios will affect your business. You may prepare this form as either a monthly, quarterly, or annual projection. To prepare this form, use the data that you have collected for your Business Financial Worksheet.

1. The first figure that you will need will be your Estimated Gross Sales Income. If your business is a pure service business, put your estimated income on the *Estimated Service Income Total* line. If your business income comes from part sales and part service, place the appropriate figures on the correct lines.

2. If your business will sell items from inventory, you will need to calculate your Estimated Cost of Goods Sold. In order to have the necessary figures to make

this computation, you will need to prepare a projection of your inventory costs and how many items you expect to sell. Fill in the Estimated Cost of Goods Sold figure on the Estimated Profit and Loss Statement. If your business is a pure service business, skip this line. Determine your Estimated Net Sales Income Total by subtracting your Estimated Cost of Goods Sold from your Estimated Gross Sales Income.

3. Calculate your Estimated Total Income for the period by adding your Estimated Net Sales Income Total and your Estimated Service Income Total and any Estimated Miscellaneous Income (for example: interest earned on a checking account).

4. Fill in the appropriate Estimated Expense account categories on the Estimated Profit and Loss Statement. If you have a large number of categories, you may need to prepare a second sheet. Based on your future projections, fill in the totals for each of your separate expense accounts. Add in any Estimated Miscellaneous Expenses.

5. Total all of your expenses and subtract your Estimated Total Expenses figure from your Estimated Total Income figure to determine your Estimated Pre-Tax Profit for the time period.

Estimated Profit and Loss Statement

For the period of:

	ESTIMATED INCOME		
Income	Estimated Gross Sales Income		
	Less Estimated Cost of Goods Sold		
	Estimated Net Sales Income Total		0.00
	Estimated Service Income Total		
	Estimated Miscellaneous Income Total		
	Estimated Total Income		0.00
	ESTIMATED EXPENSES		
Expenses	Advertising expenses		
	Auto expenses		
	Cleaning and maintenance expenses		
	Charitable contributions		
	Dues and publications		
	Office equipment expenses		
	Freight and shipping expenses		
	Business insurance expenses		
	Business interest expenses		
	Legal and accounting expenses		
	Business meals and lodging		
	Miscellaneous expenses		
	Postage expenses		
	Office rent/mortgage expenses		
	Repair expenses		
	Office supplies		
	Sales taxes		
	Federal unemployment taxes		

State unemployment taxes	
Telephone/Internet expenses	
Utility expenses	
Wages and commissions	
Estimated General Expenses Total	
Estimated Miscellaneous Expenses	
Estimated Total Expenses	

Estimated Pre-Tax Profit (Income less Expenses)	

Preparing a Balance Sheet

A Profit and Loss Statement provides a view of business operations over a particular period of time. It allows a look at the income and expenses and profits or losses of the business during the time period. In contrast, a Balance Sheet is designed to be a look at the financial position of a company on a specific date. It shows what the business owns and owes on a fixed date. Its purpose is to depict the financial strength of a company as shown by its assets and liabilities. It is merely a visual representation of the basic business financial equation: assets – liabilities = equity (or *net worth*). Essentially, the Balance Sheet shows what the company would be worth if all of the assets were sold and all the liabilities were paid off. A value is placed on each asset and on each liability. These figures are then balanced by adjusting the value of the owner's equity figure in the equation. Your Balance Sheet will total your current and fixed assets and your current and long-term liabilities. Even if your business is very new, you will need to prepare a Balance Sheet of where the business currently stands financially. Use the figures that you have gathered for the previous Business Financial Worksheet to complete your Current Balance Sheet. Please follow the instructions below to prepare your Current Balance Sheet for your Business Financial Plan:

1. Your Current Assets consist of the following items:

    *   Cash in Bank (from your business bank account balance)
    *   Cash on Hand
    *   Accounts Receivable (if you have any yet)
    *   Inventory (if you have any yet)
    *   Prepaid Expenses (these may be rent, insurance, prepaid supplies, or similar items that have been paid for prior to their actual use)

2. Total all of your Current Assets on your Current Balance Sheet.

3. Your Fixed Assets consist of the following items, which should be valued at your actual cost:

    *   Equipment
    *   Autos and Trucks
    *   Buildings

4. Total your Fixed Assets (except land) on your Current Balance Sheet. Total all of the depreciation that you have previously deducted for all of your fixed assets (except land). Include in this figure any business deductions that you have taken

for Section 179 write-offs on business equipment. *Note*: If you are just starting a business, you will not have any depreciation or Section 179 deductions as yet. Enter this total depreciation figure under "Less Depreciation" and subtract this figure from the figure for Total Fixed Assets (except land).

5. Enter the value for any land that your business owns. Land may not be depreciated. Add Total Fixed Assets (except land) amount, minus the (less depreciation) figure, and the value of the land. This is your Total Fixed Assets value.

6. Add any Miscellaneous Assets not yet included. These may consist of stocks, bonds, or other business investments. Total your Current, Fixed, and Miscellaneous Assets to arrive at your Total Assets figure.

7. Your Current Liabilities consist of the following items:

   • Accounts Payable (if you have any yet)
   • Miscellaneous Payable (include here the principal due on any short-term notes payable. Also include any interest on credit purchases, notes, or loans that has accrued but not been paid. Also list the current amounts due on any long-term liabilities. Finally, list any payroll or taxes that have accrued but not yet been paid)

8. Your Fixed Liabilities consist of Loans Payable (the principal of any long-term note, loan, or mortgage due). Any current amounts due should be listed as "Current Liabilities."

9. Total your Current and Fixed Liabilities to arrive at Total Liabilities.

10. Subtract your Total Liabilities from your Total Assets to arrive at your Owner's Equity. For a corporation, this figure represents the total of contributions by the owners or stockholders plus earnings after paying any dividends. Total Liabilities and Owner's Equity will always equal Total Assets.

Current Balance Sheet

As of:

ASSETS			
Current Assets	Cash in Bank		
	Cash on Hand		
	Accounts Receivable		
	Inventory		
	Prepaid Expenses		
	Total Current Assets		
Fixed Assets	Equipment (actual cost)		
	Autos and Trucks (actual cost)		
	Buildings (actual cost)		
	Total Fixed Assets (except land)		
	(less depreciation)		
	Net Total		
	Add Land (actual cost)		
	Total Fixed Assets		
	Total Miscellaneous Assets		
	Total Assets		
LIABILITIES			
Current Liabilities	Accounts Payable		
	Miscellaneous Payable		
	Total Current Liabilities		
Fixed Liabilities	Loans Payable (long-term)		
	Total Fixed Liabilities		
	Total Liabilities		
Owner's Equity	Net Worth or Capital Surplus + Stock Value		

Chapter 6

Operating a Sole Proprietorship

Having completed your Business Plan, including the Marketing and Financial Plans, you are ready to begin to understand, in detail, the type of business entity that you have chosen: the sole proprietorship. As noted earlier, there are numerous advantages to operating a business as a sole proprietorship, but there are also pitfalls. By understanding the actual operation of a sole proprietorship and the framework of laws within which sole proprietorships operate, it is easier to avoid the difficulties that come with the sole proprietorship form of business.

Sole proprietorships are the most common form of business operation. This is due, primarily, to the simplicity of this form of business. They are the easiest to set up. They are flexible. The taxation of sole proprietorships is relatively easy to understand. They allow the business to be under the complete control of the owner, and, unlike corporations or limited liability companies, they have very few paperwork requirements for compliance with state regulations.

Formation of a Sole Proprietorship

The formation of a sole proprietorship requires no special registration requirements in any state, beyond the registration of the use of a fictitious name for the business. There may, of course, be particular registration requirements that apply to the particular business that the sole proprietorship may be engaged in, for example, the sale of firearms or the packaging of food products. Thus, the formation of a sole proprietorship is a relatively simple matter and is accomplished by the act of beginning to engage in a business. Each year thousands of individuals begin their sole proprietorship businesses with little or no preparation or planning. Although this type of business is simple to begin, it is also prone to failure for the same reason. Starting a business as a corporation, a limited liability company, or even a partnership requires more paperwork and planning, and thus allows the business owners a greater opportunity to make careful, well thought out decisions at the planning stages of the business. The step-by-step planning process in this book for starting a sole proprietorship will take you through a similar planning process and provide opportunities to foresee and avoid some of the potential problems that you may encounter as a sole proprietor.

⚡ Warning!

A sole proprietorship is not a separate legal entity and you will be liable for all debts and liabilities of the company.

Sole Proprietorship Property

There are a few general rules that govern sole proprietorship property. Property acquired by a sole proprietorship is the property of the owner of the sole proprietorship. Unlike a corporation, limited liability company, or partnership, the sole proprietorship is not, itself, a legal entity for the purpose of holding property. This means that the sole proprietorship is ignored for property purposes and the general laws relating to the ownership of property will apply. Thus, if a sole proprietor is married, the particular state laws that apply to the acquisition of property by a married person will apply. In many ways, this simplifies the issue of property ownership for the sole-owner business. It allows for easy transfer or sale of any business property by the sole owner. However, it also means that in order to obtain financing, the sole proprietor must be personally liable for any mortgages or debts incurred for the purchase of business property.

Sole Proprietorship Liability

In general, the owner of a sole proprietorship is personally liable for any loss or injury caused to any person in the course of the business. The owner of a sole proprietorship is also personally liable for any debts and obligations of the sole proprietorship. This issue is the major difference between operating a business as a sole proprietorship and operating as a corporation or limited liability company. In both corporations and limited liability companies, most states now allow one person to own and operate the company as a sole owner. However, as long as they comply with the extensive paperwork requirements of operating the corporation or limited liability company, the sole owners of those types of businesses do not place their personal assets at risk in the company's business. What this means is that if the sole owner of a corporation defaults on a loan that was made in the name of the corporation, only the assets of the corporation itself may be reached by the creditor in a court proceeding and judgement. If a sole proprietor defaults on a business loan, all of the personal assets (including the sole proprietor's own home) are at risk to collection and enforcement of a claim by a creditor.

> ⚡ **Warning!**
>
> If a sole proprietor defaults on a business loan, all of the personal assets (including the sole proprietor's own home) are at risk to collection and enforcement of a claim by a creditor.

This seemingly great disparity in liability is, in fact, not so great in the real world of business. Unless a corporation or limited liability company has sufficient other assets to offer as collateral for a business loan, virtually all financial institutions will require that the owners of a corporation or limited liability company personally obligate themselves to pay back the loan, thus putting their personal assets at risk in the same way as a sole proprietor. Regarding liability for injuries sustained by customers or employees, business liability insurance can provide security from the loss of personal assets for a sole proprietor. The actual day-to-day difference for a business caused by the personal liability of a sole proprietor is, in fact, minimal.

Sole Proprietorship Books And Records

⚡Toolkit Tip!

Although the owners of sole proprietorships are not required by state law to keep books and records it is a sound business practice to do so.

Unlike corporations, partnerships, and limited liability companies, the owners of sole proprietorships are not required by state law to keep books and records. Although there are no state regulations relating to record-keeping, every sole proprietorship is required to keep sufficient records to comply with Federal tax requirements regarding business records. Taxation of sole proprietorships will be discussed in Chapter 15.

In general, the laws that relate to the affairs and conduct of an individual apply equally to the affairs and conduct of the owner of a sole proprietorship. Because the sole proprietorship form of business is not a legal entity itself, there is no effect from this type of business structure on the operation of laws relating to liability, property, taxation, or any other laws.

Chapter 7

Sole Proprietorship Paperwork

The business arena in America operates on a daily assortment of legal forms. There are more legal forms in use in American business than are used in the operations and governments of many foreign countries. The sole proprietorship is not immune to this flood of legal forms. While large corporations are able to obtain and pay expensive lawyers to deal with their legal problems and paperwork, most small businesses cannot afford such a course of action. The small business sole proprietorship must deal with a variety of legal documents, usually without the aid of an attorney.

Unfortunately, many businesspeople who are confronted with such forms do not understand the legal ramifications of the use of these forms. They simply sign them with the expectation that they are fairly standard documents, without any unusual legal provisions. They trust that the details of the particular document will fall within what is generally accepted within the industry or trade. In most cases, this may be true. In many situations, however, it is not. Our court system is clogged with cases in which two businesses are battling over what was really intended by the incomprehensible legal language in a certain legal document. Much of the confusion over company paperwork comes from two areas: First, there is a general lack of understanding among many in business regarding the framework of law. Second, many business documents are written in antiquated legal

> **Toolkit Tip!**
>
> Most large corporations are able to obtain and pay expensive lawyers to deal with their legal problems and paperwork while most small businesses cannot afford such a luxury.

jargon that is difficult for even most lawyers to understand and nearly impossible for a layperson to comprehend.

> **☼ Toolkit Tip!**
>
> If you are unclear about the definition of any term or word used in this book, please check the Glossary at the end of this book.

The various legal documents that are used in this book are, however, written in plain English. Standard legal jargon, as used in most lawyer-prepared documents, is, for most people, totally incomprehensible. Despite the lofty arguments by attorneys regarding the need for such strained and difficult language, the vast majority of legalese is absolutely unnecessary. As with any form of communication, clarity, simplicity, and readability should be the goal in legal documents.

Unfortunately, in some specific instances, certain obscure legal terms are the only words that accurately and precisely describe some things in certain legal contexts. In those few cases, the unfamiliar legal term will be defined when first used. Generally, however, simple terms are used throughout this book. In most cases, masculine and feminine terms have been eliminated and the generic "it," "they," or "them" have been used instead. In the few situations in which this leads to awkward sentence construction, her/his or she/he may be used instead.

All of the legal documents contained in this book have been prepared in essentially the same manner by which attorneys create legal forms. Many people believe that lawyers prepare each legal document that they compose entirely from scratch. Nothing could be further from the truth. Invariably, lawyers begin their preparation of a legal document with a standardized legal form book. Every law library has multivolume sets of these encyclopedic texts that contain blank forms for virtually every conceivable legal situation. Armed with these pre-prepared legal forms, lawyers, in many cases, simply fill in the blanks and have their secretaries retype the form for the client. Of course, the client is generally unaware of this process. As lawyers begin to specialize in a certain area of legal expertise, they compile their own files containing such blank forms.

This book provides those businesspersons who wish to form a sole proprietorship with a set of forms that have been prepared with the problems and normal legal requirements of the typical small business in mind. They are intended to be used in those situations that are clearly described by their terms. Of course, while most document use will fall within the bounds of standard business practices, some legal circumstances will present nonstandard situations. The forms in this book are designed to be readily adaptable to most usual business situations. They may be carefully altered to conform to the particular transaction that confronts your business. However, if you are faced with a complex or tangled business situation, the advice of a competent lawyer is highly recommended. If you wish, you may also create forms for certain standard situations for your company and have your lawyer check them for compliance with any local legal circumstances.

The proper and cautious use of the forms provided in this book will allow the typical company to save considerable money on legal costs over the course of the life of the business, while enabling the business to comply with legal and governmental regulations. Perhaps more importantly, these forms will provide a method by which the businessperson can avoid costly misunderstandings about what exactly was intended in a particular situation. By using the forms provided to clearly document the proceedings of everyday company operations, disputes over what was really meant can be avoided. This protection will allow the business to avoid many potential lawsuits and operate more efficiently and in compliance with the law.

> **🔆 Toolkit Tip!**
>
> Every business should set up a clear system of filing so that all required paperwork can be easily accessed when necessary.

All businesses, even non-corporation forms, need to be certain that their paperwork and recordkeeping practices are clear and consistent. Paperwork may be necessary to present to a bank loan officer, your own tax preparer, an IRS auditor, or an investor. Establishing an organized filing system that will allow you to find and use any paperwork when needed will go a long way towards keeping your business running as smoothly as possible. The following checklist provides a simple list of the major paperwork requirements needed for a Sole Proprietorship. The paperwork should be kept on file for the life of the business.

Sole Proprietorship Paperwork Checklist

- ☐ Sole Proprietorship Checklist
- ☐ Statement of Intention to Conduct Business Under an Assumed Name (filed with state and county if required or desired. Check Appendix.)
- ☐ Business insurance or health benefit plans
- ☐ Sole proprietorship accounting books
- ☐ Annual financial reports
- ☐ Sole proprietorship tax records (filed with state and federal tax authorities)

Chapter 8

Pre-Start-Up Activities

The planning stage is vital to the success of any sole proprietorship. The structure of a new sole proprietorship must be carefully tailored to the specific needs of the business. By filling out a Pre-Start-up Worksheet, potential business owners will be able to have before them all of the basic data to use in preparing the necessary sole proprietorship paperwork. The process of preparing this worksheet will also help uncover any potential problems that the business may face.

Please take the time to carefully and completely fill in all of the spaces. Following the worksheet, there is a Pre-Start-up checklist that provides a clear listing of all of the required actions necessary to begin a sole proprietorship business. Follow this checklist carefully as the sole proprietorship start-up process proceeds. Unfamiliar terms relating to business are explained in the glossary of this book. As the worksheet is filled in, please refer to the following explanations:

Sole proprietorship name: The selection of a name is often crucial to the success of a sole proprietorship. The name must not conflict with any existing company names, nor must it be deceptively similar to other names. Most states require or allow the registration of the use of a fictitious sole proprietorship name. Please refer to the Appendix in the back of the book to see if your state offers a form specifically for this registration.

Owner: This listing should provide the name, address, and phone number of the proposed owner of the sole proprietorship.

Principal place of business: This must be the address of the actual physical location of the main business. It may not be a post office box. If the sole proprietorship is home-based, this address should be the home address.

Purpose of the sole proprietorship: Here you may note the specific business purpose of the sole proprietorship. In your Sole Proprietorship Plan, you will also note that your sole proprietorship has a general purpose of engaging in any and all lawful businesses in the state in which you operate.

State/local licenses required: Here you should note any specific requirements for licenses to operate your type of business. Most states require obtaining a tax ID number and a retail, wholesale, or sales tax license. A Federal tax ID number must be obtained by all sole proprietorships that will be employing any additional persons. Additionally, certain types of businesses will require health department approvals, state board licensing, or other forms of licenses: If necessary, check with a competent local attorney for details regarding the types of licenses required for your locality and business type. Please check your state's listing in the appendix for any specific state requirements.

> **☼ Toolkit Tip!**
>
> Your sole proprietorship can have employees. You will need to obtain a federal employer identification number if you choose to do so.

Patents/copyrights/trademarks: If patents, copyrights, or trademarks will be part of the business of the sole proprietorship, they should be noted here.

State of sole proprietorship: In general, the sole proprietorship should be begun in the state in which it will conduct business.

Proposed date to begin sole proprietorship business: This should be the date on which you expect the sole proprietorship to begin its legal existence.

Initial investment: This figure is the total amount of money that will be invested in the business by the sole owner.

Initial indebtedness: If there is to be any initial indebtedness for the sole proprietorship, please list it here.

Proposed bank for sole proprietorship bank account: In advance of conducting sole proprietorship business, you should determine the bank that will handle the sole proprietorship accounts. Obtain from the bank the necessary bank paperwork, which will be signed by the owner.

Cost of setting up sole proprietorship: This cost should reflect the cost of obtaining professional assistance (legal or accounting); the cost of procuring the necessary supplies; and any other direct costs of the sole proprietorship process.

Fiscal year and accounting type: For accounting purposes, the fiscal year and accounting type (cash or accrual) of the sole proprietorship should be chosen in advance. Please consult with a competent accounting professional.

Insurance: Under this heading, consider the types of insurance that you will need, ranging from general casualty to various business liability policies. Also consider the need for the owner of the sole proprietorship to secure life and/or disability insurance.

> **⚘Toolkit Tip!**
>
> Prior to conducting sole proprietorship business, you should determine the bank that will handle the sole proprietorship accounts.

Pre-Start-up Worksheet

Name, address and phone of owner

Name_____

Address_____

_____

Phone_____

Proposed name of the company

First choice: _____

_____

Alternate choices: _____

_____

_____

Location of Business

Address of principal place of business: _____

_____

Description of principal place of business: _____

_____

_____

_____

Ownership of principal place of business (own or lease?): _____

_____

Other places of business: _____

_____

_____

_____

Type of Business

Purpose of company: _____

_____

State/local licenses required: _____

_____

Patents/copyrights/trademarks: _____

_____

State of formation: _____

Proposed date to begin company business: _____

Initial investment total: $ _____

       Date when due: _____

Initial indebtedness: $ _____

Proposed bank for company bank account: _____

_____

Cost of setting up company: _____

Fiscal year: _____

Accounting type (cash or accrual?): _____

Insurance needs: _____

_____

Sole Proprietorship Pre-Start-up Checklist

☐ Check your state's website for information regarding registration of business name (see Appendix)

☐ Complete Pre-Start-up Worksheet

☐ Prepare and file Statement of Intention to Conduct Business Under an Assumed or Fictitious Name (if required - check Appendix)

☐ Prepare Sole Proprietorship Plan

☐ Open company business bank account

☐ Prepare annual financial reports (in company record book)

☐ Maintain company tax records (filed with state and Federal authorities)

☐ Check state tax, employment, licensing, unemployment, and workers' compensation requirements

☐ Check insurance requirements

☐ Prepare company accounting ledgers

☐ Prepare company record book (looseleaf binder)

Chapter 9

Sole Proprietorship Plan

Next, you will prepare your Sole Proprietorship Plan. The Sole Proprietorship Plan provides the framework for the operation of the sole proprietorship business. Although not re- quired by any state or local law, this plan will provide you with a record of your intentions and plans for your business. It mirrors documents that are prepared by partnerships, corporations, and limited liability companies. The purpose of this plan is different from the Business Plan that you prepared in Chapters 3-5. That plan was for the purpose of presenting your business plans to others for financing or other reasons. The plan in this chapter is to provide you, the owner of the sole proprietorship, with the details of how your business will be operated. Although the preparation of this plan may seem overly formal for a simple business, it will provide you with a written plan for how to set up your business in the most beneficial manner for its suc- cess. Have your completed Pre-Start-up Worksheet before you as you prepare your plan. If you are using a computer and word-processing program, simply select those clauses from the Forms-on-CD that you wish to use in your Sole Proprietorship Plan and print out a completed plan.

☼ Toolkit Tip!

A simple sole proprietor- ship plan is for your own benefit in understand- ing how you are setting up your small business.

Sole Proprietorship Plan Checklist

- ❏ The name and address of the sole proprietor
- ❏ The main office of the sole proprietorship
- ❏ The purpose of the sole proprietorship
- ❏ Amount of initial capital and contributions to the sole proprietorship
- ❏ Cash or accrual accounting
- ❏ Life insurance
- ❏ Disability insurance
- ❏ Accounting matters
- ❏ Calendar or other accounting periods
- ❏ Insurance
- ❏ Bank account
- ❏ Business liability insurance
- ❏ Additional provisions

Sole Proprietorship Plan

This Sole Proprietorship Plan is made on _____ , 20 ___ , by
_____ , of _____ , City of _____ ,
State of _____ .

Sole Proprietorship Name

The sole proprietorship shall be known as: _____

This name shall be property of the sole proprietorship.

Sole Proprietorship Office

The sole proprietorship's principal place of business shall be:

_____

Purpose of the Sole Proprietorship

The purpose of this sole proprietorship is to:_____

_____

In addition, the sole proprietorship may also engage in any lawful business
under the laws of the State of _____ .

Start-up Capital

The start-up capital will be a total of $ _____ . The owner of the company
agrees to dedicate the following property, services, or cash to the use of the
company:

Property/Services/Cash

_____

Accounting Matters

The company will maintain accounting records on the (cash or accrual) basis
and on a calendar year basis.

Bank Account

The business will maintain a business checking bank account at: _____
_____

Insurance

The owner shall buy and maintain life insurance on his or her life in the amount of $ _____ .

The owner shall buy and maintain disability insurance in the amount of $ _____ .

The owner shall buy and maintain business liability insurance on the operations of the business in the amount of $ _____ .

Additional Provisions

The following additional provisions are part of this Plan:

Dated _____

_____
Owner Signature

_____
Printed Name of Owner

Chapter 10

Registration of Sole Proprietorship Name

The choice of a name for a business is an important aspect in the success of the business. Many business owners choose business names that contain their own names, for example: Mary and Bill's Restaurant or Smith and Jones Furniture Refinishing Company. As long as the owners' own names are the main designation of the business name, no registration of the name is generally required. If, however, the owner of a sole proprietorship chooses a name that is fictitious, many states require some type of registration of the assumed name. Examples of fictitious names might be The Landing Restaurant or Imperial Furniture Refinishing Company: names that do not identify the owners of the businesses. The main rationale for such fictitious name registration is to provide a public record of who owns businesses; owners that cannot be identified solely by the business name. This allows for a central registry of some kind, should a third party need to file a lawsuit or claim of some kind against the unidentified owner.

Some states do not require registration but simply allow business owners to register their business names as a method to prevent infringement of others upon the use of a particular name, in the manner of registering the trademark or tradename of a business. The Appendix in the back of this book provides a listing

> **⊘ Definition:**
>
> **Fictitious Name:**
> Any business name—other than one using your own given name—is considered a fictitious name and must be registered as such with either state or local authorities.

of each state's business name registration requirements. Note that some states require registration with state authorities, often the Secretary of State, while other states provide for registration in the county in which the business intends to do business. Note that most states now require the use of their own state mandated forms for name registration. Also note that a few states only provide for name registration via the internet. Finally note that some states provide for name registration as part of a "one-stop" online business registration process.

☀️ Toolkit Tip!

Some states require the publication of a state-ment in local newspapers that provides a notice to the public. Check the Appendix in the back of this book for your state's requirement.

In all states, there are either statutory rules or judge-decided case law that prevent a business from adopting a name that is deceptive to the public. Thus, for example, a business cannot imply that it is owned or operated by a licensed practitioner in a state-regulated profession if such is not, in fact, the case. Nor may a business adopt a name that is deceptively similar to the name of another business.

In many states, there is a method by which to check a registry of business names that are in use. This allows potential conflicts with other business names to be resolved prior to the adoption of a name. In addition, some states provide for the reservation of a business name even before the actual operation of the business has commenced.

Finally, some states require the publication of a statement in local newspapers that provides a notice to the public that a certain business will be operating in a community under an assumed or fictitious name. This allows the public to be notified of the names and addresses of the actual owners of the business. Please carefully check the listing for your state in the Appendix in the back of this book for the requirements that you will need to follow in the registration of your business name. Following is a standard form for registering a business name. Although this form should suffice in most locales, your own state or local authorities may proscribe a mandatory form for such registration. Please check with your particular registration authorities and check the appendix for your state's specific requirements.

Statement of Intention to Conduct Business Under an Assumed or Fictitious Name

The undersigned party does hereby state his/her intention to carry on the business of _____ , at the business location of
_____ , in the City of _____ , in the State
of _____ , under the assumed or fictitious name of:

_____

The owner's name, home address, and percentage of ownership of the
above-named business are as follows:

Name

_____

Address

_____

Percentage of Ownership : 100 percent

Signed on _____ , 20 _____

_____
Business Owner Signature

_____
Business Owner Printed Name

Chapter 11

Employee Documents

The legal forms in this chapter cover a variety of situations that arise in the area of employment. From hiring an employee to subcontracting work on a job, written documents that outline each person's responsibilities and duties are important for keeping an employment situation on an even keel. The employment contract contained in this chapter may be used and adapted for virtually any employment situation. As job skills and salaries rise and employees are allowed access to sensitive and confidential business information, written employment contracts are often a prudent business practice. An independent contractor may also be hired to perform a particular task. As opposed to an employee, this type of worker is defined as one who maintains his or her own independent business, uses his or her own tools, and does not work under the direct supervision of the person who has hired him or her. A contract for hiring an independent contractor is provided in this chapter.

General Employment Contract

This form may be used for any situation in which an employee is hired for a specific job. The issues addressed by this contract are as follows:

- That the employee will perform a certain job and any inci-

dental further duties
- That the employee will be hired for a certain period and for a certain salary
- That the employee will be given certain job benefits (for example: sick pay, vacations, etc.)
- That the employee agrees to abide by the employer's rules and regulations
- That the employee agrees to sign agreements regarding confidentiality and inventions
- That the employee agrees to submit any employment disputes to mediation and arbitration

The information necessary to complete this form is as follows:

- The names and addresses of the employer and employee
- A complete description of the job
- The date the job is to begin and the length of time that the job will last
- The amount of compensation and benefits for the employee (salary, sick pay, vacation, bonuses, and retirement and insurance benefits)
- Any additional documents to be signed
- Any additional terms
- The state whose laws will govern the contract
- Signatures of employer and employee

> **♀ Toolkit Tip!**
> An independent contractor may also be hired to perform a particular task. As opposed to an employee

Independent Contractor Agreement

This form should be used when hiring an independent contractor. It provides a standard form for the hiring out of specific work to be performed within a set time period for a particular payment. It also provides a method for authorizing extra work under the contract. Finally, this document provides that the contractor agrees to indemnify (reimburse or compensate) the owner against any claims or liabilities arising from the performance of the work. To complete this form, fill in a detailed description of the work; dates by which certain portions of the job are to be completed; the pay for the job; the terms and dates of payment; and the state whose laws will govern the contract.

Contractor/Subcontractor Agreement

This form is intended to be used by an independent contractor to hire a subcontractor to perform certain work on a job that the contractor has agreed to perform. It provides for the "farming out" of specific work to be performed by the subcontractor within a set time period for a particular payment. It also provides a method for authorizing extra work under the contract. Finally, this document provides that the subcontractor agrees to indemnify the contractor against any claims or liabilities arising from the performance of the work. To complete this form, fill in a detailed description of the work; dates by which portions of the job are to be completed; the pay for the job; the terms and dates of payment; and the state whose laws will govern the contract.

General Employment Contract

This contract is made on _____ , 20 _____ , between
_____ , employer,
of _____ , City of _____ ,
State of _____ , and _____
_____ , employee, of _____ , City of
_____ , State of _____ .

For valuable consideration, the employer and employee agree as follows:

1. The employee agrees to perform the following duties and job description:

    The employee also agrees to perform further duties incidental to the general
    job description. This is considered a full-time position.

2. The employee will begin work on _____ , 20 _____ .

    This position shall continue for a period of _____ .

3. The employee will be paid the following:

    Weekly salary: $ _____

    The employee will also be given the following benefits:

    Sick pay: $ _____
    Vacations: $ _____
    Bonuses: $ _____
    Retirement benefits: $ _____
    Insurance benefits: $ _____

4. The employee agrees to abide by all rules and regulations of the employer
    at all times while employed.

5. This contract may be terminated by:

(a) Breach of this contract by the employee
(b) The expiration of this contract without renewal
(c) Death of the employee
(d) Incapacitation of the employee for over _____ days in any one (1) year

6. The employee agrees to sign the following additional documents as a condition to obtaining employment:

7. Any dispute between the employer and employee related to this contract will be settled by voluntary mediation. If mediation is unsuccessful, the dispute will be settled by binding arbitration using an arbitrator of the American Arbitration Association.

8. Any additional terms of this contract:

9. No modification of this contract will be effective unless it is in writing and is signed by both the employer and employee. This contract binds and benefits both parties and any successors. Time is of the essence of this contract. This document is the entire agreement between the parties. This contract is governed by the laws of the State of _____ .

Dated: _____ , 20 _____

_____
Signature of Employer

_____
Printed Name of Employer

_____
Signature of Employee

_____
Printed Name of Employee

Independent Contractor Agreement

This agreement is made on _____ , 20 _____ , between _____
_____ , owner, of _____
, City of _____ , State of _____ , and _____
_____ , contractor, of _____
_____ , City of _____ , State of _____ .

For valuable consideration, the owner and contractor agree as follows:

1. The contractor agrees to furnish all of the labor and materials to do the following work for the owner as an independent contractor:

2. The contractor agrees that the following portions of the total work will be completed by the dates specified:

Work:

Dates: _____

3. The contractor agrees to perform this work in a workmanlike manner according to standard practices. If any plans or specifications are part of this job, they are attached to and are part of this agreement.

4. The owner agrees to pay the contractor as full payment $ _____ , for doing the work outlined above. This price will be paid to the contractor on satisfactory completion of the work in the following manner and on the following dates:

Work:

Dates: _____

5. The contractor and the owner may agree to extra services and work, but any such extras must be set out and agreed to in writing by both the contractor and the owner.

6. The contractor agrees to indemnify and hold the owner harmless from any claims or liability arising from the contractor's work under this agreement.

7. No modification of this agreement will be effective unless it is in writing and is signed by both parties. This agreement binds and benefits both parties and any successors. Time is of the essence of this agreement. This document, including any attachments, is the entire agreement between the parties. This agreement is governed by the laws of the State of _____.

Dated: _____ , 20 _____

_____
Signature of Owner

_____
Printed Name of Owner

_____
Signature of Contractor

_____
Printed Name of Contractor

Contractor/Subcontractor Agreement

This agreement is made on_____ , 20_____ , between
_____, contractor, of _____ ,
City of _____State of _____ , and _____ ,
subcontractor, of _____ , City of _____ ,
State of _____ .

1. The subcontractor, as an independent contractor, agrees to furnish all of the labor and materials to do the following portions of the work specified in the agreement between the contractor and the owner dated _____, 20 _____ .

2. The subcontractor agrees that the following portions of the total work will be completed by the dates specified:

   Work:

   Dates: _____

3. The subcontractor agrees to perform this work in a workmanlike manner according to standard practices. If any plans or specifications are part of this job, they are attached to and are part of this agreement.

4. The contractor agrees to pay the subcontractor as full payment $ _____ , for doing the work outlined above. This price will be paid to the subcontractor on satisfactory completion of the work in the following manner and on the following dates:

   Work:

   Dates: _____

5. The contractor and subcontractor may agree to extra services and work, but any such extras must be set out and agreed to in writing by both the contractor and the subcontractor.

6. The subcontractor agrees to indemnify and hold the contractor harmless from any claims or liability arising from the subcontractor's work under this agreement.

7. No modification of this agreement will be effective unless it is in writing and is signed by both parties. This agreement binds and benefits both parties and any successors. Time is of the essence of this agreement. This document, including any attachments, is the entire agreement between the parties. This agreement is governed by the laws of the State of _____ .

Dated: _____ , 20 _____

_____
Signature of Contractor

_____
Printed Name of Contractor

_____
Signature of Subcontractor

_____
Printed Name of Subcontractor

Chapter 12

Business Financial Recordkeeping

Each year, thousands of small businesses fail because their owners have lost control of their finances. Many of these failures are brought on by the inability of the business owners to understand the complex accounting processes and systems that have become relatively standard in modern business. Accounting and bookkeeping have, in most businesses, been removed from the direct control and, therefore, understanding of the business owners themselves. If business owners cannot understand the financial situation of their own businesses, they have little chance of succeeding. The purpose of this book is to present a simplified system of business recordkeeping that small business owners themselves can use to track their company's financial situation.

The purpose of any business financial recordkeeping system is to provide a clear vision of the relative health of the business, both on a day-to-day basis and periodically. Business owners themselves need to know whether they are making a profit, why they are making a profit, which parts of the business are profitable and which are not. This information is only available if the business owner has a clear and straightforward recordkeeping system. Business owners also need to be able to produce accurate financial statements for income tax purposes, for loan proposals, and for the purpose of selling the business. Clear, understandable, and accurate business records are vital to the success of any small business. In order to design a good recordkeeping system for a particular business, an understanding of certain fundamental ideas of accounting is necessary. For those unfamiliar with the terms and concepts of accounting, grasping these basic ideas may be the most difficult part of accounting, even simplified accounting.

Recordkeeping Terminology

First, let's get some of the terminology clarified. *Accounting* is the design of the recordkeeping system that a business uses and the preparation and interpretation of reports based on the information that is gathered and put into the system. *Bookkeeping* is the actual input of the financial information into the recordkeeping system. In this book, these two activities will be combined to allow the small business owner to understand how the records are organized, how to keep the records, and how to prepare and interpret summarized reports of the records.

The purpose of any business recordkeeping system is to allow the business owner to easily understand and use the information gathered. Certain accounting principles and terms have been adopted as standard over the years to make it easier to understand a wide range of business transactions. In order to understand what a recordkeeping system is trying to accomplish, it is necessary to define some of the standard ways of looking at a business. There are two standard reports which are the main sources of business financial information and which will be the focus of this book: the *balance sheet* and the *profit and loss statement*.

The Balance Sheet

The purpose of the balance sheet is to look at what the business owns and owes on a specific date. By seeing what a business owns and owes, anyone looking at a balance sheet can tell the relative financial position of the business at that point in time. If the business owns more than it owes, it is in good shape financially. On the other hand, if it owes more than it owns, the business may be in trouble. The balance sheet is the universal financial document used to view this aspect of a business. It provides this information by laying out the value of the assets and the liabilities of a business. One of the most critical financial tasks that a small business owner must confront is keeping track of what the business owns and owes. Before the business buys or sells anything or makes a profit or loss, the business must have some assets.

The *assets* of a business are anything that the business owns. These can be cash, on hand or in a bank account; they can be personal property, like office equipment, vehicles, tools, or supplies; they can be inventory, or material which will be sold to customers; they can be real estate, buildings and land; and they can be money that is owed to the business. Money that is owed to a business is called its *accounts receivable*, basically the money that the business hopes to eventually receive. The total of all of these things which a business owns are the business's assets.

The *liabilities* of a business are anything that the business owes to others. These consist of long-term debts, such as a mortgage on real estate or a long-term loan. It also consists of any short-term debts, such as money owed for supplies or taxes. Money that a business owes to others is called its *accounts payable*, basically the money which the business hopes to eventually pay. In addition to money owed to others, the *equity* of a business is also considered a liability. The equity of a business is the value of the ownership of the business. It is the value that would be left over if all of the debts of the business were paid off. If it is a partnership or a sole proprietorship, the business equity is referred to a the *net worth* of the business. If the business is a corporation, the owner's equity is called the *capital surplus* or *retained capital*. All of the debts of a business and its equity are together referred to as the business's liabilities.

The basic relationship between the assets and liabilities can be shown in a simple equation:

Assets = Liabilities

This simple equation is the basis of business accounting. When the books of a business are said to *balance*, it is this equation which is in balance: the assets of a business must equal the liabilities of a business. Since the liabilities of a business consists of both equity and debts, the equation can be expanded to read:

Assets = Debts + Equity

Rearranging the equation can provide a simple explanation of how to arrive at the value of a business to the owner, or its equity:

Equity = Assets – Debts

A basic tenet of recordkeeping is that both sides of this financial equation must always be equal. The formal statement of the assets and liabilities of a specific business on a specific date is called a *balance sheet*. A balance sheet is usually prepared on the last day of a month, quarter, or year. A balance sheet simply lists the amounts of the business assets and liabilities in a standardized format.

On a balance sheet, the assets of a business are generally broken down into two groups: *current assets* and *fixed assets*. Current assets consist of cash, accounts receivable (remember, money which the business intends to receive; basically, bills owed to the business); and inventory. Current assets are generally considered anything that could be converted into cash within one year. Fixed assets are more permanent-type assets and include vehicles, equipment, machinery, land, and buildings owned by the business.

The liabilities of a business are broken down into three groups: *current liabilities*, *long-term liabilities*, and *owner's equity*. Current liabilities are short-term debts, generally those that a business must pay off within one year. This includes accounts payable (remember, money that the business intends to pay; basically, bills the business owes), and taxes that are due. Long-term liabilities are long-term debts such as mortgages or long-term business loans. Owner's equity is whatever is left after debts are deducted from assets. Thus the owner's equity is what the owner would have left after all of the debts of the business are paid off. Owner's equity is the figure that is adjusted to make the equation of assets and liabilities balance.

Let's look at a simple example. Later on in the following chapters, we'll look at a more complicated example. But for now let's look at a basic sales business.

Smith's Gourmet Foods has the following assets: Smith has $500.00 in a bank account, is owed $70.00 by customers who pay for their food monthly, has $200.00 worth of food supplies, and owns food preparation equipment worth $1,300.00.

These are the assets of Smith's Gourmet Foods and they are shown on a balance sheet as follows:

Cash	*$500.00*
+ Accounts owed to it	*$70.00*
+ Inventory	*$200.00*
+ Equipment	*$1,300.00*
= Total Assets	*$ 2,070.00*

Smith also has owes the following debts: $100.00 owed to the supplier of the food, $200.00 owed to the person from whom she bought the food equipment, and $100.00 owed to the state for sales taxes that have been collected on food sales. Thus, the debts of Smith's Gourmet Foods are shown as follows:

Accounts it owes	*$100.00*
+ Loans it owes	*$200.00*
+ Taxes it owes	*$ 100.00*
= Total Debts	*$400.00*

To find what Smith's equity in this business is, we need to subtract the amount of the debts from the amount of the assets. Remember: Assets – debts = equity. Thus, the owner's equity in Smith's Gourmet Foods is as follows:

Total Assets	*$2,070.00*
– Total Debts	*$ 400.00*
= Owner's Equity	*$1,670.00*

That's it. The business of Smith's Gourmet Foods has a net worth of $1,670.00. If Smith paid off all of the debts of the business, there would be $1,670.00 left. This basic method is used to determine the net worth of businesses worldwide, from the smallest to the largest. Assets = debts + equity or Assets – debts = equity. Remember, both sides of the equation always have to be equal.

The Profit and Loss Statement

The other main business report is called the *profit and loss statement*. This report is a summary of the income and expenses of the business during a certain period. Profit and loss statements are generally prepared monthly, quarterly, or annually, depending on the type of business. Profit and loss statements are sometimes referred to as *income statements* or as *operating statements*.

Generally, *income* for a business is any money that it has received or will receive during a certain period. *Expenses* are any money that the business has paid or will pay out during a certain period. Simply put, if it has more income than expenses during a certain period, it has made a profit. If it has more expenses than income, then the business has a loss for that period of time.

Income can be broken down into two basic types: service income and sales income. The difference between the two types of income lies in the need to consider inventory costs. Service income is income derived from performing a service for someone (cutting hair, for example). Sales income is revenue derived from selling a product of some type. With service income, the profit can be determined simply by deducting the expenses that are associated with making the income. With sales income, however, in addition to deducting the expenses of making the income, the cost of the product that was sold must also be taken into account. This is done through inventory costs. Thus, for sales income, the actual income from selling a product is actually the sales income minus the cost of the product to the seller. This inventory cost is referred to as the *cost of goods sold*.

A profit and loss statement begins with a sale. Back to the food business. Smith had the following transactions during the month of July: $250.00 worth of food was sold, the wholesale cost of the food that was sold was $50.00, the cost of napkins, condiments, other supplies, and rent amounted to $100.00, and interest payments on the equipment loan were $50.00. Thus, Smith's profit and loss statement would be prepared as follows:

Gross sales income	*$250.00*
– Cost of food	*$ 50.00*
= Net sales income	*$200.00*
Operating expenses	*$100.00*
+ Interest payments	*$ 50.00*
= Net expenses	*$150.00*

Thus, for the month of July, Smith's business performed as follows:

Net sales income	*$200.00*
– Net expenses	*$150.00*
= Net profit	*$50.00*

Again, this simple set-up reflects the basics of profit and loss statements for all types of businesses, no matter their size. For a pure service business, with no inventory of any type sold to customers: Income – expenses = net profit. For a sales-type business or a sales/service-combined business: Income – cost of goods sold – expenses = profit.

These two types of summary reports, the balance sheet and the profit and loss statement are the basic tools for understanding the financial health of any business. The figures on them can be used for many purposes to understand the operations of a business. The balance sheet shows what proportion of a business's assets are actually owned by the business owner and what proportion is owned by or owed to someone else.

Looking at Smith's balance sheet, we can see that the owner's equity is $1,670.00 of assets of $2,070.00. Thus, we can see that the owner has over 80 percent ownership of the business, a very healthy situation. There are numerous ways to analyze the figures on these two financial statements. Understanding what these figures mean and how they represent the health of a business are keys to keeping control of a business's finances.

Accounting Methods

There are a few more items that must be understood regarding financial recordkeeping. First is the method for recording the records. There are two basic methods for measuring transactions: the *cash method* and the *accrual method*. Cash method accounting is a system that records income when it is received and records expenses when they are paid. Beginning in 2000, IRS regulations allow the cash method of accounting for a business with a gross annual revenue of less than $1 million for the previous three tax years (or less if the business has been operating for fewer years). (If you have been an "accrual" taxpayer, you must file IRS Form 3115: *Application for Change in Accounting Period* to change your accounting method.) Thus the IRS now allows the cash method of accounting for most small businesses. However, if your business has inventory, it is still wise to use the accrual method in order to accurately track your inventory.

The accrual method of accounting counts income and expenses when they are due to the business. Income is recorded when the business has a right to receive the income. In other words, accounts receivable (bills owed to the business) are considered as income that has already been received by the business. Expenses are considered and recorded when they are due, even if they are not yet paid. In other words, accounts payable (bills owed by the business) are considered expenses to the business when they are received, not when they are actually paid. The recordkeeping system in this book provides a simplified method of keeping accrual-method books.

Accounting Systems

In addition, there are two basic types of recordkeeping systems: *single-entry* or *double-entry*. Both types can be used to keep accurate records, although the double-entry system has more ways available to double-check calculations. Double-entry recordkeeping is, however, much more difficult to master, in that each and every transaction must be entered in two separate places in the records. The system that is used in this book is a modified form of single-entry accounting. The benefits of ease of use of a single-entry system far outweigh the disadvantages of this system. The Internal Revenue Service recommends single-entry records for beginning small businesses, and states that this type of system can be "relatively simple...used effectively...and is adequate for income tax purposes." Many accountants will disagree with this and insist that only double-entry accounting is acceptable. For the small business owner who wishes to understand his or her own company's finances, the advantages of single-entry accounting far outweigh the disadvantages.

Accounting Periods

A final item to consider is the accounting period for your business. A business is allowed to choose between a *fiscal year* accounting period and a *calendar year* period. A fiscal year consists of 12 consecutive months that *do not* end on December

31st. A calendar year consists of 12 consecutive months that *do* end on December 31st. There are complex rules relating to the choice of fiscal year accounting. If a sole-proprietorship reports income on a fiscal year, then all non-business income must also be reported on the same fiscal year. This most often unnecessarily complicates tax reporting and should generally be avoided. Partnerships and S-corporations may generally only choose to report on a fiscal year basis if there is a valid business purpose that supports the use of a fiscal year. This, again, generally, complicates the reporting of income and should be avoided unless there is an important reason to choose a fiscal year accounting period. If a fiscal year period is considered necessary, please consult a tax or accounting professional as there are complicated rules to comply with.

For the majority of small businesses, the choice of a calendar year period is perfectly adequate and, in most cases, will simplify the tax reporting and accounting recordkeeping. In the year in which a business is either started or ended, the business year for reporting may not be a full year. Thus, even for those who choose to use a calendar year, the first year may actually start on a date other than January 1st.

Recordkeeping Review

The purpose of a business financial recordkeeping system is to provide a method for the owner to keep track of the ongoing health of the business. This is done primarily by providing the owner with information on two basic financial statements. The balance sheet provides the business owner with a quick look at the assets and debts of the business and at the equity or ownership value of the business. The profit and loss statement furnishes the owner with an immediate view of the current flow of income and expenses of the business.

The business recordkeeping system that is provided in this book will detail how to set up the books for a small business. The method of reporting for this system is the accrual method. The type of system used is a single-entry system of accounting. The time period used for the system is a calendar year.

Accounting Software

The CD which accompanies this book contains computer-fillable PDF-format versions of the forms that are included in this book. They can be filled in on any computer or they may be printed out and filled in by hand. These forms do *not* comprise an integrated accounting software program. They are meant to be used by small business owners that have little or no knowledge of accounting practices. There are many fine accounting software programs on the market that may be used for small business accounting when you have acquired sufficient knowledge to use them.

Quickbooks is the most widely-used accounting software and is a full-featured fully-integrated accounting software program. As such, it does take a working knowledge of small business accounting to set up and use correctly. *Peachtree Accounting* also produces a fine full-featured accounting software program. Microsoft recently discontinued its production of its small business accounting software. There are also dozens of other accounting software programs on the market that range from very simple glorified checkbook registers to very high-level advanced accounting software.

In using any of these software products, however, an good understanding of the fundamentals of bookkeeping and accounting are necessary for their use. This book is designed to provide its readers with a working understanding of an accrual single-entry accounting system, one of the simplest small business accounting methods available to the novice business owner. Once you feel comfortable with the terms and methods that are used in this system of accounting, and if you are relatively comfortable navigating complex computer programs, you may wish to move on to a full-featured integrated accounting software program.

Simplified Accounting System

The simplified small business accounting system that is provided in this book is a modified single-entry accounting system. It is presented as a system for accrual-basis accounting for small businesses. The records are designed to be used on a calendar-year basis. Within these basic parameters, the system can be individually tailored to meet the needs of most small businesses. In Chapter 13, how to actually set up and operate the financial recordkeeping system will be explained. Clear schedules of tasks will be outlined for your use as you work with the forms. The preparation of your payroll will be covered Chapter 14. And federal tax forms for Sole Proprietorships will be covered in the last Chapter 15. Following is a checklist for setting up your business financial recordkeeping using this book:

Financial Recordkeeping Checklist

❏ Set up your business chart of accounts

❏ Open a business checking account

❏ Prepare a check register

❏ Set up a business petty cash fund

❏ Prepare a petty cash box

❏ Set up asset accounts

❏ Prepare current asset account records

❏ Prepare fixed asset account records

❏ Set up expense account records

❏ Set up income account records

❏ Set up payroll system

❏ Prepare payroll time sheets

❏ Prepare payroll depository records

❏ Determine proper tax forms for use in the business

Chapter 13

Business Accounts

The financial recordkeeping system that you will set up using this book is designed to be adaptable to any type of business. Whether your business is a service business, a manufacturing business, a retail business, a wholesale distributorship, or combination of any of these, you will be able to easily adapt this simplified system to work with your particular situation. A key to designing the most useful recordkeeping system for your particular needs is to examine your type of business in depth. After a close examination of the particular needs and operations of your type of business, you will need to set up an array of specific accounts to handle your financial records. This set of general accounts is called a chart of accounts.

A chart of accounts will list all of the various categories of financial transactions which you will need to track. There will be an account for each general type of expense which you want to keep track of. You will also have separate accounts for each type of income your business will receive. Accounts will also be set up for your business assets and liabilities. Setting up an account for each of these categories consists of the simple task of deciding which items you will need to categorize, selecting a name for the account, and assigning a number for the account.

Before you can set up your accounts, you need to understand the reason for setting up these separate accounts. It is possible, although definitely not recommended, to run a business and merely keep track of your income and expenses without any itemization at all. However, you would be unable to analyze how the business is performing beyond a simple check to see if you have any money left after paying the expenses. You would also be unable to properly fill in the necessary information for business income tax returns.

A major reason for setting up separate accounts for many business's expense and income transactions is to separate and itemize the amounts spent in each category so that this information is available at tax time. This insures that a business is taking all of its allowable business deductions. The main reason, however, to set up individual accounts is to allow the business owner to have a clear view of the financial health of the business. With separate accounts for each type of transaction, a business owner can analyze the proportional costs and revenues of each aspect of the business. Is advertising costing more than labor expenses? Is the income derived from sales items worth the discounts of the sale? Only by using the figures obtained from separate itemized accounts can these questions be answered.

In the following sections, you will select and number the various accounts for use in your business chart of accounts. You will select various income accounts, expense accounts, asset accounts, and liability accounts. For each account, you will also assign it a number. For ease of use, you should assign a particular number value to all accounts of one type. For example, all income accounts may be assigned numbers 10–29. Sales income may be account number 11; service income may be assigned account number 12, interest income may be account number 13. Similarly, expenses may be assigned numbers 30–79. Balance sheet accounts for assets and liabilities may be numbers 80–99. Be sure to leave enough numbers for future expansion of your list of accounts. There will normally be far more expense accounts than any other type of account.

If you have income or expenses from many sources, you may wish to use three-digit numbers to identify each separate category. For example, if your business consists of renting out residential houses and you have 10 properties, you may wish to set up a separate income and expense account for each property. You may wish to assign accounts numbers 110–119 to income from all properties. Thus, for example, you could then assign rental income from property number 1 to account number 111, rental income from property number 2 to account number 112, rental income from property number 3 to account number 113 and so on. Similarly, expenses can be broken down into separate accounts for individual properties. Advertising expenses might all be account numbers 510–519, thus advertising expenses for property number 1 might then be assigned number 511, advertising expenses for property number 2 would be assigned account number 512, etc.

How your individual chart of accounts will be organized will be specific to your particular business. If you have a simple business with all income coming from one source, you will probably desire a two-digit number from, perhaps, 10–29 assigned to that income account. On the other hand a more complex business with many sources of income and many different types of expenses may wish to use a system of three-digit numbers. Take some time to analyze your specific business to decide how you wish to set up your accounts. Ask yourself what type of information will you want to extract from your financial records. Do you need more details of your income sources? Then you should set up several income accounts for each type and possibly even each source of your income. Would you like more specific information on your expenses? Then you would most likely wish to set up clear and detailed expense accounts for each type of expense that you must pay.

Be aware that you may wish to alter your chart of accounts as your business grows. You may find that you have set up too many accounts and unnecessarily complicated your recordkeeping tasks. You may wish to set up more accounts once you see how your balance sheets and profit and loss statements look. You may change, add, or delete accounts at any time. Remember, however, that any transactions that have been recorded in an account must be transferred to any new account or accounts that take the place of the old account.

Income Accounts

These are accounts that are used to track the various sources of your company's income. There may be only a few sources of income for your business, or you may wish to track your income in more detail. The information which you collect in your income accounts will be used to prepare your profit and loss statements periodically. Recall that a profit and loss statement is also referred to as an income and expense statement.

On the chart of accounts that is used in this book, income is separated into several categories. You can choose the income account categories which best suit your type of business. If your business is a service business, you may wish to set up accounts for labor income and for materials income. Or you may wish to set up income accounts in more detail, for example: sales income, markup income, income from separate properties, or income from separate sources in your business, etc. Non-sales income such as bank account interest income or income on the sale of business equipment should be placed in separate individual income accounts. You may also wish to set up separate income accounts for income from different ongoing projects or income from separate portions of your business.

Following is a list of various general income accounts. Decide how much detail you will want in your financial records regarding income and then choose the appropriate accounts. You may wish to name and create different accounts than are listed here. After you have chosen your income accounts, assign a number to each account.

Income Chart of Accounts

Account #	Account Name and Description
	Income from sale of goods
	Income from services
	Income from labor charges
	Income from sales discounts
	Income from interest revenue
	Income from consulting
	Miscellaneous income

Expense Accounts

These are the accounts that you will use to keep track of your expenses. Each separate category of expense should have its own account. Many of the types of accounts are dictated by the types of expenses which should be itemized for tax purposes. You will generally have separate accounts for advertising costs, utility expenses, rent, phone costs, etc. One or more separate accounts should also be set up to keep track of inventory expenses. These should be kept separate from other expense accounts as they must be itemized for tax purposes.

Following is a list of various general expense accounts. Please analyze your business and determine which accounts would be best suited to select for your particular situation. You will then number these accounts, as you did the income accounts. The categories presented are general categories which match most IRS forms. You may, of course, set up separate accounts which are not listed to suit your particular needs. Try not to set up too many accounts or you will have a hard time trying to remember all of them. Also note that you may add or delete accounts as you need them. If you delete an account, however, you must shift any transactions that you have recorded in that account to the new account.

Expense Chart of Accounts

Account #	Account Name and Description
	Advertising expenses
	Auto expenses
	Cleaning and maintenance expenses
	Charitable contributions
	Dues and publications
	Office equipment expenses
	Freight and shipping expenses
	Business insurance expenses
	Business interest expenses
	Legal expenses
	Business meals and lodging
	Miscellaneous expenses
	Postage expenses
	Office rent expenses
	Repair expenses
	Office supplies
	Sales taxes paid
	Federal unemployment taxes paid
	State unemployment taxes paid
	Telephone expenses
	Utility expenses
	Wages and commissions

Asset and Liability Accounts

Asset and liability accounts are collectively referred to as *balance sheet accounts*. This is because the information collected on them is used to prepare your business balance sheets. You will set up current and fixed asset accounts and current and long-term liability accounts. Types of current asset accounts are cash, short-term notes receivable, accounts receivable, inventory, and pre-paid expenses. Fixed assets may include equipment, vehicles, buildings, land, long-term notes receivable, and long-term loans receivable.

Types of current liability accounts are short-term notes payable (money due within one year), short-term loans payable (money due on loan within one year), unpaid taxes, and unpaid wages. Long-term liability accounts may be long-term notes payable (money due over one year) or long-term loans payable (money due over one year). Finally, you will need an owner's equity account to tally the ownership value of your business.

Choose the asset and liability accounts which best suit your business and assign appropriate numbers to each account.

Balance Sheet Chart of Accounts

Account #	Account Name and Description
	Accounts receivable (current asset)
	Bank checking account (current asset)
	Bank savings account (current asset)
	Cash on hand (current asset)
	Notes receivable (current asset, if short-term)
	Loans receivable (current asset, if short-term)
	Inventory (current asset)
	Land (fixed asset)
	Buildings (fixed asset)
	Vehicles (fixed asset)
	Equipment (fixed asset)
	Machinery (fixed asset)
	Accounts payable (current debt)
	Notes payable (current, if due within 1 year)
	Loans payable (current, if due within 1 year)
	Notes payable (long-term debt, if over 1 year)
	Loans payable (long-term debt, if over 1 year)
	Mortgage payable (long-term debt, if over 1 year)
	Retained capital

Sample Chart of Accounts

After you have selected and numbered each of your accounts, you should prepare your chart of accounts. Simply type the number and name of each account in a numerical list. You will refer to this chart often as you prepare your financial records. Following is a sample completed chart of accounts.

This sample chart is set up to reflect the business operations of our sample company: Smith's Gourmet Foods. This is a sole proprietorship company which prepares and packages food products and delivers the products directly to consumers in their homes.

The chart reflects that the income will primarily come from one source: direct customer payments for the products which are sold. The expense accounts are chosen to cover most of the standard types of business expenses which a small business will encounter. The balance sheet accounts reflect that the business will only have as assets a bank account, some accounts receivable, inventory, and some equipment. The only liabilities that this business will have, at least initially, will be a loan for equipment and accounts payable.

Although this sample chart of accounts is fairly brief, it covers all of the basic accounts which the business will need as it begins. There is sufficient room in the numbering system chosen to add additional accounts as the business expands.

Sample Chart of Accounts

Account #	Account Name and Description
11	Income from sale of goods
12	Miscellaneous income
31	Advertising expenses
32	Auto expenses
33	Cleaning and maintenance expenses
34	Office equipment expenses
35	Business insurance expenses
36	Business meals and lodging
37	Miscellaneous expenses
38	Postage expenses
39	Repair expenses
40	Office supplies
41	Sales taxes paid
42	Telephone expenses
43	Office rent expense
51	Cash on hand (current asset)
52	Accounts receivable (current asset)
53	Bank checking account (current asset)
54	Inventory (current asset)
61	Equipment (fixed asset)
71	Accounts payable (current debt)
81	Loans payable (long-term debt)
91	Retained capital

Current Assets

After setting up a chart of accounts, you will need to open a bank account for your corporation. Then, the next financial recordkeeping task for a business will consist of preparing a method to keep track of the assets of the business. Recall that the assets of a business are everything that is owned by the business. They are either current assets that can be converted to cash within a year or fixed assets that are more long-term in nature. Each of these two main categories of assets will be discussed separately.

Following is a list of typical current assets for a business:

- Business bank checking account
- Business bank savings account
- Cash (petty cash fund and cash on hand)
- Accounts receivable (money owed to the company)
- Inventory

A company may have other types of current assets such as notes or loans receivable, but the five listed above are the basic ones for most small businesses. In complex double-entry accounting systems, the current asset account balances are constantly being changed. In a double-entry system, each time an item of inventory is sold, for example, the account balance for the inventory account must be adjusted to reflect the sale. In the type of single-entry system that is presented in this book, all asset and liability accounts are only updated when the business owner wishes to prepare a balance sheet. This may be done monthly, quarterly, or annually. At a minimum, this updating must take place at the end of the year in order to have the necessary figures available for tax purposes. The forms and instructions in this book provide a simple method for tracking and updating the required information for business assets and liabilities.

The main form for tracking your current business assets will be a Current Asset Account Record. A copy of this form follows this discussion. On this form, you will periodically track of the value of the current asset that you are following, except for your inventory. (For inventory, you will use specialized inventory records.) You should prepare a separate Current Asset Account Record for each asset. For example, if your current assets consist of a business checking account, cash on hand, and accounts receivable, you will have three separate Current Asset Accounts, one for each category of asset. These forms are very simple to use. Follow the instructions below:

① Simply fill in the Account Number for the Current Asset Account for which you are setting up the form. You will get this number from your Chart of Accounts. Also, fill in a description of the account. For example: Account Number 53: Business Banking Account.

② You must then decide how often you will be preparing a balance sheet and updating your balance sheet account balances. If you wish to keep close track of your finances, you may wish to do this on a monthly basis. For many businesses, a quarterly balance sheet may be sufficient. All businesses, no matter how small, must prepare a balance sheet at least annually, at the end of the year. Decide how often you wish to update the balances and enter the period in the space provided.

③ Next enter the date that you open the account. Under description, enter "Opening Balance." Under the "Balance" column, enter the opening value. The amount to enter for an opening balance will be as follows:
- For a bank account, this will be the opening balance of the account
- For cash on hand, this will be the opening balance of the petty cash fund and cash on hand for sales, such as the cash used in a cash register
- For accounts receivable, this will be the total amount due from all accounts

④ Periodically, you will enter a date and new balance. You will enter these new balances from the following sources:
- For bank accounts, this figure will come from your Check Register balance column on a particular date
- For cash, this new figure will come from your petty cash box balance and your Monthly Cash Summary on a certain date
- For accounts receivable, the balance will come from your Monthly Credit Sales Aging Report

⑤ After you have entered the balances on the appropriate Current Asset Account Record, you will transfer the balances to your Balance Sheet.

Current Asset Account

Account #:
Account Name: Period:

Date	Description of Asset	Balance

Inventory

Any business which sells an item of merchandise to a customer must have a system in place to keep track of inventory. *Inventory* is considered any merchandise or materials which are held for sale during the normal course of your business. Inventory costs include the costs of the merchandise or products themselves and the costs of the materials and paid labor which goes into creating a finished product. Inventory does not include the costs of the equipment or machinery that you need to create the finished product.

There are several reasons you will need a system of inventory control. First, if you are stocking parts or supplies to sell, you will need to keep track of what you have ordered, what is in stock, and when you will need to reorder. You will also need to keep track of the cost of your inventory for tax purposes. The amount of money which you spend on your inventory is not immediately deductible in the year spent as a business deduction. The only portion of your inventory costs which will reduce your gross profit for tax purposes is the actual cost of the goods which you have sold during the tax year.

The basic method for keeping track of inventory costs for tax purposes is to determine the cost of goods sold. First, you will need to know how much inventory is on hand at the beginning of the year. To this amount, you add the cost of any additional inventory you purchased during the year. Finally, you determine how much inventory is left at the end of the year. The difference is essentially the cost (to you) of the inventory which you sold during the year. This amount is referred to as the *Cost of Goods Sold.* Every year at tax time, you will need to figure the Cost of Goods Sold. Additionally, you may need to determine your Cost of Goods Sold monthly or quarterly for various business purposes.

Four inventory control records are provided for use in tracking inventory costs: Physical Inventory Record, Periodic Inventory Record, Perpetual Inventory Record, and Cost of Goods Sold Record.

Using our sample company, Smith Gourmet Foods, we will start her first year in business with an inventory of $0.00. When her business begins, there is no inventory. During the first year, she purchases $17,500.00 worth of products which are for selling to customers. At the end of the year, she counts all of the items which are left in her possession and determines her cost for these items. The cost of the items left unsold at the end of the year is $3,700.00.

The calculation of the Cost of Goods Sold for the first year in business is as follows:

Inventory at beginning of first year	*$ 00.00*
+ Plus cost of inventory added during year	*$ 17,500.00*
= Equals cost of inventory	*$ 17,500.00*
– Less inventory at end of first year	*$ 3,700.00*
= Equals cost of goods sold for first year	*$ 13,800.00*

For the second year in business, the figure for the inventory at the beginning of the year is the value of the inventory at the end of the previous year. Thus, if Smith Gourmet Foods added $25,000.00 additional inventory during the second year of operation and the value of the inventory at the end of the second year was $4,800.00, the cost-of-goods-sold calculations for the second year would be as follows:

Inventory at beginning of second year	*$ 3,700.00*
+ Plus cost of inventory added during year	*$ 25,000.00*
= Equals cost of inventory	*$ 28,700.00*
– Less inventory at end of second year	*$ 4,800.00*
= Equals cost of goods sold for second year	*$ 23,900.00*

Thus for the second year in operation the cost of goods sold would be $23,900.00. This amount would be deducted from the gross revenues that Smith's Gourmet Foods took in for the year to determine the gross profit for the second year in business.

Physical Inventory Report

This form should be used to record the results of an actual physical counting of the inventory at the end of the year and at whatever other times during the year you decide to take a physical inventory. If you decide that you will need to track your inventory monthly or quarterly, you may need to prepare this form for those time periods. To prepare this form, take the following steps:

① The quantity and description of each item of inventory should be listed, along with an item number if applicable.

② The cost (to you) of each item should be then listed under "Unit Price." A total per item cost is then calculated by multiplying the quantity of units times the unit price. This total per item cost should be listed in the far right-hand column. You will need to extract this per item unit price from your Periodic or Perpetual Inventory forms (explained next).

③ The total inventory cost should be figured by adding all the figures in the far right-hand column. The form should be dated and signed by the person doing the inventory.

Physical Inventory Report

Date: Taken by:

Quantity	Description	Item #	Unit Price	Total
			TOTAL	

Periodic Inventory Record

This is the form which you will use to keep continual track of your inventory if you have a relatively small inventory. If you have an extensive inventory, you will need to use the Perpetual Inventory Record which is supplied next. You will use the Periodic Inventory form for the purposes of keeping track of the costs of your inventory and of any orders of additional inventory. You will refer to this report when you need to order additional inventory, when you need to determine when an order should be received, and when you need to determine the cost of your inventory items at the end of the year, or other times, if desired.

① Prepare a separate Periodic Inventory Record for each item of inventory. Identify the type of item that is being tracked by description and by item number, if applicable. You may also wish to list the supplier of the item.

② The first entry on the Periodic Inventory Record should be the initial purchase of inventory. On the right-hand side of the record, list the following items:
- ✦ Date purchased
- ✦ Quantity purchased
- ✦ Price per item
- ✦ Total price paid
- ✦ *Note:* Shipping charges should not be included in the prices entered. Only the actual costs of the goods should be listed

③ When you are running low on a particular item and place an order, on the left-hand side of the record enter the following information:
- ✦ Date of the order
- ✦ Order number
- ✦ Quantity ordered
- ✦ Date the order is due to arrive

④ When the order arrives, enter the actual details about the order on the right-hand side of the page. This will allow you to keep track of your order of inventory items and also allow you to keep track of the cost of your items of inventory.

Periodic Inventory Record

Item: Item #:
Supplier:

INVENTORY ORDERED			
Date	Order #	Quantity	Due

INVENTORY RECEIVED			
Date	Quantity	Price	Total

Perpetual Inventory Record

This is the form that you will use to keep continual track of your inventory if you have a relatively extensive inventory. You will refer to this record when you need to order additional inventory, determine when an order should be received, and determine the cost of your inventory items at the end of the year. Additionally, on this form you will keep track of the number of items of each type of inventory that have been sold.

① Prepare a separate Perpetual Inventory Record for each item of inventory. Identify the type of item which is being tracked by description and by item number, if applicable. You may also wish to list the supplier for the item.

② The first entry on the Perpetual Inventory Record should be the initial purchase of inventory. On the lower left-hand side of the record, under "Inventory Received," list the following information:
   ◆ Date purchased
   ◆ Quantity purchased
   ◆ Price per item
   ◆ Total price paid
   ◆ *Note*: Shipping charges should not be included in the amounts entered

③ When you are running low on a particular item and place an order, enter the following information on the upper left-hand side of the record:
   ◆ Date of the order
   ◆ Order number
   ◆ Quantity ordered
   ◆ Date the ordered inventory is due

④ When the order arrives, enter the actual details on the lower left-hand side of the page, under "Inventory Received."

⑤ On the right-hand side of the record, keep a running total of the number of items of inventory sold. Decide how often you will be checking your stocks to update your inventory counts and stick to the schedule: weekly, monthly, or quarterly. Enter the number of items sold at each count and figure the totals. This will give you a running total of the amount of inventory you have in stock at any given time. You will, however, still need to take a physical inventory count at the end of the year (or more often) to check for lost, stolen, miscounted, or missing items, and as a check against your calculations.

Perpetual Inventory Record

Item: Item #:
Supplier:

INVENTORY ORDERED

Date	Order #	Quantity	Due

INVENTORY RECEIVED

Date	Order #	Quantity	Due

INVENTORY IN STOCK

Date	Quantity	Price	Total

Cost of Goods Sold Record

The final record for inventory control is the *Cost of Goods Sold Record*. It is on this record that you will determine the actual cost to your business of the goods which were sold during a particular time period. There are numerous methods to determine the value of your inventory at the end of a time period. The three most important are the Specific Identification method, the First-In First-Out method (called FIFO), and the Last-In First-Out method (called LIFO).

Specific Identification is the easiest to use if you have only a few items of inventory, or one-of-a-kind types of merchandise. With this method, you actually keep track of each specific item of inventory. You keep track of when you obtained the item, its cost, and when you sold the specific item.

With the FIFO method, you keep track only of general quantities of your inventory. Your inventory costs are calculated as though the oldest inventory merchandise was sold first: the first items that you purchased are the first items that you sell.

With the LIFO method, the cost values are calculated as though you sell your most-recently purchased inventory first. It is important to note that you do not necessarily have to actually sell your first item first to use the FIFO method and you do not have to actually sell your last item first to use the LIFO method of calculation.

Although there may be significant advantages in some cases to using the LIFO method, it is also a far more complicated system than the FIFO. The Specific Identification method allows you to simply track each item of inventory and deduct the actual cost of the goods which you sold during the year. The FIFO method allows you to value your inventory on hand at the end of a time period based on the cost of your most recent purchases. Using either your Periodic or Perpetual Inventory Records, valuing your inventory is a simple matter.

① At the end of your chosen time period (monthly, quarterly, or annually), take an actual physical inventory count on your Physical Inventory Record.

② Using the most recent purchases as listed on your Periodic or Perpetual Inventory Record, determine the unit price of the items left in your inventory and enter this under the Unit Price column on your Physical Inventory Record.

③ Once all of your items of inventory have been checked, counted, and a unit price determined, simply total each item and then total the value of the entire inventory. If you are conducting your final annual inventory, this final figure is your Inventory Value at year's end.

④ On the Cost of Goods Sold Record, enter this number on the line titled "Inventory Value at End of Period." If this is your first year in business, enter zero as the Inventory Value at Beginning of Period. For later periods, the Inventory Value at Beginning of Period will be the Inventory Value at End of Period for the previous period.

⑤ Using either your Periodic Inventory or your Perpetual Inventory Record sheets, total the amounts of orders during the period which are listed under the Inventory Received column. This total will be entered on the Inventory Added During Period line. Now simply perform the calculations. You will use the figures on this sheet at tax time to prepare your taxes.

NOTE: This type of inventory calculation is not intended for manufacturing companies that manufacture finished goods from raw materials or for those with gross annual receipts over $10 million. For those type of companies, an additional calculation is necessary because of uniform capitalization rules. This tax rule requires that manufacturing inventory values include the overhead associated with the manufacturing process. Please consult an accounting professional if you fall into this category of business.

Cost of Goods Sold

Period Ending:

Inventory Value at Beginning of Period	
+ Inventory Added during Period	
= Total Inventory Value	
− Inventory Value at End of Period	
= Cost of Goods Sold	

Beginning Inventory Value for Next Period
(Take from Inventory Value at End of This Period)

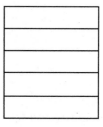

Fixed Assets

The final category of assets which you will need to track are your fixed assets. Fixed assets are the more permanent assets of your business: generally the assets which are not for sale to customers. The main categories of these fixed assets are:

- Buildings
- Land
- Machinery
- Tools
- Furniture and equipment
- Vehicles

There are many more types of fixed assets such as patents, copyrights, and goodwill. However, the six listed above are the basic ones for most small businesses. If your business includes other types of fixed assets, please consult an accounting professional. For those with basic fixed assets, you will need to keep track of the actual total costs to you to acquire them. These costs include sales taxes, transportation charges, installation costs, etc. The total cost of a fixed asset to you is referred to as the asset's *cost basis*. With a major exception explained below, the cost of fixed assets are, generally, not immediately deductible as a business expense. Rather, except for the cost of land, their costs are deductible proportionately over a period of time. This proportionate deduction is referred to as *depreciation*. Since these assets generally wear out over time (except for land), each year you are allowed to deduct a portion of the initial cost as a legitimate business expense. Each type of fixed asset is given a specific time period for dividing up the cost into proportional amounts. This time period is called the *recovery period* of the asset. Depreciation is a very complex subject and one whose rules change nearly every year. The full details of depreciation are beyond the scope of this book. What follows is a general outline of depreciation rules only. It will allow you to begin to set up your fixed asset account records. However, you will need to either consult an accounting or tax professional, or consult specific tax preparation manuals for details on how your specific assets should be depreciated.

The major exception to depreciation rules is that, under the rules of IRS Code Section 179, every year a total of $125,000.00 (Note: This amount has been subject to change many times in recent years. For example, for tax years 2009 and 2010, this amount was temporarily raised to $250,000.00 as part of the overall business stimulus legislation. Check with a tax professional for the current amounts)) of your fixed asset costs can be immediately used as a business deduction. This means that if your total purchases of equipment, tools, vehicles, etc. during a year amounted to less than $125,000.00, you can deduct all of the costs as current expenses. If your total fixed asset costs are over $125,000.00 (but not greater than $500,000.00), you can still deduct the first $125,000.00 in costs and then depreciate the remaining costs over time. Here are some basic rules relating to depreciation:

① The depreciation rules which were in effect at the time of the purchase of the asset will be the rules which apply to that particular asset.

② The actual cost to you of the asset is the cost basis that you use to compute your depreciation amount each year.

③ Used assets which you purchase for use in your business can be depreciated in the same manner as new assets.

④ Assets which you owned prior to going into business and which you will use in your business can be depreciated. The cost basis will be the lower of their actual market value when you begin to use them in your business or their actual cost to you. For example, you start a carpentry business and use your personal power saw in the business. It cost $150.00 new, but is now worth about $90.00. You can depreciate $90.00 (or deduct this amount as an expense if the total of your fixed asset deductions is under $125,000.00).

⑤ You may depreciate proportionately those assets which you use partially for business and partially for personal use. In the above example, if you use your saw 70 percent of the time in your business and 30 percent for personal use, you may deduct or depreciate 70 percent of $90.00, or $63.00.

The tax depreciation rules set up several categories of asset types for the purpose of deciding how long a period you must use to depreciate the asset. Cars, trucks, computer equipment, copiers, and similar equipment are referred to as five-year property. Most machinery, equipment, and office furniture is referred to as seven-year property. This means that for these types of property the actual costs are spread out and depreciated over five or seven years; that is, the costs are deducted over a period of five or seven years.

There are also several different ways to compute how much of the cost can be depreciated each year. There are three basic methods: Straight Line, MACRS, and ACRS. Straight line depreciation spreads the deductible amount equally over the recovery period. Thus, for the power saw which is worth $90.00 and is used 70 percent of the time in a business, the cost basis which can be depreciated is $63.00. This asset has a recovery period of seven years. Spreading the $63.00 over the seven-year period allows you to deduct a total of $9.00 per year as depreciation of the saw. After the first year, the saw will be valued on your books at $54.00. Thus, after seven years, the value of the saw on your books will be $0.00. It will have been fully depreciated. You will have finally been allowed to fully deduct its cost as a business expense. Of course, if you have fixed asset costs of less than $125,000.00 for the year you put the saw in service, you will be allowed to claim the entire $63.00 deduction that first year. Other methods of depreciation have more complicated rules which must be applied. For full details, please refer to a tax preparation manual or consult a tax or accounting professional.

Below are listed various types of property which are depreciable or deductible. Consult this list to determine which of your business purchases may be depreciated and which of them may be written off as an immediately deductible expense. Also, don't forget the special IRS Section 179 deduction.

DEDUCTIBLE EXPENSES

Advertising
Bad debts
Bank charges
Books and periodicals
Car and truck expenses:
    Gas, repairs, licenses,
      insurance, maintenance
Commissions to salespersons
Independent contractor costs
Donations
Dues to professional groups
Educational expenses
Entertainment of clients
Freight costs
Improvements worth less than $100
Insurance
Interest costs
Laundry and cleaning
Licenses for business
Legal and professional fees

Maintenance
Office equipment worth less than $100
Office furniture worth less than $100
Office supplies
Pension plans
Postage
Printing costs
Property taxes
Rent
Repairs
Refunds, returns, and allowances
Sales taxes collected
Sales taxes paid on purchases
Telephone
Tools worth less than $100
Uniforms
Utilities
Wages paid

DEPRECIABLE PROPERTY

Business buildings (not land)
Office furniture worth over $100
Office equipment worth over $100

Business machinery
Tools worth over $100
Vehicles used in business

Fixed Asset Account Record

Recall that fixed assets are business purchases which are depreciable, unless you elect to deduct fixed asset expenses up to $125,000.00 per year. For recordkeeping purposes, you will prepare a Fixed Asset Account Record for each fixed asset which you have if you have acquired over $125,000.00 in a calendar year. If you have acquired less than $125,000.00 worth in a year, you may put all of your fixed asset records on one Fixed Asset Account Record sheet.

To prepare your Fixed Asset Account Record sheet, follow the following instructions:

① List the date on which you acquired the property. If the property was formerly personal property, list the date on which you converted it to business property.

② Then list the property by description. Enter the actual cost of the property. If the property is used, enter the lower amount of the cost of the property or the actual market value of the property. If the property is part business and part personal, enter the value of the business portion of the property.

③ If you will have more than $125,000.00 worth of depreciable business property during the year, additionally you will need to enter information in the last three columns on the record. First, you will need to enter the recovery period for each asset. For most property other than buildings, this will be either five or seven years. Please consult a tax manual or tax professional.

④ You will need to enter the method of depreciation. Again, check a tax manual or with a tax professional.

⑤ Finally, you will need to determine the amount of the deduction for the first year (*Hint:* tax manual or tax professional).

⑥ Once you have set up a method for each fixed asset, each year you will determine the additional deduction and update the balance. You will then use that figure on your business tax return and in the preparation of your Balance Sheet

Fixed Asset Account

Date	Item	Cost	Years	Method	Annual	Balance

Tracking Business Debts

Business debts are also referred to as business liabilities. However, technically, business liabilities also includes the value of the owner's equity in the business.

Business debts can be divided into two general categories. First are current debts, those which will normally be paid within one year. The second general category is long-term debts. These are generally more long-term debts or those that will not be paid off within one year.

Current debts for most small businesses consist primarily of accounts payable and taxes which are due during the year. For small businesses, the taxes which are due during a year fall into three main categories: estimated income tax payments, payment of collected sales taxes, and payroll taxes. Estimated income tax payments will be discussed in Chapter 15 when we look more closely at taxes. Payroll tax recordkeeping will be explained in Chapter 14 when we discuss payroll in depth. Since the collection and payment of sales taxes are handled differently in virtually every state, you will need to contact your state's department of revenue or similar body to determine the specific necessary recordkeeping requirements for that business debt. Later in this chapter, when we discuss the records you will need to track your income, you will be shown how to handle the recordkeeping to keep track of your sales taxes.

That leaves us only with accounts payable to track as a current debt. You will have only one simple form to use to keep track of this important category. Accounts payable are the current bills which your business owes. They may be for equipment or supplies which you have purchased on credit or they may be for items which you have ordered on account. Regardless of the source of the debt, you will need a clear system to record the debt and keep track of how much you still owe on the debt.

Long-term debts of a business are those debts which will not be paid off within one year. These can either be debts based on business loans for equipment, inventory, business-owned vehicles, or business property. In the accounting system outlined in this book, you will only keep track of the current principal and interest for these debts. For long-term debts of your business, you will fill in the Long-Term Debt Record, which is explained later in this chapter.

Accounts Payable Record

On the following form, you will enter any bills or short-term debts which you do not pay immediately. If you pay the bill off upon receipt of the bill, you need not enter the amount on this sheet. Your records for expenses will take care of the necessary documentation for those particular debts. Follow these instructions to prepare and fill in this particular form:

① For those debts that you do not pay off immediately, you will need to record the following information in the left-hand column of the record:
   - ✦ The date the debt was incurred
   - ✦ To whom you owe the money
   - ✦ Payment terms (for instance: due within 30, 60, or 90 days)
   - ✦ The amount of the debt

② In the right-hand column of the Accounts Payable Record, you will record the following information:
   - ✦ The date of any payments
   - ✦ To whom the payments were made
   - ✦ The amount of any payments made

③ By periodically totaling the left- and right-hand columns, you will be able to take a look at the total amount of your unpaid accounts payable. You may wish to do this weekly, monthly, or quarterly. You will also need the figure for your total unpaid accounts payable for the preparation of your Balance Sheet.

④ When you have totaled your accounts payable at the end of your chosen periodic interval, you should start a new record and carry the unpaid accounts over to it. Using this simple record, you will be able to check your accounts payable at a glance and also have enough information available to use to prepare a Balance Sheet for your business.

Accounts Payable Record

Period from: to:

UNPAID ACCOUNTS			
Date	Due to	Terms	Amount
		TOTAL	

PAYMENTS		
Date	Paid to	Amount
	TOTAL	

Total Unpaid Accounts

− Total Payments

= Total Accounts Payable

Long-Term Debt Record

If your business has any outstanding loans which will not be paid off within one year, you will prepare a Long-Term Debt Record for each loan. You will track the principal and interest paid on each long-term debt of your business. This information will enable you to have long-term debt figures for use in preparing your Balance Sheet and interest-paid figures for use in preparing your Profit and Loss Statements. On the following page, you will find a sheet to be used for this purpose. In order to fill in this sheet, follow these directions:

① You will need to enter the following information for each company to whom a loan is outstanding:
  ◆ Name
  ◆ Address
  ◆ Contact person
  ◆ Phone number
  ◆ Loan account number
  ◆ Loan interest rate
  ◆ Original principal amount of the loan
  ◆ Term of the loan

② You will need a loan payment book or amortization schedule in order to obtain the necessary information regarding the portions of each of your payments that are principal and interest. As you make a payment, enter the following information:
  ◆ Date of payment
  ◆ Amount of principal paid
  ◆ Amount of interest paid
  ◆ Balance due (previous balance minus payment)

③ Total the balance due after each payment. Using this method of tracking accounts payable will allow you to always have a running total of your long-term liability for each long-term debt.

④ To prepare a Balance Sheet entry for long-term debts, you will simply need to total all of the various account balances for all of your long-term debts.

⑤ You should also periodically total all of the columns on your Long-Term Debt Record. You will need the totals for interest paid for your Monthly and Annual Expense Summaries.

Long-Term Debt Record

Company:
Address:
Contact Person   Phone:
Loan Account #:   Loan Interest Rate:
Original Loan Amount: Term:

Date	Payment		Principal		Interest		Balance	
TOTALS								

Tracking Business Expenses

The expenses of a business are all of the transactions of the business in which money is paid out of the business, with two general exceptions. Money paid out of the business to the owner (as a draw rather than as a salary) and money paid out of the business to pay off the principal of a loan are not considered expenses of a business. Very often, the bulk of a small business's recordkeeping will consist of tracking its expenses. Because of the tax deductibility of the cost of most business expenses, it is crucial for a business to keep careful records of what has been spent to operate the business. But even beyond the need for detailed expense records for tax purposes, a small business needs a clear system which will allow for a quick examination of where business money is being spent. The tracking of business expenses will allow you to see at a glance where your money is flowing. With detailed records, it will also be an easy task to apply various financial formulas to analyze and understand your expense/income ratios in greater depth. This will allow you to see if certain costs are out-of-line, if certain expenses are increasing or decreasing, and if your business expenses make clear business sense.

In order to track your business expenses, you will use a Weekly Expense Record and a Monthly Expense Summary. You may also need to use a number of additional specialized forms if your business needs dictate their use, such as to document travel expenses, meals and entertainment expenses, and vehicle expenses. There is also an Annual Expense Summary provided for totaling your expense payments.

Travel, Auto, and Meals and Entertainment Expenses

Travel, auto, and meals and entertainment expenses are treated slightly differently than other business expenses because you are required by the Internal Revenue Service to support your expenses with adequate additional records or evidence. These records can be in the form of trip diaries, account books, or similar items. The following list is a general guide to those travel, auto, meals, and entertainment expenses which can be deducted as legitimate business expenses:

- **Transportation**: the cost of plane, train, or bus travel to the business destination. Also the cost of a taxi, bus, or limousine between airports, stations, hotels, and business locations. This includes any costs for baggage transfers.
- **Car**: The cost of operating your car when away from home on business. You can deduct your actual expenses or you may use the standard mileage rate. If you use the standard rate, you can also deduct tolls and parking expenses. For 2010, the standard mileage rate is 50 cents per mile, but is generally changed for each tax year.

- **Lodging**: If your business trip is overnight, you can deduct the cost of your lodging.
- **Meals**: If your business trip is overnight, you can deduct the cost of meals, beverages, and tips. You may also choose instead to use a standard meal allowance. For 2010, the standard meal allowance is, generally, $65 per day for meals, depending where your business trip is located. For complete information on this, please refer to IRS Publication 463: *Travel, Entertainment, Gift, and Car Expenses* and IRS Publication 1542: *Per Diem Rates*. Whether you choose to deduct the actual cost or the standard allowance, your deduction is limited to 50 percent of your expenses.
- **Entertainment**: You can deduct the cost of business-related entertainment if you entertain a client, customer, or employee and it is directly related to your business. As with meals, entertainment expense deductions are limited to 50 percent of your actual expenses.

For travel, car, and meals and entertainment expenses, you should also keep additional records that indicate the dates the expenses were incurred, the location of the expenses, and the business reason for the expenses. These can be noted on any receipts for the expenses.

Tracking Expenses

All of your expenses will initially be recorded on the Weekly Expense Record sheet. On your expense record sheet, you will record all of your business expenses in chronological order. The expense transactions will generally come from two main sources: your business bank account check register and your petty cash register. You will transfer all of the expenses from these two sources to the main expense record sheets. This will provide you with a central listing of all of the expenditures for your business.

From this record sheet, you will transfer your expenses to a Monthly Expense Summary sheet. On the Monthly Expense Summary sheet, you will enter a line for each expense type which you have listed on your business Chart of Accounts. You will then go through your Weekly Expense Record sheets for each month and total the expenses for each account. You will enter this total in the column for the specific type of expense.

Finally, on a monthly basis, you will transfer the totals for your various expense categories to the Annual Expense Summary sheet. On this sheet, you collect and record the total monthly expenses. With these figures, you will be able to easily total your expense amounts to ascertain your quarterly and annual expenses. By recording your business expenses in this manner, you should have little difficulty being able to keep track of the money flowing out of your business on a weekly, monthly, quarterly, and annual basis. You will have all of the information that you will need to easily provide the necessary expenditure figures for preparing a Profit and Loss Statement. On the next few pages you will be given a detailed explanation of how to fill in these various simplified forms. Remember that you must tailor the forms to fit your particular business.

Weekly Expense Record

① Fill in the date or dates that the form will cover at the top where indicated.

② Beginning with your Bank Account Check Register, transfer the following information from the register to the Expense Record:
   + The date of the transaction
   + The check number
   + To whom the amount was paid
   + The expense account number (off your Chart of Accounts)
   + The amount of the transaction

③ Next, using your Petty Cash Register, transfer the following information from your Petty Cash Register to the Expense Record:
   + The date of the transaction
   + In the column for "Check Number," put "PC" to indicate that the expense was a petty cash expense
   + To whom the amount was paid
   + The expense account number (off your Chart of Accounts)
   + The amount of the transaction
   + *Note*: Do not list the checks that you make out to "Petty Cash" as an expense

④ For credit card transactions, follow these rules:
   + Do not list the payment to a credit card company as an expense
   + List the monthly amount on the credit card bill for interest as an interest expense
   + Individually, list each of the business purchases on the credit card as a separate expense item, assigning an account number to each separate business charge. Make a notation for the date, to whom the expense was paid, and the amount. In the column for "Check Number," provide the type of credit card (for example: "V" for Visa)

✦ Do not list any personal charge items as business expenses
✦ If a charged item is used partially for business and partially for personal reasons, list only that portion that is used for business reasons as a business expense

⑤ At the end of the period, total the Amount column. You will use this weekly total expense amount to cross-check your later calculations.

⑥ It is a good idea to keep all of your various business expense receipts for at least three years after the tax period to which they relate. You may wish to buy envelopes for each weekly period, label each appropriately, and file your weekly business expense receipts in them. This will make it easy to find each specific receipt, if necessary.

Weekly Expense Record

Week of:

Date	Check #	To Whom Paid	Account #	Amount
			TOTALS	

Monthly Expense Summary

Using this record sheet, you will compile and transfer the total expense amount for each expense category. In this way, you will be able to keep a monthly total of all of the expenses, broken down by category of expense. To fill in this form, do the following:

① Indicate the month that the Summary will cover where indicated at the top.

② In the first column on the left-hand side, list all of your expense account numbers from your business Chart of Accounts.

③ In the next column, using your Weekly Expense Records, transfer the amounts for each expense. If you have more than four expense amounts for any account, use a second Monthly Expense Record to record additional amounts.

④ In the Total column, list the total expenses in each category for the month.

⑤ At the bottom of the page, total the amount for all of the categories for the month. Don't forget to include any amounts from any additional records in your totals.

⑥ To double-check your transfers and your calculations, total all of your Weekly Expense Record total amounts. This figure should equal your Monthly Expense Summary total for that month. If there is a discrepancy, check each of your figures until you discover the error.

Monthly Expense Summary

Month of:

Account Name/#	Amount	Amount	Amount	Amount	Total
					TOTAL	

Annual Expense Summary

① Fill in the year. Fill in your account numbers from your Chart of Accounts across the top row. If you have more than nine expense accounts, use a second and third page, if necessary.

② On a monthly basis, carry the totals from all of the rows on your Monthly Expense Summaries to the appropriate column of the Annual Expense Summary.

③ At the end of each quarter, total all of the monthly entries to arrive at your quarterly totals for each category.

④ To double-check your monthly calculations, total your categories across each month and put this total in the final column. Compare this total with the total on your Monthly Expense Summaries. If there is a discrepancy, check each of your figures until you discover the error. Don't forget to include your extra records if you have more than nine expense accounts to list.

⑤ To double-check your quarterly calculations, total your monthly totals in the final quarterly column. This figure should equal the total of the quarterly category totals across the quarterly row. If there is a discrepancy, check each of your figures until you discover the error.

⑥ Finally, total each of your quarterly amounts to arrive at the annual totals. To cross- check your calculations, total the quarterly totals in the final column. This figure should equal the total for all of the annual totals in each category across the Annual Total row. If there is a discrepancy, check each of your. figures until you discover the error.

Annual Expense Summary

Year of:

Account # ⇨									Total
January									
February									
March									
1st Quarter									
April									
May									
June									
2nd Quarter									
July									
August									
September									
3rd Quarter									
October									
November									
December									
4th Quarter									
Annual TOTAL									

Tracking Business Income

The careful tracking of your business's income is one of the most important accounting activities you will perform. It is essential for your business that you know intimately where your income comes from. Failure to accurately track income and cash is one of the most frequent causes of business failure. You must have in place a clear and easily-understood system to track your business income. There are three separate features of tracking business income that must be incorporated into your accounting system. You will need a system in place to handle cash, track all of your sales and service income, and handle credit sales.

The first system you will need is a clear method for handling cash on a daily or weekly basis. This is true no matter how large or small your business may be and regardless of how much or how little cash is actually handled. You must have a clear record of how much cash is on hand and of how much cash is taken in during a particular time period. You will also need to have a method to tally this cash flow on a monthly basis. For these purposes, two forms are provided: a Weekly Cash Report and a Monthly Cash Report Summary.

The second feature of your business income tracking system should be a method to track your actual income from sales or services. This differs from your cash-tracking. With these records you will track taxable and nontaxable income whether the income is in the form of cash, check, credit card payment, or on account. Please note that when *nontaxable income* is referred to, it means only income that is not subject to any state or local sales tax (generally, this will be income from the performance of a service). These records will also track your intake of sales taxes, if applicable. For this segment of your income tracking, you will have a Weekly Income Record. You will also track your income on Monthly and Annual Income Summaries, which will provide you with a monthly, quarterly, and annual report of your taxable income, non-taxable income, and sales taxes collection.

The third feature of your business income tracking consists of a method to track and bill credit sales. With this portion of income-tracking, you will list and track all of your sales to customers which are made on account or on credit. The accounts that owe you money are referred to as your *accounts receivable*. They are the accounts from whom you hope to receive payment. The tracking of these credit sales will take place on either Weekly or Monthly Credit Sales Record. You will also use a Credit Sales Aging Report to see how your customers are doing over time. The actual billing of these credit sales will incorporate an Invoice, Statement, and Past Due Statement. Finally, a Credit Memo will be used to track those instances when a customer is given credit for any returned items.

Tracking Your Cash

Most businesses will have to handle cash in some form. Here we are not talking about the use of petty cash. Petty cash is the cash that a business has on hand for the payment of minor expenses which may crop up and for which the use of a business check is not convenient. The cash handling discussed in this section is the daily handling of cash used to take money in from customers or clients and the use of a cash drawer or some equivalent. You must have some method to accurately account for the cash used in your business in this regard. Two forms are provided: a Weekly Cash Report and a Monthly Cash Report Summary. The use of these forms is explained below.

Weekly Cash Reports

This form is used each week to track the cash received in the business from customer payments to the business, not petty cash. The cash may be in a cash box or some type of cash register. Regardless of how your cash is held, you need a method to account for the cash. Please follow these instructions:

① You must decide how much cash you will need to begin each period with sufficient cash to meet your needs and make change for cash sales. Usually $100.00 should be sufficient for most needs. Choose a figure and begin each period with that amount in your cash drawer. Excess cash that has been collected should be deposited in your business bank account. Each period, fill in the date and the cash on hand on your Cash Report.

② As you take in cash and checks throughout the period, record each item of cash taken in, checks taken in, and any instances of cash paid out. "Cash Out" does not mean change that has been made, but rather cash paid out for business purposes (for example, a refund).

③ Your business may have so much daily cash flow that it will be burdensome to record each item of cash flow on your sheet. In that case, you will need a cash register of some type. Simply total the cash register at the end of the day and record the total cash in, checks in, and cash out in the appropriate places on the weekly Cash Report.

④ At the end of each period, total your Cash In and Checks In. Add these two amounts to your Cash on Hand at the beginning of the period. This equals your Total Receipts for the period. Subtract any Cash Out from this amount. This figure should equal your actual cash on hand at the end of the period. Make a bank deposit for all of the checks and for all of the cash in excess of the amount that you will need to begin the next period.

⑤   In the space for deposits, note the following: a deposit number, if applicable; the date of the deposit; the deposit amount; and the name and signature of the person who made the deposit. Don't forget to also record your deposit in your business Bank Account Check Register.

Weekly Cash Report

Week of: Cash on Hand Beginning:

Week	CASH IN Name	Amount	CHECKS IN Name	Amount	CASH OUT Name	Amount
1						
2						
3						
4						
5						
6						
7						
8						
9						
10						
11						
12						
TOTAL						

Deposit #:	
Deposit Date:	
Deposit Amount:	
Deposited by:	
Signed:	

Total Cash in

+ Total Checks in

+ Cash on Hand Beginning

= Total Receipts

− Total Cash Out

= Balance on Hand

− Bank Deposit

= Cash on Hand Ending

Monthly Cash Report Summary

This form will be used to keep a monthly record of your Weekly Cash Reports. It serves as a monthly listing of your cash flow and of your business bank account deposits. You will, of course, also record your bank deposits in your business Bank Account Check Register. To use this form, follow these instructions:

① On a monthly basis, collect your Weekly Cash Reports. From each Record, record the following information:
   ◆ Cash on hand at the beginning of the period
   ◆ Cash taken in
   ◆ Checks taken in
   ◆ Cash paid out
   ◆ The amount of the daily or weekly bank deposit
   ◆ Cash on hand at the end of the period and after the bank deposit

② You can total the Deposit column as a cross-check against your Bank Account Check Register record of deposits.

Monthly Cash Report Summary

Month:

Date	On Hand	Cash in	Checks in	Cash out	Deposit	On Hand
1						
2						
3						
4						
5						
6						
7						
8						
9						
10						
11						
12						
13						
14						
15						
16						
17						
18						
19						
20						
21						
22						
23						
24						
25						
26						
27						
28						
29						

Tracking Income

The second feature of your business income tracking system should be a method to keep track of your actual income. This portion of the system will provide you with a list of all taxable and non-taxable income and of any sales taxes collected, if applicable. For sales tax information, please contact your state's sales tax revenue collection agency. If your state has a sales tax on the product or service which you provide, you will need accurate records to determine your total taxable and non-taxable income and the amount of sales tax which is due. For this purpose and for the purpose of tracking all of your income for your own business analysis, you should prepare a Weekly Income Record. The information from these reports will then be used to prepare Monthly and Annual Income Summaries.

Weekly Income Records

① You will need to contact your state taxing agency for information on how to determine if a sale or the provision of a service is taxable or nontaxable. You also will need to determine the appropriate rates for sales tax collection.

② For each item, record the following information:
  ◆ Invoice number
  ◆ Taxable income amount
  ◆ Sales tax amount
  ◆ Nontaxable income amount
  ◆ Total income (Taxable, sales tax, and nontaxable amounts combined)

③ On a weekly basis, total the amounts in each column to determine the totals for the particular time period. These figures will be carried over to the Monthly and Annual Income Summary sheets that will be explained next.

Weekly Income Record

Week of:

Invoice #	Taxable Income	Sales Tax	Nontaxable Income	Total Income
Weekly TOTAL				

Monthly Income Summary

To use this form, do the following:

① Fill in the appropriate month.

② Using your Weekly Income Records, record the following information for each day or week:
   ✦ Total taxable income amount
   ✦ Total sales tax amount
   ✦ Total nontaxable income amount
   ✦ Total income (taxable, sales tax, and nontaxable amounts combined)

③ On a monthly basis, total the amounts in each column to determine the totals for the particular month. These figures will be carried over to the Annual Income Summary that will be explained next.

Monthly Income Summary

Month of:

Invoice #	Taxable Income	Sales Tax	Nontaxable Income	Total Income
Monthly TOTAL				

Annual Income Summary

① Fill in the year.

② On a monthly basis, carry the totals from all of the columns on your Monthly Income Summary form to the appropriate column of the Annual Income Summary form.

③ At the end of each quarter, total all of the monthly entries to arrive at your quarterly totals for each category.

④ To double-check your monthly calculations, total your categories across each month and put this total in the final column. Compare this total with the total on your Monthly Income Summary sheets. If there is a discrepancy, check each of your figures until you discover the error.

⑤ To double-check your quarterly calculations, total your monthly totals in the final quarterly column. This figure should equal the total of the quarterly category totals across the quarterly row. If there is a discrepancy, check each of your figures until you discover the error.

⑥ Finally, total each of your quarterly amounts to arrive at the annual totals. To cross check your calculations, total the quarterly totals in the final column. This figure should equal the total for all of the annual totals in each category across the Annual Total row. If there is a discrepancy, check each of your figures until you discover the error.

Annual Income Summary

Year of:

Date	Taxable Income	Sales Tax	Nontaxable Income	Total Income
January				
February				
March				
1st Quarter				
April				
May				
June				
2nd Quarter				
July				
August				
September				
3rd Quarter				
October				
November				
December				
4th Quarter				
Annual TOTAL				

Tracking Credit Sales

The final component of your business income tracking system will be a logical method to track your credit sales. You will use a Weekly or Monthly Credit Sales Record to track the actual sales on credit and a Credit Sales Aging Report to track the payment on these sales. In addition, several forms are provided for the billing of these credit sales: an Invoice, Statement, Past Due Statement, and Credit Memo.

Weekly or Monthly Credit Sales Records

To keep track of sales made to customers on credit or on account, follow these directions:

① Fill in the appropriate date or time period.

② For each sale that is made on credit, fill in the following information from the customer Invoice (see Invoice instructions later in this chapter):
   ◆ Invoice number
   ◆ Date of sale
   ◆ Customer name
   ◆ Total sale amount

③ The final column is for recording the date that the credit sale has been paid in full.

④ The information from your Weekly or Monthly Credit Sales Record will also be used to prepare your Credit Sales Aging Report on a monthly basis.

Weekly Credit Sales Record

Week of:

Invoice #	Sale Date	Customer	Sale Total	Date Paid

Monthly Credit Sales Record

Month:

Invoice #	Sale Date	Customer	Sale Total	Date Paid

Credit Sales Aging Report

This report is used to track the current status of your credit sales or accounts receivables. Through the use of this form you will be able to track whether or not the people or companies that owe you money are falling behind on their payments. With this information, you will be able to determine how to handle these accounts: sending past due notices, halting sales to them, turning them over to a collection agency, etc. To use this form, do the following:

① Decide on which day of the month you would like to perform your credit sales aging calculations. Enter this date on the first line of the form.

② For each credit sales account, enter the name of the account from your Weekly or Monthly Credit Sales Records.

③ In the Total column, enter the total current amount that is owed to you. If this figure is based on credit sales during the current month, enter this figure again in the Current column. Do this for each credit account.

④ Each month you will prepare a new Credit Sales Aging Report on a new sheet. On the same date in the next month, determine how much of the originally-owed balance has been paid off. Enter the amount of the unpaid balance from the previous month in the 30–60 days column. Enter any new credit sales for the month under the Current column. The figure in the Total column should be the total of all of the columns to the right of the Total column.

⑤ Each month, determine how much was paid on the account, deduct that amount from the oldest amount due, and shift the amounts due over one column to the right. Add any new credit sales to the Current column and put the total of the amounts in the Total column.

⑥ After entering the information for each month, total each of the columns across the Total line at the bottom of the report. The Total column is 100 percent of the amount due. Calculate what percentage of 100 percent each of the other columns is to determine how much of your accounts receivable are 30, 60, 90, or more than 90 days overdue.

Credit Sales Aging Report

Account Name	Total	Current	30–60 Days	60–90 Days	90 Days +
TOTALS					
PERCENT	100%				

Invoices and Statements

For credit sales, you will need to provide each customer with a current Invoice. You will also need to send them a Statement if the balance is not paid within the first 30 days. You will also need to send a Past Due Statement if the balance becomes overdue. Finally, a form is provided to record instances when a customer is given credit for a returned item. You will need to provide two copies of each of these forms: one for your records and one for the customer.

Invoice

The invoice is your key credit sales document. To prepare and track invoices, follow these directions:

① For each order, fill in the following information:
  ✦ Date
  ✦ The name and address of who will be billed for the order
  ✦ The name and address where the order will be shipped
  ✦ The item number of the product or service sold
  ✦ The quantity ordered
  ✦ The description of the item
  ✦ The per unit price of the item
  ✦ The total amount billed (quantity times per unit price)

② Subtotal all of the items where shown. Add any sales taxes and shipping costs and total the Balance.

③ Record the pertinent information from the Invoice on the appropriate Weekly or Monthly Credit Sales Record.

④ Record the pertinent information from the Invoice on the appropriate Weekly Income Record or Monthly Income Summary.

⑤ Send one copy of the Invoice to the customer with the order and file the other copy in a file for your invoices.

Invoice

Date:

Invoice No.:

Bill to:

Ship to:

Item #	Qty.	Description	Price Each	Total
				0.00
				0.00
				0.00
				0.00
				0.00
				0.00
				0.00
				0.00
				0.00
				0.00
				0.00
				0.00
				0.00
				0.00
				0.00

Subtotal	0.00
Tax	
Shipping	
BALANCE	0.00

Statement and Past Due Statement

Statements are used to send your credit customers a notice of the amount that is currently due. Statements are generally sent at 30-day intervals, beginning either 30 days after the invoice is sent, or at the beginning of the next month or the next cycle for sending statements. Follow these instructions for preparing your statements:

① You should decide on a statement billing cycle. Generally, this is a specific date each month (for example: the first, tenth, or fifteenth of each month).

② Fill in the date and the account name and address.

③ In the body of the form, enter information from any Invoice that is still unpaid as of the date you are completing the Statement. You should enter the following items for each unpaid Invoice:
  ✦ The date of the Invoice
  ✦ A description (including Invoice number) of the Invoice
  ✦ Any payments received since the last statement or since the sale
  ✦ The amount still owed on that Invoice

④ When all of the invoice information for all of the customer's invoices has been entered, total the Amounts column and enter in Balance.

⑤ The information on the Statement then can be used to enter information on your Credit Sales Aging Report.

⑥ The Past Due Statement is simply a version of the basic Statement that includes a notice that the account is past due. This Past Due Statement should be sent when the account becomes overdue. Fill it out in the same manner used for Statements.

Statement

Date:

Account:

Date	Description	Payment	Amount Due

Please pay this BALANCE

Past Due Statement

Date:

Account:

This account is now past due. Please pay upon receipt to avoid collection costs

Date	Description	Payment	Amount Due

Please pay this BALANCE

Credit Memo

The final form for tracking your business income is the Credit Memo. This form is used to provide you and your customer with a written record of any credit given for goods that have been returned by the customer. You will need to set a policy regarding when such credit will be given, (for example: whether only for a certain time period after the sale, or for defects, or other limitations). To use the Credit Memo, follow these instructions:

①　Fill in the date, the number of the original Invoice, and the customer's name and address.

②　Fill in the following information in the body of the Credit Memo:
- ✦ Item number of item returned
- ✦ Quantity of items returned
- ✦ Description of item returned
- ✦ Unit price of item returned
- ✦ Total amount of credit (quantity times unit price)

③　Subtotal the credit for all items. Add any appropriate sales tax credit and total the amount in the Credit box. This is the amount that will be credited or refunded to the customer.

④　In the lower-left box, indicate the reason for the return, any necessary approval, and the date of the approval.

⑤　Handle the Credit Memo like a negative Invoice. Record the amount of credit as a negative on the Weekly Income Record.

⑥　Record the pertinent information from the Credit Memo as a negative amount on the appropriate Weekly, or Monthly Credit Sales Record, if the Credit Memo applies to a previous sale on credit that was recorded on a Credit Sales Record.

Credit Memo

Date:

Invoice #:

Credit to:

GOODS RETURNED

Item #	Qty.	Description	Price Each	Total

Reason for return:

Approved by:

Date:

Subtotal

Tax

CREDIT

Chapter 14

Business Payroll

One of the most difficult and complex accounting functions that small businesses face is their payroll. Because of the various state and federal taxes that must be applied and the myriad government forms that must be prepared, the handling of a business payroll often causes accounting nightmares. Even if there is only one employee, there is a potential for problems.

First, let's examine the basics. If your business is a corporation or limited liability company, all pay must be handled as payroll, even if you are the only employee. The corporation is a separate entity and the corporation or limited liability company itself will be the employer. You and any other people that you hire will be the employees. If you are operating as a sole proprietorship, you may still hire employees. A business payroll entails a great deal of paperwork and has numerous government tax filing deadlines. You will be required to make payroll tax deposits, file various quarterly payroll tax returns, and make additional end-of-the-year reports.

Initially, you must take certain steps to set up your payroll and official status as an employer. The following information contains the instructions only for meeting federal requirements. Please check with your particular state and local governments for information regarding any additional payroll tax, state unemployment insurance, or workers' compensation requirements.

Setting up Your Payroll

1. The first step in becoming an employer is to file Internal Revenue Service Form SS-4: Application for Employer Identification Number. This will officially register your business with the Federal government as an employer. This form and instructions are included on the Forms-on-CD.

2. Next, each employee must fill in an IRS Form W-4: Employee's Withholding Allowance Certificate. This will provide you with the necessary information regarding withholding allowances to enable you to prepare your payroll.

3. You must then determine the gross salary or wage that each employee will earn. For each employee, complete an Employee Payroll Record and prepare a Quarterly Payroll Time Sheet as explained later in this chapter.

> **⋇ Toolkit Tip!**
>
> Every business that hires employees must have an federal employer identification number that you will receive by filing IRS Form SS-4.

4. You will then need to consult the tables in IRS Circular E: Employer's Tax Guide. From the tables in this publication, you will be able to determine the proper deductions for each employee for each pay period. If your employees are paid on an hourly basis and the number of hours worked is different each pay period, you will have to perform these calculations for each pay period. You will need to obtain the latest version of this guide from www.irs.gov.

5. Before you pay your employee, you should open a separate business bank account for handling your business payroll tax deductions and payments. This will allow you to immediately deposit all taxes due into this separate account and help prevent the lack of sufficient money available when the taxes are due.

6. Next you will pay your employee and record the deduction information on the Employee Payroll Record.

7. When you have completed paying all of your employees for the pay period, you will write a separate check for the total amount of all of your employees' deductions and any employer's share of taxes. You will then deposit this check

into your business payroll tax bank account that you set up following the instructions above.

8. At the end of every month, you will need to transfer the information regarding employee deductions to your Payroll Depository Record and Annual Payroll Summary. Copies of these forms and instructions are included later in this chapter. You will then calculate your employer share of Social Security and Medicare taxes. Each month (or quarter if your tax liability is more than $2,500 per quarter), you will need to deposit the correct amount of taxes due to the Federal government. This is done by making a monthly payment to your bank for the taxes due using IRS Form 8109: Federal Tax Deposit Coupon (If your liability is below $2500 per quarter then you make the payment on a quarterly basis when you file IRS Form 941: Employer's Quarterly Federal Tax Return. Copies of these forms are contained on the Forms-on-CD.

9. On a quarterly or annual basis, you will also need to make a tax payment for Federal Unemployment Tax, using IRS Form 940: Employer's Annual Federal Unemployment (FUTA) Tax Return. This tax is solely the responsibility of the employer and is not deducted from the employee's pay. Also on a quarterly basis, you will need to file IRS Form 941: Employer's Quarterly Federal Tax Return. If you have made monthly deposits of your taxes due, there will be no quarterly taxes to pay, but you will still need to file these forms quarterly.

10. Finally, to complete your payroll, at the end of the year you must do the following:

   • Prepare IRS Form W-2: Wage and Tax Statement for each employee
   • File IRS Form W-3: Transmittal of Wage and Tax Statements

Remember that your state and local tax authorities will generally have additional requirements and taxes that will need to be paid. In many jurisdictions, these requirements are tailored after the Federal requirements and the procedures and due dates are similar.

Payroll Checklist

☐ File IRS Form SS-4: Application for Employer Identification Number and obtain Federal Employer Identification Number.

☐ Obtain IRS Form W-4: Employee's Withholding Allowance Certificate for each employee.

☐ Set up Payroll Record and Quarterly Payroll Time sheet for each employee.

☐ Open separate business Payroll Tax Bank Account.

☐ Consult IRS Circular E: Employer's Tax Guide and use tables to determine withholding tax amounts.

☐ Obtain information on any applicable state or local taxes.

☐ List withholding, Social Security, Medicare and any state or local deductions on employee's Payroll Record.

☐ Pay employees and deposit appropriate taxes in your Payroll Tax Bank Account.

☐ Fill in Payroll Depository Record and Annual Payroll Summary.

☐ Pay payroll taxes:

    ☐ Monthly using IRS Form 8109: Federal Tax Deposit Coupon, if your payroll tax liability is more than $2500 per quarter.

    ☐ Quarterly using IRS Form 941: Employer's Quarterly Federal Tax Return, if your payroll tax liability is less than $2500 per quarter.

    ☐ Annually, file IRS Form 940: Employer's Annual Federal Unemployment (FUTA) Tax Return.

☐ Annually, prepare and file IRS W-2 Forms: Wage and Tax Statement for each employee, and IRS Form W-3: Transmittal of Wage and Tax Statements.

Quarterly Payroll Time Sheet

On the following page is a Quarterly Payroll Time Sheet. If your employees are paid an hourly wage, you will prepare a sheet like this for each employee for each quarter during the year. On this sheet you will keep track of the following information:

- Number of hours worked (daily, weekly, and quarterly)
- Number of regular and overtime hours worked

The information from this Quarterly Payroll Time Sheet will be transferred to your individual Employee Payroll Record in order to calculate the employee's paycheck amounts. This is explained following the Quarterly Payroll Time Sheet.

Quarterly Payroll Time Sheet

Employee:

Week of	Sun	Mon	Tue	Wed	Thu	Fri	Sat	Reg	OT	Total
Quarterly TOTAL										

Employee Payroll Record

1. For each employee, fill in the following information at the top of the form:

    - Name and address of employee
    - Employee's Social Security number
    - Number of exemptions claimed by employee on Form W-4
    - Regular and overtime wage rates
    - Pay period (i.e.., weekly, biweekly, monthly, etc.)
    - Date check is written
    - Payroll check number

2. For each pay period, fill in the number of regular and overtime ("OT") hours worked by the employee from his or her Quarterly Payroll Time Sheet. Multiply this amount by the employee's wage rate to determine the gross pay. For example: 40 hours at the regular wage of $8.00/hour = $320.00; plus five hours at the overtime wage rate of $12.00/hour = $60.00. Gross pay for the period is $320.00 + $60.00 = $380.00.

3. Determine the Federal withholding tax deduction for the pay amount by consulting the withholding tax tables in IRS Circular E: Employer's Tax Guide. Enter this figure on the form in the "Fed. W/H" column.

4. Determine the employee's share of Social Security and Medicare deductions. As of 2008, the employee's Social Security share rate is 6.2 percent and the employee's Medicare share rate is 1.45 percent. Multiply these rates times the employee's gross wages and enter the figures in the appropriate places; the "S/S Ded." and "Medic. Ded." columns. For example: for $380.00, the Social Security deduction would be $380.00 x .062 = $23.56 and the Medicare deduction would be $380.00 x .0145 = $5.51.

5. Determine any state taxes and enter in the appropriate column.

6. Subtract all of the deductions from the employee's gross wages to determine the employee's net pay. Enter this figure in the final column and prepare the employee's paycheck using the deduction information from this sheet. Also prepare a check to your payroll tax bank account for a total of the Federal withholding amount and two times the Social Security and Medicare amounts. This includes your employer share of these taxes. The employer's share of Social Security and Medicare taxes is equal to the employee's share.

Employee Payroll Record

Employee:

Address:

Social Security #:

Number of Exemptions:

Rate of Pay: Overtime Rate:

Pay Period:

Date	Check #	Pay Period	Reg. Hours	OT Hours	Gross Pay	Fed. W/H	S/S Ded.	Medic. Ded.	State Taxes	Net Pay
Pay Period TOTAL										

Payroll Depository Record

You will be required to deposit taxes with the IRS on a monthly or quarterly basis (unless your total employment taxes totaled more than $50,000.00 for the previous year, in which case you should obviously consult an accountant). If your employment taxes total less than $2,500.00 per quarter, you may pay your payroll tax liability when you quarterly file your Federal Form 941: Employer's Quarterly Federal Tax Return. If your payroll tax liability is more than $2,500.00 per quarter, you must deposit your payroll taxes on a monthly basis with a bank using IRS Form 8109: Federal Tax Deposit Coupon. Sample copies of these two Federal forms are contained on the Forms-on-CD. To track your payroll tax liability, use the Payroll Depository Record which follows these instructions:

1. On a monthly basis, total each column on all of your Employee Payroll Records. This will give you a figure for each employee's Federal withholding, Social Security, and Medicare taxes for the month.

2. Total all of the Federal withholding taxes for all employees for the month and enter this figure in the appropriate column on the Payroll Depository Record.

3. Total Social Security and Medicare taxes for all of your employees for the entire month and enter this figure in the appropriate columns on the Payroll Depository Record. Note that "SS/EE" refers to Social Security/Employee's Share and that "MC/EE" refers to Medicare/Employee's Share.

4. Enter identical amounts in the SS/ER and MC/ER columns as you have entered in the SS/EE and MC/EE columns. "ER" refers to the employer's share. The employer's share of Social Security and Medicare is the same as the employee's share, but is not deducted from the employee's pay.

5. Total all of the deductions for the month. This is the amount of your total monthly Federal payroll tax liability. If necessary, write a check to your local bank for this amount and deposit it using IRS Form 8109: Federal Tax Deposit Coupon.

6. If you must file only quarterly, total all three of your monthly amounts on a quarterly basis and pay this amount when you file your IRS Form 941: Employer's Quarterly Federal Tax Return. On a yearly basis, total all of the quarterly columns to arrive at your total annual Federal payroll tax liability.

Payroll Depository Record

Month	Fed. W/H	SS/EE	SS/ER	MC/EE	MC/ER	Total
January						
February						
March						
1st Quarter						

1st Quarter Total Number of Employees:　　　　Total Wages Paid:

Month	Fed. W/H	SS/EE	SS/ER	MC/EE	MC/ER	Total
April						
May						
June						
2nd Quarter						

2nd Quarter Total Number of Employees:　　　　Total Wages Paid:

Month	Fed. W/H	SS/EE	SS/ER	MC/EE	MC/ER	Total
July						
August						
September						
3rd Quarter						

3rd Quarter Total Number of Employees:　　　　Total Wages Paid:

Month	Fed. W/H	SS/EE	SS/ER	MC/EE	MC/ER	Total
October						
November						
December						
4th Quarter						

4th Quarter Total Number of Employees:　　　　Total Wages Paid:

Yearly TOTAL						

Yearly Total Number of Employees:　　　　Total Wages Paid:

Annual Payroll Summary

The final payroll form is used to total all of the payroll amounts for all employees on a monthly, quarterly, and annual basis. Much of the information on this form is similar to the information that you compiled for the Payroll Depository Record. However, the purpose of this form is to provide you with a record of all of your payroll costs, including the payroll deduction costs. This form will be useful for both tax and planning purposes as you examine your business profitability on a quarterly and annual basis. Follow these directions to prepare this form:

1. For each month, total all of your employees' gross and net pay amounts from their individual Employee Payroll Records and transfer these totals to this form.

2. For each month, transfer the amounts for Federal withholding from the Payroll Depository Record to this form.

3 For each month, total both columns on your Payroll Depository Record for SS/EE ("Social Security/Employee") and SS/ER ("Social Security/Employer") and transfer this total to the "S/S Taxes" column on this summary. Total the MC/EE ("Medicare/Employee") and MC/ER ("Medicare/Employer") columns also and enter the total in the "Medicare Taxes" column on this form.

4. On a quarterly basis, total the columns to determine your quarterly payroll costs. Annually, total the quarterly amounts to determine your annual costs.

Annual Payroll Summary

	Gross Pay	Federal W/H	S/S Taxes	Medicare Taxes	State Taxes	Net Pay
January						
February						
March						
1st Quarter Total						
April						
May						
June						
2nd Quarter Total						
July						
August						
September						
3rd Quarter Total						
October						
November						
December						
4th Quarter Total						
Yearly TOTAL						

Chapter 15

Taxation of Sole Proprietorship

A basic comprehension of the information required on federal tax forms will help you understand why certain financial records are necessary. Understanding tax reporting will also assist you as you decide how to organize your business financial records. A checklist of tax forms is provided that details which IRS forms are necessary for each type of business. In addition, various schedules of tax filing are also provided to assist you in keeping your tax reporting timely. Finally, a sample of each form is included on the Forms-on-CD. Taxation details for all five basic business entities follow:

Taxation of Sole Proprietorships

The taxation of sole proprietorships is a relatively easy concept to understand. The sole proprietorship is not considered a separate entity for federal tax purposes. Thus, all of the profits and losses of the business are simply reported as personal profits or losses of the sole owner. They are reported on IRS Schedule C: Profits or Losses of a Business or on IRS Schedule C-EZ: Net Profits of a Business and are included in the calculations for completing the owner's joint or single IRS Form 1040.

Please note that many of the tax forms in this chapter will only apply to a sole proprietorship that actually hires employees. Simply because a sole proprietorship business is owned by one owner does not in any way restrict the sole owner from hiring employees or independent contractors to assist in the operation of the business. In fact, there have been sole proprietorships that have operated with many, many employees and at different locations and even in many states.

Sole Proprietorship Tax Forms Checklist

❏ IRS Form 1040: U.S. Individual Income Tax Return

❏ IRS Schedule C: Profit or Loss From Business. Must be filed with IRS Form 1040 by all sole proprietorships, unless Schedule IRS Schedule C-EZ is filed

❏ IRS Schedule C-EZ: Net Profit From Business. May be filed if expenses are under $5,000 and other qualifications are met (See Schedule C-EZ)

❏ IRS Form 1040-SS: Self-Employment Tax. Required for any sole proprietor who shows $400 income from his or her business on IRS Schedule C or C-EZ

❏ IRS Form 1040-ES: Estimated Tax for Individuals. Must be used by all sole proprietors who expect to make a profit requiring estimated taxes

❏ IRS Form SS-4: Application for Employer Identification Number. Must be filed by all sole proprietors who will hire one or more employees

❏ IRS Form W-2: Wage and Tax Statement. Must be filed by all sole proprietors who have one or more employees

❏ IRS Form W-3: Transmittal of Wage and Tax Statement .Must be filed by all sole proprietors who have one or more employees

❏ IRS Form W-4: Employee's Withholding Allowance Certificate. Must be provided to employees of sole proprietors. Not filed with the IRS

❏ IRS Form 940: Employer's Annual Federal Unemployment Tax Return (FUTA). Must be filed by all sole proprietors who have employees

❏ IRS Form 941: Employer's Quarterly Federal Tax Return. Must be filed by all sole proprietors who have one or more employees

❏ IRS Form 8109: Federal Tax Deposit Coupon. Used by all employers with quarterly employee tax liability over $2,500.00 (Obtain from IRS)

❏ IRS Form 8829: Expenses for Business Use of Your Home. Filed with annual IRS Form 1040, if necessary

❏ Any required state and local income and sales tax forms

Sole Proprietorship Monthly Tax Schedule

❑ If you have employees, and your payroll tax liability is over $2,500.00 quarterly, you must make monthly tax payments using IRS Form 8109

❑ If required, file and pay any necessary state or local sales tax

Sole Proprietorship Quarterly Tax Schedule

❑ Pay any required estimated taxes using vouchers from IRS Form 1040-ES

❑ If you have employees, file IRS Form 941 and make any required payments of FICA and withholding taxes

❑ If you have employees and your unpaid FUTA tax liability is over $500.00, make FUTA deposit using IRS Form 8109

❑ If required, file and pay any necessary state or local sales tax

Sole Proprietorship Annual Tax Schedule

❑ If you have employees, prepare IRS Forms W-2 and provide to employees by January 31

❑ File IRS Form W-3 and copies of all IRS Forms W-2 with IRS by January 31

❑ If you have paid any independent contractors over $600 annually, prepare IRS Forms 1099 and provide to recipients by January 31; and file IRS Form 1096 and copies of all IRS Forms 1099 with IRS by January 31

❑ Make required unemployment tax payment and file IRS Form 940

❑ File IRS Form 1040-SS with your annual IRS Form 1040

❑ File IRS Schedule C and IRS Form 1040

❑ If you are required, file and pay any necessary state or local sales, income, or unemployment taxes

❑ File IRS Form 8829 with your annual IRS Form 1040, if necessary

Order Forms and Publications from the IRS

* .Braille materials available for people with visual impairments
  - Download accessible tax products at IRS.gov
  - Call 1-800-829-3676 to request by mail

* Conventional mail (within U.S., Puerto Rico and Virgin Islands)
  - Online orders for forms and publications by mail
  - Call 1-800-TAX-FORM (1-800-829-3676) to order tax products by mail

* Forms and Publications webpage (access/acquire electronic and print media)
  - Download IRS forms and publications at IRS.gov

* Tax Products DVD
  - Order the Tax Product DVD through the official distributor, National Technichal Information
    Service (NTIS)

* State Tax Forms
  - State tax forms information available on the Federation of Tax Administrators website

The following are "sample" IRS forms and not intended for use. The most current IRS forms that were available at the time of this book's publication date are provided on the Forms-on-CD. We advise that you check for current forms at www.IRS.gov or your local IRS office.

Sole Proprietorship: Small Business Start-Up Kit

Form **1040**

Department of the Treasury—Internal Revenue Service

U.S. Individual Income Tax Return 2009

(99)　IRS Use Only—Do not write or staple in this space.

Label (See instructions on page 14.) **Use the IRS label.** Otherwise, please print or type.	For the year Jan. 1–Dec. 31, 2009, or other tax year beginning　　, 2009, ending　　, 20

OMB No. 1545-0074

Your first name and initial　　Last name

Your social security number

If a joint return, spouse's first name and initial　　Last name

Spouse's social security number

Home address (number and street). If you have a P.O. box, see page 14.　　Apt. no.

City, town or post office, state, and ZIP code. If you have a foreign address, see page 14.

▲ You **must** enter your SSN(s) above. ▲

Checking a box below will not change your tax or refund.

Presidential Election Campaign ▶ Check here if you, or your spouse if filing jointly, want $3 to go to this fund (see page 14) ▶ ☐ **You**　☐ **Spouse**

Filing Status

Check only one box.

1 ☐ Single
2 ☐ Married filing jointly (even if only one had income)
3 ☐ Married filing separately. Enter spouse's SSN above and full name here. ▶
4 ☐ Head of household (with qualifying person). (See page 15.) If the qualifying person is a child but not your dependent, enter this child's name here. ▶
5 ☐ Qualifying widow(er) with dependent child (see page 16)

Exemptions

6a ☐ **Yourself.** If someone can claim you as a dependent, **do not** check box 6a . . . . . .
b ☐ **Spouse** . . . .

Boxes checked on 6a and 6b　_____

No. of children on 6c who:
• lived with you
• did not live with you due to divorce or separation (see page 18)

Dependents on 6c not entered above

Add numbers on lines above ▶

c **Dependents:**

(1) First name　　Last name	(2) Dependent's social security number	(3) Dependent's relationship to you	(4) ✔ if qualifying child for child tax credit (see page 17)
			☐
			☐
			☐
			☐

If more than four dependents, see page 17 and check here ▶ ☐

d Total number of exemptions claimed . . . .

Income

Attach Form(s) W-2 here. Also attach Forms W-2G and 1099-R if tax was withheld.

If you did not get a W-2, see page 22.

Enclose, but do not attach, any payment. Also, please use Form 1040-V.

7	Wages, salaries, tips, etc. Attach Form(s) W-2	**7**	
8a	**Taxable** interest. Attach Schedule B if required	**8a**	
b	Tax-exempt interest. **Do not** include on line 8a . . .	8b		
9a	Ordinary dividends. Attach Schedule B if required	**9a**	
b	Qualified dividends (see page 22)	9b		
10	Taxable refunds, credits, or offsets of state and local income taxes (see page 23) . .	**10**	
11	Alimony received	**11**	
12	Business income or (loss). Attach Schedule C or C-EZ	**12**	
13	Capital gain or (loss). Attach Schedule D if required. If not required, check here ▶ ☐	**13**	
14	Other gains or (losses). Attach Form 4797	**14**	
15a	IRA distributions . 15a	**b** Taxable amount (see page 24)	**15b**	
16a	Pensions and annuities 16a	**b** Taxable amount (see page 25)	**16b**	
17	Rental real estate, royalties, partnerships, S corporations, trusts, etc. Attach Schedule E	**17**	
18	Farm income or (loss). Attach Schedule F	**18**	
19	Unemployment compensation in excess of $2,400 per recipient (see page 27) . .	**19**	
20a	Social security benefits 20a	**b** Taxable amount (see page 27)	**20b**	
21	Other income. List type and amount (see page 29) _____	**21**	
22	Add the amounts in the far right column for lines 7 through 21. This is your **total income** ▶	**22**	

Adjusted Gross Income

23	Educator expenses (see page 29)	23	
24	Certain business expenses of reservists, performing artists, and fee-basis government officials. Attach Form 2106 or 2106-EZ	24	
25	Health savings account deduction. Attach Form 8889 .	25	
26	Moving expenses. Attach Form 3903	26	
27	One-half of self-employment tax. Attach Schedule SE .	27	
28	Self-employed SEP, SIMPLE, and qualified plans . .	28	
29	Self-employed health insurance deduction (see page 30)	29	
30	Penalty on early withdrawal of savings	30	
31a	Alimony paid **b** Recipient's SSN ▶	31a	
32	IRA deduction (see page 31)	32	
33	Student loan interest deduction (see page 34) . . .	33	
34	Tuition and fees deduction. Attach Form 8917 . . .	34	
35	Domestic production activities deduction. Attach Form 8903	35	
36	Add lines 23 through 31a and 32 through 35	36	
37	Subtract line 36 from line 22. This is your **adjusted gross income** . . . . . ▶	37	

For Disclosure, Privacy Act, and Paperwork Reduction Act Notice, see page 97.　　Cat. No. 11320B　　Form **1040** (2009)

Form 1040 (2009)   Page **2**

Tax and Credits	38	Amount from line 37 (adjusted gross income)	38
	39a	Check { □ **You** were born before January 2, 1945, □ Blind. } **Total boxes**	
		if: { □ **Spouse** was born before January 2, 1945, □ Blind. } checked ► 39a	
Standard Deduction for—	b	If your spouse itemizes on a separate return or you were a dual-status alien, see page 35 and check here ► 39b□	
	40a	**Itemized deductions** (from Schedule A) **or** your **standard deduction** (see left margin) . .	40a
• People who check any box on line 39a, 39b, or 40b **or** who can be claimed as a dependent, see page 35.	b	If you are increasing your standard deduction by certain real estate taxes, new motor vehicle taxes, or a net disaster loss, attach Schedule L and check here (see page 35) . ► 40b□	
	41	Subtract line 40a from line 38	41
	42	**Exemptions.** If line 38 is $125,100 or less and you did not provide housing to a Midwestern displaced individual, multiply $3,650 by the number on line 6d. Otherwise, see page 37 . .	42
• All others:	43	**Taxable income.** Subtract line 42 from line 41. If line 42 is more than line 41, enter -0- . .	43
Single or Married filing separately, $5,700	44	**Tax** (see page 37). Check if any tax is from: **a** □ Form(s) 8814 **b** □ Form 4972 .	44
	45	**Alternative minimum tax** (see page 40). Attach Form 6251	45
Married filing jointly or Qualifying widow(er), $11,400	46	Add lines 44 and 45 . . . . ►	46
	47	Foreign tax credit. Attach Form 1116 if required	47	
	48	Credit for child and dependent care expenses. Attach Form 2441	48	
Head of household, $8,350	49	Education credits from Form 8863, line 29	49	
	50	Retirement savings contributions credit. Attach Form 8880	50	
	51	Child tax credit (see page 42)	51	
	52	Credits from Form: **a** □ 8396 **b** □ 8839 **c** □ 5695	52	
	53	Other credits from Form: **a** □ 3800 **b** □ 8801 **c** □	53	
	54	Add lines 47 through 53. These are your **total credits**	54
	55	Subtract line 54 from line 46. If line 54 is more than line 46, enter -0- . . . . . ►	55
Other Taxes	56	Self-employment tax. Attach Schedule SE	56
	57	Unreported social security and Medicare tax from Form: **a** □ 4137 **b** □ 8919 . .	57
	58	Additional tax on IRAs, other qualified retirement plans, etc. Attach Form 5329 if required . .	58
	59	Additional taxes: **a** □ AEIC payments **b** □ Household employment taxes. Attach Schedule H	59
	60	Add lines 55 through 59. This is your **total tax** . . . . ►	60
Payments	61	Federal income tax withheld from Forms W-2 and 1099 . .	61	
	62	2009 estimated tax payments and amount applied from 2008 return	62	
	63	Making work pay and government retiree credits. Attach Schedule M	63	
If you have a qualifying child, attach Schedule EIC.	64a	**Earned income credit (EIC)**	64a	
	b	Nontaxable combat pay election ▶ 64b		
	65	Additional child tax credit. Attach Form 8812	65	
	66	Refundable education credit from Form 8863, line 16 . . .	66	
	67	First-time homebuyer credit. Attach Form 5405	67	
	68	Amount paid with request for extension to file (see page 72) .	68	
	69	Excess social security and tier 1 RRTA tax withheld (see page 72)	69	
	70	Credits from Form: **a** □ 2439 **b** □ 4136 **c** □ 8801 **d** □ 8885	70	
	71	Add lines 61, 62, 63, 64a, and 65 through 70. These are your **total payments** . . . . ►	71
Refund	72	If line 71 is more than line 60, subtract line 60 from line 71. This is the amount you **overpaid**	72
Direct deposit? See page 73 and fill in 73b, 73c, and 73d, or Form 8888.	73a	Amount of line 72 you want **refunded to you.** If Form 8888 is attached, check here . ► □	73a
	▶ b	Routing number [ ] ▶ c Type: □ Checking □ Savings	
	▶ d	Account number [ ]	
	74	Amount of line 72 you want **applied to your 2010 estimated tax** ► 74	
Amount You Owe	75	**Amount you owe.** Subtract line 71 from line 60. For details on how to pay, see page 74 . ►	75
	76	Estimated tax penalty (see page 74) 76	

Third Party Designee	Do you want to allow another person to discuss this return with the IRS (see page 75)? □ **Yes.** Complete the following. □ **No**
	Designee's name ► Phone no. ► Personal identification number (PIN) ► [ ]

Sign Here

Joint return? See page 15. Keep a copy for your records.

Under penalties of perjury, I declare that I have examined this return and accompanying schedules and statements, and to the best of my knowledge and belief, they are true, correct, and complete. Declaration of preparer (other than taxpayer) is based on all information of which preparer has any knowledge.

Your signature	Date	Your occupation	Daytime phone number
Spouse's signature. If a joint return, **both** must sign.	Date	Spouse's occupation	

Paid Preparer's Use Only

Preparer's signature ▶	Date	Check if self-employed □	Preparer's SSN or PTIN
Firm's name (or yours if self-employed), address, and ZIP code ▶		EIN	
		Phone no.	

Form **1040** (2009)

SCHEDULE C
(Form 1040)

Department of the Treasury
Internal Revenue Service (99)

Profit or Loss From Business
(Sole Proprietorship)

▶ Partnerships, joint ventures, etc., generally must file Form 1065 or 1065-B.
▶ Attach to Form 1040, 1040NR, or 1041.   ▶ See Instructions for Schedule C (Form 1040).

OMB No. 1545-0074

20**09**

Attachment
Sequence No. **09**

Name of proprietor | Social security number (SSN)

A Principal business or profession, including product or service (see page C-2 of the instructions) | **B** Enter code from pages C-9, 10, & 11 ▶

C Business name. If no separate business name, leave blank. | **D** Employer ID number (EIN), if any

E Business address (including suite or room no.) ▶
City, town or post office, state, and ZIP code

F Accounting method: **(1)** ☐ Cash **(2)** ☐ Accrual **(3)** ☐ Other (specify) ▶

G Did you "materially participate" in the operation of this business during 2009? If "No," see page C-3 for limit on losses   ☐ Yes ☐ No

H If you started or acquired this business during 2009, check here . . . . ▶ ☐

Part I Income

1	Gross receipts or sales. **Caution.** See page C-4 and check the box if:	
	• This income was reported to you on Form W-2 and the "Statutory employee" box on that form was checked, or	
	• You are a member of a qualified joint venture reporting only rental real estate income not subject to self-employment tax. Also see page C-3 for limit on losses. ▶ ☐	**1**
2	Returns and allowances	**2**
3	Subtract line 2 from line 1	**3**
4	Cost of goods sold (from line 42 on page 2)	**4**
5	**Gross profit.** Subtract line 4 from line 3	**5**
6	Other income, including federal and state gasoline or fuel tax credit or refund (see page C-4) .	**6**
7	**Gross income.** Add lines 5 and 6 . . . . ▶	**7**

Part II Expenses. Enter expenses for business use of your home **only** on line 30.

8	Advertising	**8**		**18**	Office expense	**18**
9	Car and truck expenses (see page C-4)	**9**		**19**	Pension and profit-sharing plans .	**19**
10	Commissions and fees .	**10**		**20**	Rent or lease (see page C-6):	
11	Contract labor (see page C-4)	**11**		**a**	Vehicles, machinery, and equipment	**20a**
12	Depletion	**12**		**b**	Other business property . . .	**20b**
13	Depreciation and section 179 expense deduction (not included in Part III) (see page C-5)	**13**		**21**	Repairs and maintenance . . .	**21**
				22	Supplies (not included in Part III) .	**22**
				23	Taxes and licenses	**23**
				24	Travel, meals, and entertainment:	
14	Employee benefit programs (other than on line 19) . .	**14**		**a**	Travel	**24a**
15	Insurance (other than health)	**15**		**b**	Deductible meals and entertainment (see page C-6) . .	**24b**
16	Interest:			**25**	Utilities	**25**
a	Mortgage (paid to banks, etc.)	**16a**		**26**	Wages (less employment credits)	**26**
b	Other	**16b**		**27**	Other expenses (from line 48 on page 2)	**27**
17	Legal and professional services	**17**				

28	**Total expenses** before expenses for business use of home. Add lines 8 through 27 . . . . ▶	**28**
29	Tentative profit or (loss). Subtract line 28 from line 7	**29**
30	Expenses for business use of your home. Attach **Form 8829**	**30**
31	**Net profit or (loss).** Subtract line 30 from line 29.	
	• If a profit, enter on both **Form 1040**, line 12, and **Schedule SE, line 2,** or on **Form 1040NR, line 13** (if you checked the box on line 1, see page C-7). Estates and trusts, enter on **Form 1041, line 3.**	**31**
	• If a loss, you **must** go to line 32.	
32	If you have a loss, check the box that describes your investment in this activity (see page C-7).	
	• If you checked 32a, enter the loss on both **Form 1040, line 12,** and **Schedule SE, line 2,** or on **Form 1040NR, line 13** (if you checked the box on line 1, see the line 31 instructions on page C-7). Estates and trusts, enter on **Form 1041, line 3.**	**32a** ☐ All investment is at risk. **32b** ☐ Some investment is not at risk.
	• If you checked 32b, you **must** attach **Form 6198.** Your loss may be limited.	

For Paperwork Reduction Act Notice, see page C-9 of the instructions.   Cat. No. 11334P   Schedule C (Form 1040) 2009

Part III   **Cost of Goods Sold**   (see page C-8)

33	Method(s) used to value closing inventory: **a** ☐ Cost **b** ☐ Lower of cost or market **c** ☐ Other (attach explanation)		
34	Was there any change in determining quantities, costs, or valuations between opening and closing inventory? If "Yes," attach explanation . . . . ☐ **Yes** ☐ **No**		
35	Inventory at beginning of year. If different from last year's closing inventory, attach explanation . . .	**35**	
36	Purchases less cost of items withdrawn for personal use	**36**	
37	Cost of labor. Do not include any amounts paid to yourself	**37**	
38	Materials and supplies	**38**	
39	Other costs	**39**	
40	Add lines 35 through 39	**40**	
41	Inventory at end of year	**41**	
42	**Cost of goods sold.** Subtract line 41 from line 40. Enter the result here and on page 1, line 4 . . .	**42**	

Part IV   **Information on Your Vehicle.** Complete this part **only** if you are claiming car or truck expenses on line 9 and are not required to file Form 4562 for this business. See the instructions for line 13 on page C-5 to find out if you must file Form 4562.

43   When did you place your vehicle in service for business purposes? (month, day, year)   ▶ _____ / _____ / _____

44   Of the total number of miles you drove your vehicle during 2009, enter the number of miles you used your vehicle for:

   a   Business _____   **b** Commuting (see instructions) _____   **c** Other _____

45   Was your vehicle available for personal use during off-duty hours?   . . . .   ☐ **Yes**   ☐ **No**

46   Do you (or your spouse) have another vehicle available for personal use?.   . . . .   ☐ **Yes**   ☐ **No**

47a   Do you have evidence to support your deduction?   . . . .   ☐ **Yes**   ☐ **No**

   b   If "Yes," is the evidence written?   . . . .   ☐ **Yes**   ☐ **No**

Part V   **Other Expenses.** List below business expenses not included on lines 8–26 or line 30.

--		
--		
--		
--		
--		
--		
--		
48 **Total other expenses.** Enter here and on page 1, line 27	**48**	

Sole Proprietorship: Small Business Start-Up Kit

SCHEDULE C-EZ
(Form 1040)

Department of the Treasury
Internal Revenue Service (99)

Net Profit From Business
(Sole Proprietorship)

▶ Partnerships, joint ventures, etc., generally must file Form 1065 or 1065-B.

▶ Attach to Form 1040, 1040NR, or 1041. ▶ See instructions on page 2.

OMB No. 1545-0074

2009

Attachment
Sequence No. **09A**

Name of proprietor

Social security number (SSN)

Part I   General Information

You May Use Schedule C-EZ Instead of Schedule C Only If You:

- Had business expenses of $5,000 or less.
- Use the cash method of accounting.
- Did not have an inventory at any time during the year.
- Did not have a net loss from your business.
- Had only one business as either a sole proprietor, qualified joint venture, or statutory employee.

And You:

- Had no employees during the year.
- Are not required to file **Form 4562,** Depreciation and Amortization, for this business. See the instructions for Schedule C, line 13, on page C-5 to find out if you must file.
- Do not deduct expenses for business use of your home.
- Do not have prior year unallowed passive activity losses from this business.

A   Principal business or profession, including product or service

B   Enter business code (see page 2)
▶

C   Business name. If no separate business name, leave blank.

D   Enter your EIN (see page 2)

E   Business address (including suite or room no.). Address not required if same as on page 1 of your tax return.

City, town or post office, state, and ZIP code

Part II   Figure Your Net Profit

1   **Gross receipts. Caution.** See the instructions for Schedule C, line 1, on page C-4 and check the box if:

- This income was reported to you on Form W-2 and the "Statutory employee" box on that form was checked, or
- You are a member of a qualified joint venture reporting only rental real estate income not subject to self-employment tax.

▶ ☐   **1**

2   **Total expenses** (see page 2). If more than $5,000, you **must** use Schedule C **2**

3   **Net profit.** Subtract line 2 from line 1. If less than zero, you **must** use Schedule C. Enter on both **Form 1040, line 12,** and **Schedule SE, line 2,** or on **Form 1040NR, line 13.** (If you checked the box on line 1, **do not** report the amount from line 3 on Schedule SE, line 2.) Estates and trusts, enter on **Form 1041, line 3** **3**

Part III   Information on Your Vehicle. Complete this part **only** if you are claiming car or truck expenses on line 2.

4   When did you place your vehicle in service for business purposes? (month, day, year) ▶ _____ .

5   Of the total number of miles you drove your vehicle during 2009, enter the number of miles you used your vehicle for:

a   Business _____   **b**   Commuting (see page 2) _____   **c**   Other _____

6   Was your vehicle available for personal use during off-duty hours?   . . . .   ☐ Yes   ☐ No

7   Do you (or your spouse) have another vehicle available for personal use? . . . .   ☐ Yes   ☐ No

8a   Do you have evidence to support your deduction?   . . . .   ☐ Yes   ☐ No

b   If "Yes," is the evidence written?   . . . .   ☐ Yes   ☐ No

For Paperwork Reduction Act Notice, see page 2.   Cat. No. 14374D   Schedule C-EZ (Form 1040) 2009

Form **1040-SS**	**U.S. Self-Employment Tax Return (Including the Additional Child Tax Credit for Bona Fide Residents of Puerto Rico)**	OMB No. 1545-0090
Department of the Treasury Internal Revenue Service	U.S. Virgin Islands, Guam, American Samoa, the Commonwealth of the Northern Mariana Islands (CNMI), or Puerto Rico. For the year Jan. 1–Dec. 31, 2009, or other tax year beginning , 2009, and ending , 20 .	20**09**

Please type or print	Your first name and initial	Last name	Your social security number
	If a joint return, spouse's first name and initial	Last name	Spouse's social security number
	Present home address (number, street, and apt. no., or rural route)		
	City, town or post office, commonwealth or territory, and ZIP code		

Part I Total Tax and Credits

1 Filing status. Check the box for your filing status (see page SS-3).

☐ Single

☐ Married filing jointly.

☐ Married filing separately. Enter spouse's social security no. above and full name here. ▶ _____

2 Qualifying children. Complete **only** if you are a bona fide resident of Puerto Rico and you are claiming the additional child tax credit (see page SS-5).

(a) First name Last name	(b) Child's social security number	(c) Child's relationship to you

3	Self-employment tax from Part V, line 12.	3	
4	Household employment taxes (see page SS-3). Attach Schedule H (Form 1040).	4	
5	**Total tax.** Add lines 3 and 4 (see page SS-3)	5	
6	2009 estimated tax payments (see page SS-3).	6	
7	Excess social security tax withheld (see page SS-4)	7	
8	Additional child tax credit from Part II, line 3	8	
9	Health coverage tax credit. Attach Form 8885	9	
10	Government retiree credit (see page SS-4)	10	
11	**Total payments and credits.** Add lines 6 through 10	11	
12	If line 11 is more than line 5, subtract line 5 from line 11. This is the amount you **overpaid**	12	
13a	Amount of line 12 to be **refunded to you.** If Form 8888 is attached, check here ▶ ☐	13a	
b	Routing Number	▶ c Type: ☐ Checking ☐ Savings	
d	Account Number		
14	Amount of line 12 to be **applied to 2010 estimated tax.** ▶ 14		
15	**Amount you owe.** If line 5 is more than line 11, subtract line 11 from line 5. For details on how to pay, see page SS-5 ▶	15	

Third Party Designee

Do you want to allow another person to discuss this return with the IRS (see page SS-8)? ☐ **Yes.** Complete the following ☐ **No**

Designee's name ▶	Phone no. ▶	Personal Identification number (PIN) ▶

Sign Here

Joint Return?
See pg. SS-3
Keep a copy for your records.

Under penalties of perjury, I declare that I have examined this return and accompanying schedules and statements, and to the best of my knowledge and belief, they are true, correct, and complete. Declaration of preparer (other than the taxpayer) is based on all information of which the preparer has any knowledge.

Your signature	Date	Daytime phone number
Spouse's signature. If a joint return, **both** must sign.	Date	

Paid Preparer's Use Only

Preparer's signature ▶	Date	Check if self-employed ☐	Preparer's SSN or PTIN
Firm's name (or yours if self-employed), address, and Zip code ▶		EIN	
		Phone no.	

For Disclosure, Privacy Act, and Paperwork Reduction Act Notice, see page SS-9.   Cat. No. 17184B   Form **1040-SS** (2009)

Sole Proprietorship: Small Business Start-Up Kit

Part II Bona Fide Residents of Puerto Rico Claiming Additional Child Tax Credit—See page SS-5.

Caution. You must have three or more qualifying children to claim the additional child tax credit.

1	Income derived from sources within Puerto Rico	**1**	
2	Withheld social security and Medicare taxes from Forms 499R-2/W-2PR (attach copy of form(s)) . .	**2**	
3	**Additional child tax credit.** Use the worksheet on page SS-6 to figure the amount to enter here and in Part I, line 8	**3**	

Part III Profit or Loss From Farming—See the instructions for Schedule F (Form 1040).

Name of proprietor	Social security number

Note. If you are filing a joint return and both you and your spouse had a profit or loss from a farming business, see *Joint returns* and *Husband-Wife Business* beginning on page SS-2 for more information.

Section A—Farm Income—Cash Method

Complete Sections A and B. (Accrual method taxpayers, complete Sections B and C, and Section A, line 11.)

Do not include sales of livestock held for draft, breeding, sport, or dairy purposes.

1	Sales of livestock and other items you bought for resale	**1**			
2	Cost or other basis of livestock and other items reported on line 1 . .	**2**			
3	Subtract line 2 from line 1.			**3**	
4	Sales of livestock, produce, grains, and other products you raised			**4**	
5a	Total cooperative distributions (Form(s) 1099-PATR)	**5a**		**5b** Taxable amount	**5b**
6	Agricultural program payments received			**6**	
7	Commodity Credit Corporation loans reported under election (or forfeited)			**7**	
8	Crop insurance proceeds			**8**	
9	Custom hire (machine work) income			**9**	
10	Other income			**10**	
11	**Gross farm income.** Add amounts in the right column for lines 3 through 10. If accrual method taxpayer, enter the amount from Section C, line 50 . . . . ▶			**11**	

Section B—Farm Expenses—Cash and Accrual Method

Do not include personal or living expenses (such as taxes, insurance, or repairs on your home) that did not produce farm income. Reduce the amount of your farm expenses by any reimbursements before entering the expenses below.

12	Car and truck expenses (attach **Form 4562**)	**12**		25	Pension and profit-sharing plans	**25**
13	Chemicals	**13**		26	Rent or lease:	
14	Conservation expenses . .	**14**		a	Vehicles, machinery, and equipment	**26a**
15	Custom hire (machine work)	**15**		b	Other (land, animals, etc.) . .	**26b**
16	Depreciation and section 179 expense deduction not claimed elsewhere (attach **Form 4562** if required) . .	**16**		27	Repairs and maintenance . .	**27**
				28	Seeds and plants purchased .	**28**
				29	Storage and warehousing .	**29**
17	Employee benefit programs other than on line 25 . . .	**17**		30	Supplies purchased	**30**
18	Feed purchased	**18**		31	Taxes	**31**
19	Fertilizers and lime	**19**		32	Utilities	**32**
20	Freight and trucking . . .	**20**		33	Veterinary, breeding, and medicine	**33**
21	Gasoline, fuel, and oil . . .	**21**		34	Other expenses (specify):	
22	Insurance (other than health)	**22**		a	_____	**34a**
23	Interest:			b	_____	**34b**
a	Mortgage (paid to banks, etc.)	**23a**		c	_____	**34c**
b	Other	**23b**		d	_____	**34d**
24	Labor hired	**24**		e		**34e**
35	**Total expenses.** Add lines 12 through 34e . . . . ▶					**35**
36	**Net farm profit or (loss).** Subtract line 35 from line 11. Enter the result here and in Part V, line 1a					**36**

Form **1040-SS** (2009)

Section C—Farm Income—Accrual Method

Do not include sales of livestock held for draft, breeding, sport, or dairy purposes on any of the lines below.

37	Sales of livestock, produce, grains, and other products during the year.	37	
38a	Total cooperative distributions (Form(s) 1099-PATR) **38a**	**38b** Taxable amount	38b
39	Agricultural program payments received	39	
40	Commodity Credit Corporation loans reported under election (or forfeited)	40	
41	Crop insurance proceeds	41	
42	Custom hire (machine work) income	42	
43	Other farm income (specify) _____	43	
44	Add the amounts in the right column for lines 37 through 43	44	
45	Inventory of livestock, produce, grains, and other products at the beginning of the year	45	
46	Cost of livestock, produce, grains, and other products purchased during the year	46	
47	Add lines 45 and 46	47	
48	Inventory of livestock, produce, grains, and other products at the end of the year	48	
49	Cost of livestock, produce, grains, and other products sold. Subtract line 48 from line 47* . . .	49	
50	**Gross farm income.** Subtract line 49 from line 44. Enter the result here and in Part III, line 11 . ▶	50	

*If you use the unit-livestock-price method or the farm-price method of valuing inventory and the amount on line 48 is larger than the amount on line 47, subtract line 47 from line 48. Enter the result on line 49. Add lines 44 and 49. Enter the total on line 50 and in Part III, line 11.

Part IV **Profit or Loss From Business (Sole Proprietorship)**—See the instructions for Schedule C (Form 1040).

Name of proprietor	Social security number

Note. If you are filing a joint return and both you and your spouse had a profit or loss from a business, see *Joint returns* and *Husband-Wife Business* beginning on page SS-2 for more information.

Section A—Income

1	Gross receipts $ _____ Less returns and allowances $ _____ Balance ▶	1	
2a	Inventory at beginning of year	2a	
b	Purchases less cost of items withdrawn for personal use	2b	
c	Cost of labor. Do not include any amounts paid to yourself.	2c	
d	Materials and supplies.	2d	
e	Other costs (attach statement)	2e	
f	Add lines 2a through 2e	2f	
g	Inventory at end of year	2g	
h	Cost of goods sold. Subtract line 2g from line 2f	2h	
3	**Gross profit.** Subtract line 2h from line 1	3	
4	Other income.	4	
5	**Gross income.** Add lines 3 and 4 . . . . ▶	5	

Section B—Expenses

6	Advertising	6	18	Rent or lease:	
7	Car and truck expenses (attach **Form 4562**)	7	a	Vehicles, machinery, and equipment	18a
8	Commissions and fees . .	8	b	Other business property . .	18b
9	Contract labor	9	19	Repairs and maintenance . .	19
10	Depletion	10	20	Supplies (not included in Section A)	20
11	Depreciation and section 179 expense deduction (not included in Section A). (Attach **Form 4562** if required.) . .	11	21	Taxes and licenses	21
			22	Travel, meals, and entertainment:	
			a	Travel	22a
			b	Deductible meals and entertainment	22b
12	Employee benefit programs (other than on line 17) . . .	12	23	Utilities	23
13	Insurance (other than health)	13	24	Wages not included on line 2c	24
14	Interest on business indebtedness.	14	25a	Other expenses (list type and amount):	
15	Legal and professional services	15		_____	
16	Office expense	16		_____	
17	Pension and profit-sharing plans	17	25b	Total other expenses . . .	25b
26	Total expenses. Add lines 6 through 25b . . . . ▶	26			
27	**Net profit or (loss).** Subtract line 26 from line 5. Enter the result here and in Part V, line 2 . . .	27			

Form **1040-SS** (2009)

Sole Proprietorship: Small Business Start-Up Kit

Part V   **Self-Employment Tax—** If you had **church employee income**, see page SS-1 before you begin.

Name of person with **self-employment** income	Social security number of person with **self-employment** income ▶

Note. If you are filing a joint return and both you and your spouse had self-employment income, you must **each** complete a **separate** Part V.

A	If you are a minister, member of a religious order, or Christian Science practitioner **and** you filed Form 4361, but you had $400 or more of **other** net earnings from self-employment, check here and continue with Part V ▶ ☐			
1a	Net farm profit or (loss) from Part III, line 36, and your distributive share from farm partnerships. **Note.** Skip lines 1a and 1b if you use the farm optional method (see page SS-8).	**1a**		
b	If you received social security retirement or disability benefits, enter the amount of Conservation Reserve Program payments included in Part III, line 6, plus your distributive share of these payments from farm partnerships	**1b**	(	)
2	Net nonfarm profit or (loss) from Part IV, line 27, and your distributive share from nonfarm partnerships. Ministers and members of religious orders, see pages SS-1 and SS-2 for amounts to report on this line. See pages SS-6 and SS-7 for other income to report. **Note.** Skip this line if you use the nonfarm optional method (see page SS-8)	**2**		
3	Combine lines 1a, 1b, and 2	**3**		
4a	If line 3 is more than zero, multiply line 3 by 92.35% (.9235). Otherwise, enter the amount from line 3	**4a**		
b	If you elect one or both of the optional methods, enter the total of lines 2 and 4 of Part VI here	**4b**		
c	Combine lines 4a and 4b. If less than $400, **stop;** you do not owe self-employment tax. **Exception.** If less than $400 and you had **church employee income,** enter -0- and continue ▶	**4c**		

5a	Enter your **church employee income** from Form(s) W-2, W-2AS, W-2CM, W-2GU, W-2VI, or 499R-2/W-2PR. See page SS-1 for definition of church employee income.	**5a**			
b	Multiply line 5a by 92.35% (.9235). If less than $100, enter -0-		**5b**		
6	**Net earnings from self-employment.** Add lines 4c and 5b ▶		**6**		
7	Maximum amount of combined wages and self-employment earnings subject to social security tax for 2009		**7**	106,800	00
8a	Total social security wages and tips from Form(s) W-2, W-2AS, W-2CM, W-2GU, W-2VI, or 499R-2/W-2PR. If $106,800 or more, skip lines 8b through 10, and go to line 11.	**8a**			
b	Unreported tips subject to social security tax from Form 4137, line 10 (see page SS-8)	**8b**			
c	Wages subject to social security tax from Form 8919, line 10 (see page SS-8)	**8c**			
d	Add lines 8a, 8b, and 8c		**8d**		
9	Subtract line 8d from line 7. If zero or less, enter -0- here and on line 10 and go to line 11 ▶		**9**		
10	Multiply the **smaller** of line 6 or line 9 by 12.4% (.124)		**10**		
11	Multiply line 6 by 2.9% (.029)		**11**		
12	**Self-employment tax.** Add lines 10 and 11. Enter here and in Part I, line 3		**12**		

Part VI   **Optional Methods To Figure Net Earnings—** See page SS-8 for limitations.

Note. If you are filing a joint return and both you and your spouse choose to use an optional method to figure net earnings, you must **each** complete and attach a **separate** Part VI.

	Farm Optional Method			
1	Maximum income for optional methods	**1**	4,360	00
2	Enter the **smaller** of: two-thirds (²/₃) of gross farm income (Part III, line 11, plus your distributive share from farm partnerships), but not less than zero; **or** $4,360. Also include this amount in Part V, line 4b, above.	**2**		
	Nonfarm Optional Method			
3	Subtract line 2 from line 1	**3**		
4	Enter the **smaller** of: two-thirds (²/₃) of gross nonfarm income (Part IV, line 5, plus your distributive share from nonfarm partnerships), but not less than zero; **or** the amount in Part VI, line 3, above. Also include this amount in Part V, line 4b, above	**4**		

Form **1040-SS** (2009)

Pay by Credit or Debit Card

You can use your credit or debit card to make estimated tax payments. Call toll-free or visit the website of one of the service providers listed below and follow the instructions. A convenience fee will be charged by the service provider. Fees may vary between providers. You will be told what the fee is during the transaction and you will have the option to either continue or cancel the transaction. You can also find out what the fee will be by calling the provider's toll-free automated customer service number or visiting the provider's website shown below.

Link2Gov Corporation
1-888-PAY-1040™ (1-888-729-1040)
1-888-658-5465 (Customer Service)
www.PAY1040.com

RBS WorldPay, Inc.
1-888-9-PAY-TAX™ (1-888-972-9829)
1-877-517-4881 (Customer Service)
www.payUSAtax.com

Official Payments Corporation
1-888-UPAY-TAX™ (1-888-872-9829)
1-877-754-4413 (Customer Service)
www.officialpayments.com

You will be given a confirmation number at the end of the transaction. Enter the confirmation number in column (c) of the Record of Estimated Tax Payments (on page 9). Do not include the amount of the convenience fee in column (d).

Note. You can deduct the convenience fee charged by the service provider in 2010 as a miscellaneous itemized deduction (subject to the 2%-of-AGI limit) on your 2010 income tax return.

Where To File Your Estimated Tax Payment Voucher if Paying by Check or Money Order

Mail your estimated tax payment voucher and check or money order to the address shown below for the place where you live. Do not mail your tax return to this address or send an estimated tax payment without a payment voucher. Also, do not mail your estimated tax payments to the address shown in the Form 1040 or 1040A instructions. If you need more payment vouchers, you can make a copy of one of your unused vouchers.

Caution: For proper delivery of your estimated tax payment to a P.O. box, you must include the box number in the address. Also, note that only the U.S. Postal Service can deliver to P.O. boxes. Therefore, you cannot use a private delivery service to make estimated tax payments required to be sent to a P.O. box.

IF you live in . . .	THEN send it to "Internal Revenue Service" at . . .
Maine, Massachusetts, New Hampshire, New Jersey, New York, Pennsylvania, Vermont	P.O. Box 37007 Hartford, CT 06176-0007
Florida, Georgia, North Carolina, South Carolina	P.O. Box 105225 Atlanta, GA 30348-5225
Alaska, Arizona, California, Colorado, Hawaii, Nevada, New Mexico, Oregon, Utah, Washington	P.O. Box 510000 San Francisco, CA 94151-5100
Arkansas, Connecticut, Delaware, District of Columbia, Maryland, Missouri, Ohio, Rhode Island, Virginia, West Virginia	P.O. Box 970006 St. Louis, MO 63197-0006
Alabama, Kentucky, Louisiana, Mississippi, Tennessee, Texas	P.O. Box 1300 Charlotte, NC 28201-1300
Idaho, Illinois, Indiana, Iowa, Kansas, Michigan, Minnesota, Montana, Nebraska, North Dakota, Oklahoma, South Dakota, Wisconsin, Wyoming	P.O. Box 802502 Cincinnati, OH 45280-2502
All APO and FPO addresses, U.S. citizens or tax residents living in a foreign country, or filing Form 2555, 2555-EZ, or 4563. American Samoa, the Commonwealth of the Northern Mariana Islands, nonpermanent residents of Guam or the U.S. Virgin Islands, Puerto Rico (or if excluding income under Internal Revenue Code section 933), dual-status aliens	P.O. Box 1300 Charlotte, NC 28201-1300 USA
Permanent residents of Guam*	Department of Revenue and Taxation Government of Guam P.O. Box 23607 GMF, GU 96921
Permanent residents of the U.S. Virgin Islands*	V.I. Bureau of Internal Revenue 9601 Estate Thomas Charlotte Amalie St. Thomas, VI 00802

* Permanent residents must prepare separate vouchers for estimated income tax and self-employment tax payments. Send the income tax vouchers to the address for permanent residents and the self-employment tax vouchers to the address for nonpermanent residents.

Form **1040-ES**
Department of the Treasury
Internal Revenue Service

20︎10 Estimated Tax

Payment Voucher 1

OMB No. 1545-0074

File only if you are making a payment of estimated tax by check or money order. Mail this voucher with your check or money order payable to the **"United States Treasury."** Write your social security number and "2010 Form 1040-ES" on your check or money order. Do not send cash. Enclose, but do not staple or attach, your payment with this voucher.

Calendar year—Due April 15, 2010

Amount of estimated tax you are paying by check or money order.

Dollars	Cents

Print or type

Your first name and initial	Your last name	Your social security number

If joint payment, complete for spouse

Spouse's first name and initial	Spouse's last name	Spouse's social security number

Address (number, street, and apt. no.)

City, state, and ZIP code. (If a foreign address, enter city, province or state, postal code, and country.)

For Privacy Act and Paperwork Reduction Act Notice, see instructions on page 8.
Instructions for Form 1040-ES (2010)   -11-

Form **SS-4** (Rev. January 2010) Department of the Treasury Internal Revenue Service	**Application for Employer Identification Number** (For use by employers, corporations, partnerships, trusts, estates, churches, government agencies, Indian tribal entities, certain individuals, and others.) ▶ See separate instructions for each line.　▶ Keep a copy for your records.	OMB No. 1545-0003 EIN

Type or print clearly.

1	Legal name of entity (or individual) for whom the EIN is being requested

2	Trade name of business (if different from name on line 1)	3	Executor, administrator, trustee, "care of" name

4a	Mailing address (room, apt., suite no. and street, or P.O. box)	5a	Street address (if different) (Do not enter a P.O. box.)

4b	City, state, and ZIP code (if foreign, see instructions)	5b	City, state, and ZIP code (if foreign, see instructions)

6	County and state where principal business is located

7a	Name of responsible party	7b	SSN, ITIN, or EIN

8a	Is this application for a limited liability company (LLC) (or a foreign equivalent)? . . . . ☐ Yes ☐ No	8b	If 8a is "Yes," enter the number of LLC members . . . . ▶

8c If 8a is "Yes," was the LLC organized in the United States? . . . . ☐ Yes ☐ No

9a **Type of entity** (check only one box). **Caution.** If 8a is "Yes," see the instructions for the correct box to check.

☐ Sole proprietor (SSN) _____
☐ Partnership
☐ Corporation (enter form number to be filed) ▶_____
☐ Personal service corporation
☐ Church or church-controlled organization
☐ Other nonprofit organization (specify) ▶_____
☐ Other (specify) ▶

☐ Estate (SSN of decedent) _____
☐ Plan administrator (TIN) _____
☐ Trust (TIN of grantor) _____
☐ National Guard　☐ State/local government
☐ Farmers' cooperative　☐ Federal government/military
☐ REMIC　☐ Indian tribal governments/enterprises
Group Exemption Number (GEN) if any ▶

9b If a corporation, name the state or foreign country (if applicable) where incorporated

State	Foreign country

10 **Reason for applying** (check only one box)

☐ Started new business (specify type) ▶ _____
☐ Hired employees (Check the box and see line 13.)
☐ Compliance with IRS withholding regulations
☐ Other (specify) ▶

☐ Banking purpose (specify purpose) ▶_____
☐ Changed type of organization (specify new type) ▶_____
☐ Purchased going business
☐ Created a trust (specify type) ▶ _____
☐ Created a pension plan (specify type) ▶ _____

11	Date business started or acquired (month, day, year). See instructions.	12	Closing month of accounting year

13	Highest number of employees expected in the next 12 months (enter -0- if none). If no employees expected, skip line 14.	**14** If you expect your employment tax liability to be $1,000 or less in a full calendar year **and** want to file Form 944 annually instead of Forms 941 quarterly, check here. (Your employment tax liability generally will be $1,000 or less if you expect to pay $4,000 or less in total wages.) If you do not check this box, you must file Form 941 for every quarter. ☐

Agricultural	Household	Other

15 First date wages or annuities were paid (month, day, year). **Note.** If applicant is a withholding agent, enter date income will first be paid to nonresident alien (month, day, year) . . . . ▶

16 Check **one** box that best describes the principal activity of your business.
☐ Construction　☐ Rental & leasing　☐ Transportation & warehousing　☐ Accommodation & food service　☐ Wholesale-other　☐ Retail
☐ Real estate　☐ Manufacturing　☐ Finance & insurance　☐ Other (specify)
☐ Health care & social assistance　☐ Wholesale-agent/broker

17 Indicate principal line of merchandise sold, specific construction work done, products produced, or services provided.

18 Has the applicant entity shown on line 1 ever applied for and received an EIN? ☐ Yes ☐ No
If "Yes," write previous EIN here ▶

Third Party Designee	Complete this section **only** if you want to authorize the named individual to receive the entity's EIN and answer questions about the completion of this form.	
	Designee's name	Designee's telephone number (include area code) ( )
	Address and ZIP code	Designee's fax number (include area code) ( )

Under penalties of perjury, I declare that I have examined this application, and to the best of my knowledge and belief, it is true, correct, and complete.

Name and title (type or print clearly) ▶	Applicant's telephone number (include area code) ( )
Signature ▶　　　　　　　Date ▶	Applicant's fax number (include area code) ( )

For Privacy Act and Paperwork Reduction Act Notice, see separate instructions.　　　Cat. No. 16055N　　　Form **SS-4** (Rev. 1-2010)

Do I Need an EIN?

File Form SS-4 if the applicant entity does not already have an EIN but is required to show an EIN on any return, statement, or other document.[1] See also the separate instructions for each line on Form SS-4.

IF the applicant...	AND...	THEN...
Started a new business	Does not currently have (nor expect to have) employees	Complete lines 1, 2, 4a–8a, 8b–c (if applicable), 9a, 9b (if applicable), and 10–14 and 16–18.
Hired (or will hire) employees, including household employees	Does not already have an EIN	Complete lines 1, 2, 4a–6, 7a–b (if applicable), 8a, 8b–c (if applicable), 9a, 9b (if applicable), 10–18.
Opened a bank account	Needs an EIN for banking purposes only	Complete lines 1–5b, 7a–b (if applicable), 8a, 8b–c (if applicable), 9a, 9b (if applicable), 10, and 18.
Changed type of organization	Either the legal character of the organization or its ownership changed (for example, you incorporate a sole proprietorship or form a partnership) [2]	Complete lines 1–18 (as applicable). .
Purchased a going business [3]	Does not already have an EIN	Complete lines 1–18 (as applicable).
Created a trust	The trust is other than a grantor trust or an IRA trust [4]	Complete lines 1–18 (as applicable).
Created a pension plan as a plan administrator [5]	Needs an EIN for reporting purposes	Complete lines 1, 3, 4a–5b, 9a, 10, and 18.
Is a foreign person needing an EIN to comply with IRS withholding regulations	Needs an EIN to complete a Form W-8 (other than Form W-8ECI), avoid withholding on portfolio assets, or claim tax treaty benefits [6]	Complete lines 1–5b, 7a–b (SSN or ITIN optional), 8a, 8b–c (if applicable), 9a, 9b (if applicable), 10, and 18.
Is administering an estate	Needs an EIN to report estate income on Form 1041	Complete lines 1–6, 9a, 10–12, 13–17 (if applicable), and 18.
Is a withholding agent for taxes on non-wage income paid to an alien (i.e., individual, corporation, or partnership, etc.)	Is an agent, broker, fiduciary, manager, tenant, or spouse who is required to file Form 1042, Annual Withholding Tax Return for U.S. Source Income of Foreign Persons	Complete lines 1, 2, 3 (if applicable), 4a–5b, 7a–b (if applicable), 8a, 8b–c (if applicable), 9a, 9b (if applicable), 10, and 18.
Is a state or local agency	Serves as a tax reporting agent for public assistance recipients under Rev. Proc. 80-4, 1980-1 C.B. 581 [7]	Complete lines 1, 2, 4a–5b, 9a, 10, and 18.
Is a single-member LLC	Needs an EIN to file Form 8832, Classification Election, for filing employment tax returns and excise tax returns, or for state reporting purposes [8]	Complete lines 1–18 (as applicable).
Is an S corporation	Needs an EIN to file Form 2553, Election by a Small Business Corporation [9]	Complete lines 1–18 (as applicable).

[1] For example, a sole proprietorship or self-employed farmer who establishes a qualified retirement plan, or is required to file excise, employment, alcohol, tobacco, or firearms returns, must have an EIN. A partnership, corporation, REMIC (real estate mortgage investment conduit), nonprofit organization (church, club, etc.), or farmers' cooperative must use an EIN for any tax-related purpose even if the entity does not have employees.

[2] However, do not apply for a new EIN if the existing entity only (a) changed its business name, (b) elected on Form 8832 to change the way it is taxed (or is covered by the default rules), or (c) terminated its partnership status because at least 50% of the total interests in partnership capital and profits were sold or exchanged within a 12-month period. The EIN of the terminated partnership should continue to be used. See Regulations section 301.6109-1(d)(2)(iii).

[3] Do not use the EIN of the prior business unless you became the "owner" of a corporation by acquiring its stock.

[4] However, grantor trusts that do not file using Optional Method 1 and IRA trusts that are required to file Form 990-T, Exempt Organization Business Income Tax Return, must have an EIN. For more information on grantor trusts, see the Instructions for Form 1041.

[5] A plan administrator is the person or group of persons specified as the administrator by the instrument under which the plan is operated.

[6] Entities applying to be a Qualified Intermediary (QI) need a QI-EIN even if they already have an EIN. See Rev. Proc. 2000-12.

[7] See also o use o   emp oyer on page 4 of the instructions. **Note.** State or local agencies may need an EIN for other reasons, for example, hired employees.

[8] See i sregar e   eatities on page 4 of the instructions for details on completing Form SS-4 for an LLC.

[9] An existing corporation that is electing or revoking S corporation status should use its previously-assigned EIN.

Attention:

This form is provided for informational purposes only. Copy A appears in red, similar to the official IRS form. Do **not** file copy A downloaded from this website with the SSA. The official printed version of this IRS form is scannable, but the online version of it, printed from this website, is not. A penalty of $50 per information return may be imposed for filing forms that cannot be scanned.

To order official IRS forms, call 1-800-TAX-FORM (1-800-829-3676) or Order Information Returns and Employer Returns Online, and we'll mail you the scannable forms and other products.

You may file Forms W-2 and W-3 electronically on the SSA's website at Employer Reporting Instructions & Information. You can create fill-in versions of Forms W-2 and W-3 for filing with SSA. You may also print out copies for filing with state or local governments, distribution to your employees, and for your records.

See IRS Publications 1141, 1167, 1179 and other IRS resources for information about printing these tax forms.

22222	a Employee's social security number	OMB No. 1545-0008		
b Employer identification number (EIN)			1 Wages, tips, other compensation	2 Federal income tax withheld
c Employer's name, address, and ZIP code			3 Social security wages	4 Social security tax withheld
			5 Medicare wages and tips	6 Medicare tax withheld
			7 Social security tips	8 Allocated tips
d Control number			9 Advance EIC payment	10 Dependent care benefits
e Employee's first name and initial Last name Suff.			11 Nonqualified plans	12a
			13 Statutory employee Retirement plan Third-party sick pay	12b
			14 Other	12c
				12d
f Employee's address and ZIP code				

15 State	Employer's state ID number	16 State wages, tips, etc.	17 State income tax	18 Local wages, tips, etc.	19 Local income tax	20 Locality name

Form **W-2** Wage and Tax Statement   **2010**   Department of the Treasury—Internal Revenue Service

Copy 1—For State, City, or Local Tax Department

202

DO NOT STAPLE

33333	a Control number	For Official Use Only ▶ OMB No. 1545-0008		

b Kind of Payer	941 ☐ Military ☐ 943 ☐ 944 ☐ CT-1 ☐ Hshld. emp. ☐ Medicare govt. emp. ☐ Third-party sick pay ☐	1 Wages, tips, other compensation	2 Federal income tax withheld

		3 Social security wages	4 Social security tax withheld
c Total number of Forms W-2	d Establishment number	5 Medicare wages and tips	6 Medicare tax withheld
e Employer identification number (EIN)		7 Social security tips	8 Allocated tips
f Employer's name		9 Advance EIC payments	10 Dependent care benefits
		11 Nonqualified plans	12a Deferred compensation
		13 For third-party sick pay use only	12b HIRE exempt wages and tips
		14 Income tax withheld by payer of third-party sick pay	
g Employer's address and ZIP code			
h Other EIN used this year			
15 State Employer's state ID number		16 State wages, tips, etc.	17 State income tax
		18 Local wages, tips, etc.	19 Local income tax
Contact person		Telephone number ( )	For Official Use Only
Email address		Fax number ( )	

Under penalties of perjury, I declare that I have examined this return and accompanying documents, and, to the best of my knowledge and belief, they are true, correct, and complete.

Signature ▶ _____ Title ▶ _____ Date ▶ _____

Form **W-3** Transmittal of Wage and Tax Statements   **2010**   Department of the Treasury Internal Revenue Service

Send this entire page with the entire Copy A page of Form(s) W-2 to the Social Security Administration.

Do not send any payment (cash, checks, money orders, etc.) with Forms W-2 and W-3.

Reminder

Separate instructions. See the 2010 Instructions for Forms W-2 and W-3 for information on completing this form.

Purpose of Form

A Form W-3 Transmittal is completed only when paper Copy A of Form(s) W-2, Wage and Tax Statement, are being filed. Do not file Form W-3 alone. Do not file Form W-3 for Form(s) W-2 that were submitted electronically to the Social Security Administration (see below). All paper forms **must** comply with IRS standards and be machine readable. Photocopies are **not** acceptable. Use a Form W-3 even if only one paper Form W-2 is being filed. Make sure both the Form W-3 and Form(s) W-2 show the correct tax year and Employer Identification Number (EIN). Make a copy of this form and keep it with Copy D (For Employer) of Form(s) W-2 for your records.

Electronic Filing

The Social Security Administration (SSA) strongly suggests employers report Form W-3 and W-2 Copy A electronically instead of on paper. SSA provides two free options on its Business Services Online (BSO) website:

● **W-2 Online.** Use fill-in forms to create, save, print, and submit up to 20 Forms W-2 to SSA.

● **File Upload.** Upload wage files to SSA that you have created using payroll or tax software that formats the files according to SSA's *Specifications for Filing Form W-2 Electronically (EFW2)*.

For more information, go to *www.socialsecurity.gov/employer* and select "First Time Filers" or "Returning Filers" under "BEFORE YOU FILE."

When To File

Mail any paper Forms W-2 under cover of this Form W-3 Transmittal by February 28, 2011. Electronic fill-in forms or uploads are filed through SSA's Business Services Online (BSO) Internet site and will be on time if submitted by March 31, 2011.

Where To File Paper Forms

Send this entire page with the entire Copy A page of Form(s) W-2 to:

**Social Security Administration
Data Operations Center
Wilkes-Barre, PA 18769-0001**

Note. If you use "Certified Mail" to file, change the ZIP code to "18769-0002." If you use an IRS-approved private delivery service, add "ATTN: W-2 Process, 1150 E. Mountain Dr." to the address and change the ZIP code to "18702-7997." See Publication 15 (Circular E), Employer's Tax Guide, for a list of IRS-approved private delivery services.

For Privacy Act and Paperwork Reduction Act Notice, see the back of Copy D of Form W-2.
Cat. No. 10159Y

Form W-4 (2010)

Purpose. Complete Form W-4 so that your employer can withhold the correct federal income tax from your pay. Consider completing a new Form W-4 each year and when your personal or financial situation changes.

Exemption from withholding. If you are exempt, complete **only** lines 1, 2, 3, 4, and 7 and sign the form to validate it. Your exemption for 2010 expires February 16, 2011. See Pub. 505, Tax Withholding and Estimated Tax.

Note. You cannot claim exemption from withholding if (a) your income exceeds $950 and includes more than $300 of unearned income (for example, interest and dividends) and (b) another person can claim you as a dependent on his or her tax return.

Basic instructions. If you are not exempt, complete the **Personal Allowances Worksheet** below. The worksheets on page 2 further adjust your withholding allowances based on itemized deductions, certain credits, adjustments to income, or two-earners/multiple jobs situations.

Complete all worksheets that apply. However, you may claim fewer (or zero) allowances. For regular wages, withholding must be based on allowances you claimed and may not be a flat amount or percentage of wages.

Head of household. Generally, you may claim head of household filing status on your tax return only if you are unmarried and pay more than 50% of the costs of keeping up a home for yourself and your dependent(s) or other qualifying individuals. See Pub. 501, Exemptions, Standard Deduction, and Filing Information, for information.

Tax credits. You can take projected tax credits into account in figuring your allowable number of withholding allowances. Credits for child or dependent care expenses and the child tax credit may be claimed using the **Personal Allowances Worksheet** below. See Pub. 919, How Do I Adjust My Tax Withholding, for information on converting your other credits into withholding allowances.

Nonwage income. If you have a large amount of nonwage income, such as interest or dividends, consider making estimated tax

payments using Form 1040-ES, Estimated Tax for Individuals. Otherwise, you may owe additional tax. If you have pension or annuity income, see Pub. 919 to find out if you should adjust your withholding on Form W-4 or W-4P.

Two earners or multiple jobs. If you have a working spouse or more than one job, figure the total number of allowances you are entitled to claim on all jobs using worksheets from only one Form W-4. Your withholding usually will be most accurate when all allowances are claimed on the Form W-4 for the highest paying job and zero allowances are claimed on the others. See Pub. 919 for details.

Nonresident alien. If you are a nonresident alien, see Notice 1392, Supplemental Form W-4 Instructions for Nonresident Aliens, before completing this form.

Check your withholding. After your Form W-4 takes effect, use Pub. 919 to see how the amount you are having withheld compares to your projected total tax for 2010. See Pub. 919, especially if your earnings exceed $130,000 (Single) or $180,000 (Married).

Personal Allowances Worksheet (Keep for your records.)

A Enter "1" for **yourself** if no one else can claim you as a dependent . . . . **A** _____

B Enter "1" if:
- You are single and have only one job; or
- You are married, have only one job, and your spouse does not work; or
- Your wages from a second job or your spouse's wages (or the total of both) are $1,500 or less.

B _____

C Enter "1" for your **spouse.** But, you may choose to enter "-0-" if you are married and have either a working spouse or more than one job. (Entering "-0-" may help you avoid having too little tax withheld.) . . . . **C** _____

D Enter number of **dependents** (other than your spouse or yourself) you will claim on your tax return . . . . . . **D** _____

E Enter "1" if you will file as **head of household** on your tax return (see conditions under **Head of household** above) . **E** _____

F Enter "1" if you have at least $1,800 of **child or dependent care expenses** for which you plan to claim a credit . . **F** _____

(**Note.** Do **not** include child support payments. See Pub. 503, Child and Dependent Care Expenses, for details.)

G **Child Tax Credit** (including additional child tax credit). See Pub. 972, Child Tax Credit, for more information.
- If your total income will be less than $61,000 ($90,000 if married), enter "2" for each eligible child; then **less** "1" if you have three or more eligible children.
- If your total income will be between $61,000 and $84,000 ($90,000 and $119,000 if married), enter "1" for each eligible child plus "1" **additional** if you have six or more eligible children. . . . . **G** _____

H Add lines A through G and enter total here. (**Note.** This may be different from the number of exemptions you claim on your tax return.) ▶ **H** _____

For accuracy, complete all worksheets that apply.
- If you plan to **itemize or claim adjustments to income** and want to reduce your withholding, see the **Deductions and Adjustments Worksheet** on page 2.
- If you have **more than one job** or **are married and you and your spouse both work** and the combined earnings from all jobs exceed $18,000 ($32,000 if married), see the **Two-Earners/Multiple Jobs Worksheet** on page 2 to avoid having too little tax withheld.
- If **neither** of the above situations applies, **stop here** and enter the number from line H on line 5 of Form W-4 below.

- - - - - - - - - - **Cut here and give Form W-4 to your employer. Keep the top part for your records.** - - - - - - - - - -

Form **W-4**	**Employee's Withholding Allowance Certificate**	OMB No. 1545-0074
Department of the Treasury Internal Revenue Service	▶ **Whether you are entitled to claim a certain number of allowances or exemption from withholding is subject to review by the IRS. Your employer may be required to send a copy of this form to the IRS.**	20**10**

1 Type or print your first name and middle initial.	Last name	2 Your social security number
Home address (number and street or rural route)	3 ☐ Single ☐ Married ☐ Married, but withhold at higher Single rate. **Note.** If married, but legally separated, or spouse is a nonresident alien, check the "Single" box.	
City or town, state, and ZIP code	4 If your last name differs from that shown on your social security card, check here. You must call 1-800-772-1213 for a replacement card. ▶ ☐	

5 Total number of allowances you are claiming (from line **H** above **or** from the applicable worksheet on page 2) . . **5** _____

6 Additional amount, if any, you want withheld from each paycheck . . . . **6** $ _____

7 I claim exemption from withholding for 2010, and I certify that I meet **both** of the following conditions for exemption.
- Last year I had a right to a refund of **all** federal income tax withheld because I had **no** tax liability **and**
- This year I expect a refund of **all** federal income tax withheld because I expect to have **no** tax liability.

If you meet both conditions, write "Exempt" here . . . . ▶ **7** _____

Under penalties of perjury, I declare that I have examined this certificate and to the best of my knowledge and belief, it is true, correct, and complete.

Employee's signature (Form is not valid unless you sign it.) ▶ _____ **Date** ▶ _____

8 Employer's name and address (Employer: Complete lines 8 and 10 only if sending to the IRS.)	9 Office code (optional)	10 Employer identification number (EIN)

For Privacy Act and Paperwork Reduction Act Notice, see page 2.   Cat. No. 10220Q   Form **W-4** (2010)

Form **940 for 2009:** **Employer's Annual Federal Unemployment (FUTA) Tax Return**

Department of the Treasury — Internal Revenue Service

850109

OMB No. 1545-0028

(EIN)
Employer identification number ☐☐ – ☐☐☐☐☐☐☐

Name (not your trade name) _____

Trade name (if any) _____

Address _____
Number   Street   Suite or room number
_____
City   State   ZIP code

Type of Return
(Check all that apply.)

☐ **a.** Amended
☐ **b.** Successor employer
☐ **c.** No payments to employees in 2009
☐ **d.** Final: Business closed or stopped paying wages

Read the separate instructions before you fill out this form. Please type or print within the boxes.

Part 1: Tell us about your return. If any line does NOT apply, leave it blank.

1   If you were required to pay your state unemployment tax in ...

     1a One state only, write the state abbreviation . . . . . **1a** ☐☐
     - OR -
     1b More than one state (You are a multi-state employer) . . . . **1b** ☐ Check here. Fill out Schedule A.

2   If you paid wages in a state that is subject to **CREDIT REDUCTION** . . . . **2** ☐ Check here. Fill out Schedule A (Form 940), Part 2.

Part 2: Determine your FUTA tax before adjustments for 2009. If any line does NOT apply, leave it blank.

3   Total payments to all employees . . . . **3** ☐

4   Payments exempt from FUTA tax . . . . **4** ☐

     Check all that apply: **4a** ☐ Fringe benefits   **4c** ☐ Retirement/Pension   **4e** ☐ Other
     4b ☐ Group-term life insurance   **4d** ☐ Dependent care

5   Total of payments made to each employee in excess of $7,000 . . . . **5** ☐

6   **Subtotal** (line 4 + line 5 = line 6) . . . . **6** ☐

7   **Total taxable FUTA wages** (line 3 – line 6 = line 7) . . . . **7** ☐

8   **FUTA tax before adjustments** (line 7 × .008 = line 8) . . . . **8** ☐

Part 3: Determine your adjustments. If any line does NOT apply, leave it blank.

9   If ALL of the taxable FUTA wages you paid were excluded from state unemployment tax, multiply line 7 by .054 (line 7 × .054 = line 9). Then go to line 12 . . . **9** ☐

10   If SOME of the taxable FUTA wages you paid were excluded from state unemployment tax, OR you paid ANY state unemployment tax late (after the due date for filing Form 940), fill out the worksheet in the instructions. Enter the amount from line 7 of the worksheet . . . . . . **10** ☐

11   If credit reduction applies, enter the amount from line 3 of Schedule A (Form 940) . . . . . **11** ☐

Part 4: Determine your FUTA tax and balance due or overpayment for 2009. If any line does NOT apply, leave it blank.

12   **Total FUTA tax after adjustments** (lines 8 + 9 + 10 + 11 = line 12) . . . . **12** ☐

13   FUTA tax deposited for the year, including any overpayment applied from a prior year . . **13** ☐

14   Balance due (If line 12 is more than line 13, enter the difference on line 14.)
     ● If line 14 is more than $500, you must deposit your tax.
     ● If line 14 is $500 or less, you may pay with this return. For more information on how to pay, see the separate instructions . . . . **14** ☐

15   Overpayment (If line 13 is more than line 12, enter the difference on line 15 and check a box below.) . . . . **15** ☐

Check one: ☐ Apply to next return.
☐ Send a refund.

▶ You **MUST** fill out both pages of this form and **SIGN** it.

Next ➡

For Privacy Act and Paperwork Reduction Act Notice, see the back of Form 940-V, Payment Voucher.   Cat. No. 11234O   Form **940** (2009)

850209

Name (not your trade name)	Employer identification number (EIN)

Part 5: Report your FUTA tax liability by quarter only if line 12 is more than $500. If not, go to Part 6.

16 Report the amount of your FUTA tax liability for each quarter; do NOT enter the amount you deposited. If you had no liability for a quarter, leave the line blank.

16a **1st quarter** (January 1 – March 31) . . . . .16a   .

16b **2nd quarter** (April 1 – June 30) . . . . .16b   .

16c **3rd quarter** (July 1 – September 30) . . . . .16c   .

16d **4th quarter** (October 1 – December 31) . . . . . . .16d   .

17 **Total tax liability for the year** (lines 16a + 16b + 16c + 16d = line 17) 17   .   **Total must equal line 12.**

Part 6: May we speak with your third-party designee?

Do you want to allow an employee, a paid tax preparer, or another person to discuss this return with the IRS? See the instructions for details.

☐ **Yes.** Designee's name and phone number   (   )   –

Select a 5-digit Personal Identification Number (PIN) to use when talking to IRS

☐ **No.**

Part 7: Sign here. You MUST fill out both pages of this form and SIGN it.

Under penalties of perjury, I declare that I have examined this return, including accompanying schedules and statements, and to the best of my knowledge and belief, it is true, correct, and complete, and that no part of any payment made to a state unemployment fund claimed as a credit was, or is to be, deducted from the payments made to employees. Declaration of preparer (other than taxpayer) is based on all information of which preparer has any knowledge.

✘ **Sign your name here**

Print your name here

Print your title here

Date   /   /

Best daytime phone   (   )   –

Paid preparer's use only

Check if you are self-employed . . . ☐

Preparer's name		Preparer's SSN/PTIN	
Preparer's signature		Date	/ /
Firm's name (or yours if self-employed)		EIN	
Address		Phone	( ) –
City	State	ZIP code	

Form **940** (2009)

Form 940-V, Payment Voucher

What Is Form 940-V?

Form 940-V is a transmittal form for your check or money order. Using Form 940-V allows us to process your payment more accurately and efficiently. If you have any balance due of $500 or less on your 2009 Form 940, fill out Form 940-V and send it with your check or money order.

Note. If your balance is more than $500, see *When Must You Deposit Your FUTA Tax?* in the Instructions for Form 940.

How Do You Fill Out Form 940-V?

Type or print clearly.

Box 1. Enter your employer identification number (EIN). Do not enter your social security number (SSN).

Box 2. Enter the amount of your payment. Be sure to put dollars and cents in the appropriate spaces.

Box 3. Enter your business name and complete address exactly as they appear on your Form 940.

How Should You Prepare Your Payment?

- Make your check or money order payable to the *United States Treasury.* Do not send cash.
- On the memo line of your check or money order, write:
  - — your EIN,
  - — Form 940, and
  - — 2009.
- Carefully detach Form 940-V along the dotted line.
- Do not staple your payment to the voucher.
- Mail your 2009 Form 940, your payment, and Form 940-V in the envelope that came with your 2009 Form 940 instruction booklet. If you do not have that envelope, use the table in the Instructions for Form 940 to find the mailing address.

✂ ▼ **Detach Here and Mail With Your Payment and Form 940.** ▼ ✂

Form **940-V**

Department of the Treasury
Internal Revenue Service

Payment Voucher

▶ **Do not staple or attach this voucher to your payment.**

OMB No. 1545-0028

2009

1 Enter your employer identification number (EIN).	2 Enter the amount of your payment. ▶	Dollars	Cents
	3 Enter your business name (individual name if sole proprietor).		
	Enter your address.		
	Enter your city, state, and ZIP code.		

207

Form 941 for 2010: Employer's QUARTERLY Federal Tax Return
(Rev. February 2010)
Department of the Treasury — Internal Revenue Service

950110

OMB No. 1545-0029

(EIN)
Employer identification number

☐☐ – ☐☐☐☐☐☐☐

Name *(not your tr de n me)*

Trade name *(if any)*

Address

Number   Street   Suite or room number

City   State   ZIP code

Report for this Quarter of 2010
(Check one.)

☐ **1:** January, February, March

☐ **2:** April, May, June

☐ **3:** July, August, September

☐ **4:** October, November, December

Read the separate instructions before you complete Form 941. Type or print within the boxes.

Part 1: Answer these questions for this quarter.

1 Number of employees who received wages, tips, or other compensation for the pay period including: *Mar. 12* (Quarter 1), *June 12* (Quarter 2), *Sept. 12* (Quarter 3), *Dec. 12* (Quarter 4) **1** _____

2 Wages, tips, and other compensation **2** _____

3 Income tax withheld from wages, tips, and other compensation . . . . **3** _____

4 If no wages, tips, and other compensation are subject to social security or Medicare tax ☐ Check and go to line 6.

5 Taxable social security and Medicare wages and tips:

	Column 1		Column 2
5a Taxable social security wages	_____	× .124 =	_____
5b Taxable social security tips	_____	× .124 =	_____
5c Taxable Medicare wages & tips	_____	× .029 =	_____

5d Total social security and Medicare taxes (*Column 2,* lines 5a + 5b + 5c = line 5d) . . **5d** _____

6 Total taxes before adjustments (lines 3 + 5d = line 6) . . . . **6** _____

7 CURRENT QUARTER'S ADJUSTMENTS, for example, a fractions of cents adjustment. See the instructions.

7a Current quarter's fractions of cents _____

7b Current quarter's sick pay . . . . _____

7c Current quarter's adjustments for tips and group-term life insurance _____

7d TOTAL ADJUSTMENTS. Combine all amounts on lines 7a through 7c . . . . . . **7d** _____

8 Total taxes after adjustments. Combine lines 6 and 7d . . . . **8** _____

9 Advance earned income credit (EIC) payments made to employees . . . . **9** _____

10 Total taxes after adjustment for advance EIC (line 8 – line 9 = line 10) . . . . . **10** _____

11 Total deposits for this quarter, including overpayment applied from a prior quarter and overpayment applied from Form 941-X or Form 944-X . . . . _____

12a COBRA premium assistance payments (see instructions) . . . _____

12b Number of individuals provided COBRA premium assistance reported on line 12a . . . _____

13 Add lines 11 and 12a . . . . **13** _____

14 Balance due. If line 10 is more than line 13, write the difference here. For information on how to pay, see the instructions . . . . **14** _____

15 Overpayment. If line 13 is more than line 10, write the difference here _____ ☐ Apply to next return. Check one ☐ Send a refund.

▶ You MUST complete both pages of Form 941 and SIGN it.

Next ▶

For Privacy Act and Paperwork Reduction Act Notice, see the back of the Payment Voucher.   Cat. No. 17001Z   Form **941** (Rev. 2-2010)

950210

Name *(not your trade name)*	Employer identification number (EIN)

Part 2: Tell us about your deposit schedule and tax liability for this quarter.

If you are unsure about whether you are a monthly schedule depositor or a semiweekly schedule depositor, see *Pub. 15 (Circular E)*, section 11.

16 [ ] [ ] Write the state abbreviation for the state where you made your deposits OR write "MU" if you made your deposits in *multiple* states.

17 Check one: [ ] Line 10 on this return is less than $2,500 or line 10 on the return for the preceding quarter was less than $2,500, and you did not incur a $100,000 next-day deposit obligation during the current quarter. Go to Part 3.

[ ] You were a monthly schedule depositor for the entire quarter. Enter your tax liability for each month. Then go to Part 3.

Tax liability: Month 1 [.]

Month 2 [.]

Month 3 [.]

Total liability for quarter [.] Total must equal line 10.

[ ] You were a semiweekly schedule depositor for any part of this quarter. Complete *Schedule B (Form 941): Report of Tax Liability for Semiweekly Schedule Depositors,* and attach it to Form 941.

Part 3: Tell us about your business. If a question does NOT apply to your business, leave it blank.

18 If your business has closed or you stopped paying wages . . . . [ ] Check here, and

enter the final date you paid wages [/ /] .

19 If you are a seasonal employer and you do not have to file a return for every quarter of the year . . [ ] Check here.

Part 4: May we speak with your third-party designee?

Do you want to allow an employee, a paid tax preparer, or another person to discuss this return with the IRS? See the instructions for details.

[ ] Yes. Designee's name and phone number [ ] [ ]

Select a 5-digit Personal Identification Number (PIN) to use when talking to the IRS. [ ][ ][ ][ ][ ]

[ ] No.

Part 5: Sign here. You MUST complete both pages of Form 941 and SIGN it.

Under penalties of perjury, I declare that I have examined this return, including accompanying schedules and statements, and to the best of my knowledge and belief, it is true, correct, and complete. Declaration of preparer (other than taxpayer) is based on all information of which preparer has any knowledge.

X **Sign your name here**

Print your name here
Print your title here

Date [/ /] Best daytime phone

Paid preparer's use only Check if you are self-employed . . . [ ]

Preparer's name		Preparer's SSN/PTIN	
Preparer's signature		Date	/ /
Firm's name (or yours if self-employed)		EIN	
Address		Phone	
City	State	ZIP code	

Attention:

This form is provided for informational purposes and should not be reproduced on personal computer printers by individual taxpayers for filing. The printed version of this form is designed as a "machine readable" form. As such, it must be printed using special paper, special inks, and within precise specifications.

Additional information about the printing of these specialized tax forms can be found in IRS Publications 1141, 1167, 1179, and other IRS resources.

Taxpayers and authorized representatives may obtain Forms 8109-B with the taxpayer's name, address, and Employer Identification Number (EIN) entered on the forms by going to a local IRS Taxpayer Assistance Center or by calling 1-800-829-4933.

If a taxpayer or tax practitioner needs copies of blank Forms 8109-B, a request for blank copies must be made in writing on company letterhead.

These requests must be mailed to the National Distribution Center at:

Internal Revenue Service
National Distribution Center
1201 N. Mitsubishi Motorway
Bloomington, IL 61705-6613

For more information, see *Need a blank coupon?* on our web page titled *What are FTDs and why are they important?*

AMOUNT OF DEPOSIT (Do NOT type. please print.)

DOLLARS   CENTS

MONTH TAX YEAR ENDS →

EMPLOYER IDENTIFICATION NUMBER →

BANK NAME/ DATE STAMP

Name _____

Address _____

City _____

State _____ ZIP _____

Telephone number ( )

IRS USE ONLY

Darken only one TYPE OF TAX			Darken only one TAX PERIOD
⌀ ◄ 941	⌀ ◄ 945		⌀ ◄ 1st Quarter
⌀ ◄1120	⌀ ◄ 1042		⌀ ◄ 2nd Quarter
⌀ ◄ 943	⌀ ◄ 990-T		⌀ ◄ 3rd Quarter
⌀ ◄ 720	⌀ ◄990-PF		⌀ ◄ 4th Quarter
⌀ ◄ CT-1	⌀ ◄ 944		
⌀ ◄ 940			ʰᵇ

FOR BANK USE IN MICR ENCODING

Federal Tax Deposit Coupon

Form 8109-B (Rev. 12-2009)

- -

↑ SEPARATE ALONG THIS LINE AND SUBMIT TO DEPOSITARY WITH PAYMENT ↑ OMB NO. 1545-0257

What's new. For Forms CT-1, 940, 943, 944, 945, and 1042, darken only the 4th quarter space for the proper tax period.

Do not use a federal tax deposit coupon (Form 8109 or Form 8109-B) to make a payment with Forms CT-1X, 941-X, 943-X, 944-X, 945-X, or with Formulario 941-X(PR).

Note. Pen or #2 pencil can be used to complete the form. The name, address, and telephone number may be completed other than by hand. You cannot use photocopies of the coupons to make your deposits. Do not staple, tape, or fold the coupons.

The IRS encourages you to make federal tax deposits using the Electronic Federal Tax Payment System (EFTPS). For more information on EFTPS, go to *www.eftps.gov* or call 1-800-555-4477.

Purpose of form. Use Form 8109-B to make a tax deposit only in the following two situations.

1. You have not yet received your resupply of preprinted deposit coupons (Form 8109).

2. You are a new entity and have already been assigned an employer identification number (EIN), but you have not been received your initial supply of preprinted deposit coupons (Form 8109). If you have not received your EIN, see *Exceptions* below.

Note. If you do not receive your resupply of deposit coupons and a deposit is due or you do not receive your initial supply within 5–6 weeks of receipt of your EIN, call 1-800-829-4933.

Caution. Do not use these coupons to deposit delinquent taxes assessed by the IRS. Pay delinquent taxes directly to the IRS using the stub included with the notice or by using EFTPS.

How to complete the form. Enter your name as shown on your return or other IRS correspondence, address, and EIN in the spaces provided. Do not make a name or address change on this form (see Form 8822, Change of Address). If you are required to file a Form 1120, 1120-C, 990-PF (with net investment income), 990-T, or 2438, enter the month in which your tax year ends in the MONTH TAX YEAR ENDS boxes. For example, if your tax year ends in January, enter 01; if it ends in December, enter 12. Make your entries for EIN and MONTH TAX YEAR ENDS (if applicable) as shown in *Amount of deposit* below.

Exceptions. If you have applied for an EIN, have not received it, and a deposit must be made, do not use Form 8109-B. Instead, send your payment to the IRS address where you file your return. Make your check or money order payable to the United States Treasury and show on it your name (as shown on Form SS-4, Application for Employer Identification Number), address, kind of tax, period covered, and date you applied for an EIN.

Amount of deposit. Enter the amount of the deposit in the space provided. Enter the amount legibly, forming the characters as shown below:

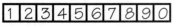

Hand print money amounts without using dollar signs, commas, a decimal point, or leading zeros. If the deposit is for whole dollars only, enter "00" in the CENTS boxes. For example, a deposit of $7,635.22 would be entered like this:

	DOLLARS	CENTS
	7 6 3 5	2 2

Caution. Darken only one space for TYPE OF TAX and only one space for TAX PERIOD. Darken the space to the left of the applicable form and tax period. Darkening the wrong space or multiple spaces may delay proper crediting to your account. See below for an explanation of *Types of Tax* and *Marking the Proper Tax Period.*

Types of Tax

Form 941 Employer's QUARTERLY Federal Tax Return (includes Forms 941-M, 941-PR, and 941-SS)

Form 943 Employer's Annual Federal Tax Return for Agricultural Employees

Form 944 Employer's ANNUAL Federal Tax Return (includes Forms 944-PR, 944(SP), and 944-SS)

Form 945 Annual Return of Withheld Federal Income Tax

Form 720 Quarterly Federal Excise Tax Return

Form CT-1 Employer's Annual Railroad Retirement Tax Return

Form 940 Employer's Annual Federal Unemployment (FUTA) Tax Return (includes Form 940-PR)

Form 1120 U.S. Corporation Income Tax Return (includes Form 1120 series of returns and Form 2438)

Form 990-T Exempt Organization Business Income Tax Return

Form 990-PF Return of Private Foundation or Section 4947(a)(1) Nonexempt Charitable Trust Treated as a Private Foundation

Form 1042 Annual Withholding Tax Return for U.S. Source Income of Foreign Persons

Marking the Proper Tax Period

Payroll taxes and withholding. For Form 941, if your liability was incurred during:

- January 1 through March 31, darken the 1st quarter space;
- April 1 through June 30, darken the 2nd quarter space;
- July 1 through September 30, darken the 3rd quarter space; and
- October 1 through December 31, darken the 4th quarter space.

For Forms CT-1, 940, 943, 944, 945, and 1042, darken only the 4th quarter space.

Do not use a federal tax deposit coupon (Form 8109 or Form 8109-B) to make a payment with Forms CT-1X, 941-X, 943-X, 944-X, 945-X, or with Formulario 941-X(PR).

Note. If the liability for Form 941 was incurred during one quarter and deposited in another quarter, darken the space for the quarter in which the tax liability was incurred. For example, if the liability was incurred in March and deposited in April, darken the 1st quarter space.

Excise taxes. For Form 720, follow the instructions above for Form 941. For Form 990-PF, with net investment income, follow the instructions on page 2 for Form 1120, 990-T, and 2438.

Department of the Treasury
Internal Revenue Service

Cat. No. 61042S

Form **8109-B** (Rev. 12-2009)

Form **8829**	**Expenses for Business Use of Your Home**	OMB No. 1545-0074
Department of the Treasury Internal Revenue Service (99)	▶ File only with Schedule C (Form 1040). Use a separate Form 8829 for each home you used for business during the year. ▶ See separate instructions.	**2009** Attachment Sequence No. **66**

Name(s) of proprietor(s)	Your social security number

Part I Part of Your Home Used for Business

1	Area used regularly and exclusively for business, regularly for daycare, or for storage of inventory or product samples (see instructions)	1	
2	Total area of home	2	
3	Divide line 1 by line 2. Enter the result as a percentage.	3	%

For daycare facilities not used exclusively for business, go to line 4. All others go to line 7.

4	Multiply days used for daycare during year by hours used per day	4		hr.		
5	Total hours available for use during the year (365 days x 24 hours) (see instructions)	5		8,760 hr.		
6	Divide line 4 by line 5. Enter the result as a decimal amount . . .	6	.			
7	Business percentage. For daycare facilities not used exclusively for business, multiply line 6 by line 3 (enter the result as a percentage). All others, enter the amount from line 3 . . . . . ▶			7		%

Part II Figure Your Allowable Deduction

8	Enter the amount from Schedule C, line 29, **plus** any net gain or (loss) derived from the business use of your home and shown on Schedule D or Form 4797. If more than one place of business, see instructions		8	

	See instructions for columns **(a)** and **(b)** before completing lines 9–21.		**(a)** Direct expenses	**(b)** Indirect expenses		
9	Casualty losses (see instructions).	9				
10	Deductible mortgage interest (see instructions) .	10				
11	Real estate taxes (see instructions)	11				
12	Add lines 9, 10, and 11	12				
13	Multiply line 12, column (b) by line 7		13			
14	Add line 12, column (a) and line 13				14	
15	Subtract line 14 from line 8. If zero or less, enter -0-				15	
16	Excess mortgage interest (see instructions) .	16				
17	Insurance	17				
18	Rent	18				
19	Repairs and maintenance	19				
20	Utilities	20				
21	Other expenses (see instructions).	21				
22	Add lines 16 through 21	22				
23	Multiply line 22, column (b) by line 7	23				
24	Carryover of operating expenses from 2008 Form 8829, line 42 . .	24				
25	Add line 22 column (a), line 23, and line 24.				25	
26	Allowable operating expenses. Enter the **smaller** of line 15 or line 25				26	
27	Limit on excess casualty losses and depreciation. Subtract line 26 from line 15				27	
28	Excess casualty losses (see instructions)	28				
29	Depreciation of your home from line 41 below	29				
30	Carryover of excess casualty losses and depreciation from 2008 Form 8829, line 43	30				
31	Add lines 28 through 30				31	
32	Allowable excess casualty losses and depreciation. Enter the **smaller** of line 27 or line 31 . .				32	
33	Add lines 14, 26, and 32.				33	
34	Casualty loss portion, if any, from lines 14 and 32. Carry amount to **Form 4684** (see instructions)				34	
35	**Allowable expenses for business use of your home.** Subtract line 34 from line 33. Enter here and on Schedule C, line 30. If your home was used for more than one business, see instructions ▶				35	

Part III Depreciation of Your Home

36	Enter the **smaller** of your home's adjusted basis or its fair market value (see instructions) . .	36	
37	Value of land included on line 36	37	
38	Basis of building. Subtract line 37 from line 36	38	
39	Business basis of building. Multiply line 38 by line 7.	39	
40	Depreciation percentage (see instructions).	40	%
41	Depreciation allowable (see instructions). Multiply line 39 by line 40. Enter here and on line 29 above	41	

Part IV Carryover of Unallowed Expenses to 2010

42	Operating expenses. Subtract line 26 from line 25. If less than zero, enter -0-	42	
43	Excess casualty losses and depreciation. Subtract line 32 from line 31. If less than zero, enter -0-	43	

For Paperwork Reduction Act Notice, see page 4 of separate instructions. Cat. No. 13232M Form **8829** (2009)

Chapter 16

Additional Legal Forms

Instructions for Releases

Releases are a method of acknowledging the satisfaction of an obligation or of releasing parties from liability or claims. Releases are used in various situations in the business world, from releasing a person or company from liability after an accident to a release of liens or claims against property. Releases can be very powerful documents. The various releases contained in this chapter are tailored to meet the most common situations in which a release is used. For a release to be valid, there must be some type of consideration received by the person who is granting the release. Releases should be used carefully as they may prevent any future claims against the party to whom it is granted. In general, a release from claims relating to an accident which causes personal injury should not be signed without a prior examination by a doctor. Also note that a release relating to damage to community property in a "community property" state must be signed by both spouses. Study the various forms provided to determine which one is proper for the use intended.

General Release: This release serves as a full blanket-release from one party to another. It should only be used when all obligations of one party are to be released. The party signing this release is discharging the other party from all of their obligations to the other party stemming from a specific incident or transaction. This form can be used when one party has a claim against another and the other agrees to waive the claim for payment. To complete this form, fill in the following information:
① Name of person granting release
② Address of person granting release
③ Name of person granted release
④ Address of person granted release

⑤ Transaction or incident for which release is being granted
⑥ Date of release
⑦ Signature of person granting release
⑧ Printed name of person granting release

Mutual Release: The mutual release form provides a method for two parties to jointly release each other from their mutual obligations or claims. This form should be used when both parties intend to discharge each other from all of their mutual obligations. It essentially serves the purpose of two reciprocal General Releases.

① Name of first person granting release
② Address of first person granting release
③ Name of second person granting release
④ Address of second person granting release
⑤ Transaction or incident for which release is being granted
⑥ Date of release
⑦ Signature of first person granting release
⑧ Printed name of first person granting release
⑨ Signature of second person granting release
⑩ Printed name of second person granting release

Specific Release: This release form should be used only when a particular claim or obligation is being released, while allowing other liabilities to continue. The obligation being released should be spelled out in careful and precise terms to prevent confusion with any other obligation or claim. In addition, the liabilities or obligations which are not being released, but will survive, should also be carefully noted.

① Name of person granting release
② Address of person granting release
③ Name of person granted release
④ Address of person granted release
⑤ Claim or obligation for which release is being granted (Also note any claims, liabilities, or obligations that are not being released)
⑥ Transaction or incident for which release is being granted
⑦ Date of release
⑧ Signature of person granting release
⑨ Printed name of person granting release

General Release

For consideration, I, ① _____ ,
address: ②

release ③ _____ ,
address: ④

from all claims and obligations, known or unknown, to this date arising from the following transaction or incident: ⑤

The party signing this release has not assigned any claims or obligations covered by this release to any other party.

The party signing this release intends that it both bind and benefit itself and any successors.

Dated ⑥ _____ , 20 ____

⑦ _____
Signature of person granting release

⑧ _____
Printed name of person granting release

Mutual Release

For consideration, ① _____ ,
address: ②

and ③ _____ ,
address: ④

release each other from all claims and obligations, known or unknown, that they may have against each other arising from the following transaction or incident: ⑤

Neither party has assigned any claims or obligations covered by this release to any other party.

Both parties signing this release intend that it both bind and benefit themselves and any successors.

Dated ⑥ _____ , 20 ____

⑦ _____
Signature of 1st person

⑨ _____
Signature of 2nd person

⑧ _____
Printed name of 1st person

⑩ _____
Printed name of 2nd person

Specific Release

For consideration, I, ①_____ ,
address: ②

release ③_____ ,
address: ④

from the following specific claims and obligations: ⑤

arising from the following transaction or incident: ⑥

Any claims or obligations that are not specifically mentioned are not released by this Specific Release.

The party signing this release has not assigned any claims or obligations covered by this release to any other party.

The party signing this release intends that it both bind and benefit itself and any successors.

Dated ⑦_____ , 20 _____

⑧_____
Signature of person granting release

⑨_____
Printed name of person granting release

Instructions for Receipts

Receipt in Full: This form should be used as a receipt for a payment that completely pays off a debt. You will need to include the amount paid, the name of the person who paid it, the date when paid, and a description of the obligation that is paid off (for example: an invoice, statement, or bill of sale). The original receipt should go to the person making the payment, but a copy should be retained.

1. Amount paid
2. Name of person paying
3. Identify what is being paid for
4. Date
5. Signature
6. Printed name

Receipt on Account: This form should be used as a receipt for a payment that does not fully pay off a debt, but, rather, is a payment on account and is credited to the total balance due. You will need to include the amount paid, the name of the person who paid it, the date when paid, and a description of the account to which the payment is to be applied. The original receipt should go to the person making the payment, but a copy should be kept by you.

1. Amount paid
2. Name of person paying
3. Identify what account
4. Date
5. Signature
6. Printed name

Receipt for Goods: This form should be used as a receipt for the acceptance of goods. It is intended to be used in conjunction with a delivery order or purchase order. It also states that the goods have been inspected and found to be in conformance with the order. The original of this receipt should be retained by the person delivering the goods and a copy should go to the person accepting delivery.

1. Date
2. Signature
3. Printed name

Receipt in Full

The undersigned acknowledges receipt of the sum of $ ①_____ paid by

②_____ .

This payment constitutes full payment and satisfaction of the following obligation: ③

Dated ④_____ , 20 _____

⑤_____
Signature of Person Receiving Payment

⑥_____
Printed Name of Person Receiving Payment

Receipt on Account

The undersigned acknowledges receipt of the sum of $ ①_____ paid by

②_____ .

This payment will be applied and credited to the following account: ③

Dated ④_____ , 20 _____

⑤_____
Signature of Person Receiving Payment

⑥_____
Printed Name of Person Receiving Payment

Receipt for Goods

The undersigned acknowledges receipt of the goods which are described on the attached purchase order. The undersigned also acknowledges that these goods have been inspected and found to be in conformance with the purchase order specifications.

Dated ①_____ , 20 _____

②_____
Signature of Person Receiving Goods

③_____
Printed Name of Person Receiving Goods

Instructions for Rental of Personal Property

Personal Property Rental Agreement:
To prepare this form, fill in the following information:
1. Date of rental agreement
2. Name of Owner
3. Address of Owner
4. Name of Renter
5. Address of Renter
6. Complete description of rental property
7. Beginning and ending date and time of rental agreement
8. Amount being charged for rental
9. period of time for payment (usually a month or day)
10. Describe payment details
11. Amount of late fee
12. Number of days the rental not paid to make it in default
13. Amount of security deposit
14. Amount of insurance coverage required
15. Additional terms
16. Which state's laws will be used
17. Signature of Owner
18. Printed name of Owner
19. Signature of Renter
20. Printed name of Renter

Bill of Sale, with Warranties: This document is used as a receipt of the sale of personal property. It is, in many respects, often used to operate as a *title* (or ownership document) to items of personal property. It verifies that the person noted in the bill of sale has obtained legal title to the property from the previous owner. This particular version also provides that the seller *warrants* (or guarantees) that he or she has the authority to transfer legal title to the buyer and that there are no outstanding debts or liabilities for the property. In addition, this form provides that the seller warrants that the property is in good working condition on the date of the sale. To complete this form, simply fill in the names and addresses of the seller and buyer, the purchase price of the item, and a description of the property.

To prepare this form, fill in the following information:
1. Date of Bill of Sale
2. Name of Seller
3. Address of Seller

④ Name of Buyer
⑤ Address of Buyer
⑥ Amount received for property
⑦ Describe property being purchased
⑧ Signature of Seller
⑨ Printed name of Seller

Bill of Sale, without Warranties: This form also provides a receipt to the buyer for the purchase of an item of personal property. However, in this form, the seller makes no warranties at all, either regarding the authority to sell the item or the condition of the item. It is sold to the buyer in "as is" condition. The buyer takes it regardless of any defects. To complete this form, fill in the names and addresses of the seller and buyer, the purchase price of the item, and a description of the property.

To prepare this form, fill in the following information:
① Date of Bill of Sale
② Name of Seller
③ Address of Seller
④ Name of Buyer
⑤ Address of Buyer
⑥ Amount received for property
⑦ Describe property being purchased
⑧ Signature of Seller
⑨ Printed name of Seller

Bill of Sale, Subject to Debt: This form also provides a receipt to the buyer for the purchase of an item of personal property. This form, however, provides that the property sold is subject to a certain prior debt. It verifies that the seller has obtained legal title to the property from the previous owner, but that the seller specifies that the property is sold subject to a certain debt which the buyer is to pay off. In addition, the buyer agrees to indemnify the seller regarding any liability on the debt. This particular bill of sale version also provides that the seller warrants that he or she has authority to transfer legal title to the buyer. In addition, this form provides that the owner warrants that the property is in good working condition on the date of the sale. To complete this form, fill in the names and addresses of the seller and buyer, the purchase price of the item, a description of the property, and a description of the debt.

Sole Proprietorship: Small Business Start-Up Kit

To prepare this form, fill in the following information:
1. Date of Bill of Sale
2. Name of Seller
3. Address of Seller
4. Name of Buyer
5. Address of Buyer
6. Amount received for property
7. Describe property being purchased
8. Describe debt
9. Signature of Seller
10. Printed name of Seller
11. Signature of Buyer
12. Printed name of Buyer

PERSONAL PROPERTY RENTAL AGREEMENT

This Agreement is made on ①_____ , 20 _____ , between
②_____ , Owner,
address:③

and ④_____ , Renter,
address:⑤

1. The Owner agrees to rent to the Renter and the Renter agrees to rent from the Owner the following property: ⑥

2. The term of this agreement will be from ⑦_____ o'clock ___ . m.,
_____ , 20 _____ , until _____ o'clock ___ . m., _____
_____ , 20 _____ .

3. The rental payments will be $ ⑧_____ per ⑨_____ and will be payable by the Renter to the Owner as follows:⑩

4. The Renter agrees to pay a late fee of $ ⑪_____ per day that the rental payment is late. If the rental payments are in default for over ⑫_____ days, the Owner may immediately demand possession of the property without advance notice to the Renter.

5. The Owner warrants that the property is free of any known faults which would affect its safe operation under normal usage and is in good working condition.

6. The Renter states that the property has been inspected and is in good working condition. The Renter agrees to use the property in a safe manner and in normal usage and to maintain the property in good repair. The Renter further agrees not to use the property in a negligent manner or for any illegal purpose.

7. The Renter agrees to fully indemnify the Owner for any damage to or loss of the property during the term of this agreement, unless such loss or damage is caused by a defect of the rented property.

8. The Owner shall not be liable for any injury, loss, or damage caused by any use of the property.

9. The Renter has paid the Owner a security deposit of $ ⑬_____ . This security deposit will be held as security for payments of the rent and for the repair of any damages to the property by the Renter. This deposit will be returned to the Renter upon the termination of this agreement, minus any rent still owed to the Owner and minus any amounts needed to repair the property, beyond normal wear and tear.

10. The Renter may not assign or transfer any rights under this agreement to any other person, nor allow the property to be used by any other person, without the written consent of the Owner.

11. Renter agrees to obtain insurance coverage for the property during the term of this rental agreement in the amount of $ ⑭_____ . Renter agrees to provide the Owner with a copy of the insurance policy and to not cancel the policy during the term of this rental agreement.

12. This agreement may be terminated by either party by giving twenty-four (24) hours written notice to the other party.

13. Any dispute related to this agreement will be settled by voluntary mediation. If mediation is unsuccessful, the dispute will be settled by binding arbitration using an arbitrator of the American Arbitration Association.

14. The following are additional terms of this agreement: ⑮

15. The parties agree that this agreement is the entire agreement between them. This agreement binds and benefits both the Owner and Renter and any successors. Time is of the essence of this agreement.

16. This agreement is governed by the laws of the State of ⑯_____ .

⑰_____
Signature of Owner

⑲_____
Signature of Renter

⑱_____
Printed Name of Owner

⑳_____
Printed Name of Renter

BILL OF SALE, WITH WARRANTIES

This Bill of Sale is made on ① _____ , 20 _____ , between

② _____ , Seller,

address: ③

and ④ _____ , Buyer,

address: ⑤

In exchange for the payment of $ ⑥ _____ , received from the Buyer, the Seller sells and transfers possession of the following property to the Buyer: ⑦

The Seller warrants that it owns this property and that it has the authority to sell the property to the Buyer. Seller also warrants that the property is sold free and clear of all liens, indebtedness, or liabilities.

The Seller also warrants that the property is in good working condition as of this date.

Signed and delivered to the Buyer on the above date.

⑧ _____

Signature of Seller

⑨ _____

Printed Name of Seller

BILL OF SALE, WITHOUT WARRANTIES

This Bill of Sale is made on ① _____ , 20 ____ , between
② _____ , Seller,
address:③

and ④ _____ , Buyer,
address:⑤

In exchange for the payment of $ ⑥ _____ , received from the Buyer, the Seller sells and transfers possession of the following property to the Buyer:⑦

The Seller disclaims any implied warranty of merchantability or fitness and the property is sold in its present condition, "as is."

Signed and delivered to the Buyer on the above date.

⑧ _____
Signature of Seller

⑨ _____
Printed Name of Seller

BILL OF SALE, SUBJECT TO DEBT

This Bill of Sale is made on ①_____ , 20 _____ , between
②_____ , Seller,
address:③

and ④_____ , Buyer,
address:⑤

In exchange for the payment of $ ⑥_____ , received from the Buyer, the Seller sells and transfers possession of the
following property to the Buyer:⑦

The Seller warrants that it owns this property and that it has the authority to sell the property to the Buyer. Seller also states
that the property is sold subject to the following debt:⑧

The Buyer buys the property subject to the above debt and agrees to pay the debt. Buyer also agrees to indemnify and hold
the Seller harmless from any claim based on failure to pay off this debt.

The Seller also warrants that the property is in good working condition as of this date.

Signed and delivered to the Buyer on the above date.

⑨_____
Signature of Seller

⑪_____
Signature of Buyer

⑩_____
Printed Name of Seller

⑫_____
Printed Name of Buyer

Promissory Note Instructions

A *promissory note* is a document by which a borrower promises to pay the holder of the note a certain amount of money under specific terms. In the forms in this chapter, the person who borrows the money is referred to as the *borrower* and the person whom the borrower is to pay is referred to as the *noteholder*. The noteholder is generally also the lender, but this need not be so. This chapter also contains various forms for demanding payments on a promissory note. *Note*: If you are at all unsure of the correct use of any forms in this chapter, please consult an attorney.

Promissory Note (Installment Repayment): This type of promissory note is a standard unsecured note. Being *unsecured* means that the noteholder has no collateral or specific property to foreclose against should the borrower default on the note. If the borrower doesn't pay, the noteholder must sue and get a general judgment against the borrower. Collection of the judgment may then be made against the borrower's assets. This particular note calls for the borrower to pay a certain annual interest rate on the note and to make periodic payments to the noteholder. It also has certain general terms:

- The borrower may prepay any amount on the note without penalty
- If the borrower is in default, the noteholder may demand full payment on the note
- The note is not assumable by anyone other than the borrower
- The borrower waives certain formalities relating to demands for payment
- The borrower agrees to pay any of the costs of collection after a default

In order to complete this form, the following information is necessary:

① Amount of Note
② Date of Note
③ Name of borrower
④ Address of borrower
⑤ Name of noteholder
⑥ Address of noteholder
⑦ Principle amount
⑧ Interest rate
⑨ Number of installments
⑩ Amount of payments
⑪ What day of the "payment period" payment is due
⑫ The period for the installments (for example, monthly or weekly)
⑬ Payment in full by this date
⑭ The number of days a payment may be late before it is considered a default
⑮ Signature of borrower
⑯ Printed name of borrower

Promissory Note (Lump Sum Repayment): This note is also an unsecured promise to pay. However, this version of a promissory note calls for the payment, including accrued interest, to be paid in one lump sum at a certain date in the future. This note has the same general conditions relating to prepayment, defaults, and assumability as the Promissory Note with Installment Payments discussed on the previous page. To prepare this form, use the following information:

① Amount of Note
② Date of Note
③ Name of borrower
④ Address of borrower
⑤ Name of noteholder
⑥ Address of noteholder
⑦ Principle amount
⑧ Interest rate
⑨ Date that lump sum is due
⑩ The number of days a payment may be late before it is considered a default
⑪ Signature of borrower
⑫ Printed name of borrower

Promissory Note (on Demand): This also is an unsecured note. This type of promissory note, however, is immediately payable in full at any time upon the demand of the noteholder. This note has the same general conditions relating to prepayment, defaults, and assumability as the Promissory Note with Installment Payments discussed previously. The following information is necessary to complete this form:

① Amount of Note
② Date of Note
③ Name of borrower
④ Address of borrower
⑤ Name of noteholder
⑥ Address of noteholder
⑦ Principle amount
⑧ Interest rate
⑨ The number of days past the demand date that payment may be made before the note is in default
⑩ Signature of borrower
⑪ Printed name of borrower

Release of Promissory Note: This release is intended to be used to release a party from obligations under a Promissory Note. There are several other methods by which to accomplish this same objective. The return of the original note to the maker, clearly marked "Paid in Full" will serve the same purpose. A Receipt in Full will also accomplish this goal (see Chapter 10: *Releases*). The Release of Promissory Note may, however, be used in those situations when the release is based on something other than payment in full of the underlying note. For example, the note may be satisfied by a gift from the bearer of the note of release from the obligation. Another situation may involve a release of the note based on a concurrent release of a claim that the maker of the note holds against the holder of the note. The following information is needed to complete this form:

① Date of original promissory note
② Amount of promissory note
③ Name of noteholder
④ Address of noteholder
⑤ Name of borrower
⑥ Address of borrower
⑦ Date of release signed
⑧ Signature of noteholder
⑨ Printed name of noteholder

Demand and Notice of Default on Installment Promissory Note: This form will be used to notify the maker of a promissory note of his or her default on an installment payment on a promissory note. Notice of default should be sent promptly to any account that falls behind in its payments on a note. This promissory note provides a legal basis for a suit for breach of the promissory note. The following information is needed to complete this form:

① Date of demand
② Name and address of borrower
③ Name of borrower
④ Date of original note
⑤ Amount of original note
⑥ Date of default payment
⑦ Amount of default payment
⑧ Signature of noteholder
⑨ Printed name of noteholder

PROMISSORY NOTE (INSTALLMENT REPAYMENT)

$ ①_____

Dated: ②_____ , 20 _____

For value received, ③_____ , Borrower, address: ④

promises to pay ⑤_____ , Noteholder, address: ⑥

the principal amount of $ ⑦_____ , with interest at the annual rate of ⑧_____ percent, on any unpaid balance.

Payments are payable to the Noteholder in ⑨____ consecutive installments of $ ⑩____ , including interest, and continuing on the ⑪___ day of each ⑫___ until paid in full. If not paid off sooner, this note is due and payable in full on ⑬___ , 20 ___ .

This note may be prepaid in whole or in part at any time without penalty. If the Borrower is in default more than ⑭_____ days with any payment, this note is payable upon demand of any Noteholder. This note is not assumable without the written consent of the Noteholder. The Borrower waives demand, presentment for payment, protest, and notice. In the event of any default, the Borrower will be responsible for any costs of collection on this note, including court costs and attorney fees.

⑮_____
Signature of Borrower

⑯_____
Printed Name of Borrower

PROMISSORY NOTE (LUMP SUM REPAYMENT)

$ ①_____

Dated: ②_____ , 20 _____

For value received, ③_____ , Borrower, address: ④

promises to pay ⑤_____ , Noteholder, address: ⑥

the principal amount of $ ⑦_____ , with interest at the annual rate of ⑧_____ percent, on any unpaid balance.

Payment on this note is due and payable to the Noteholder in full on or before ⑨_____ , 20 _____ .

This note may be prepaid in whole or in part at any time without penalty. If the Borrower is in default more than ⑩_____ days with any payment, this note is payable upon demand of any Noteholder. This note is not assumable without the written consent of the Noteholder. The Borrower waives demand, presentment for payment, protest, and notice. In the event of any default, the Borrower will be responsible for any costs of collection on this note, including court costs and attorney fees.

⑪_____
Signature of Borrower

⑫_____
Printed Name of Borrower

PROMISSORY NOTE (ON DEMAND)

$ ① _____

Dated: ② _____ , 20 ___

For value received, ③ _____ , Borrower,
address:④

promises to pay ON DEMAND to
⑤ _____ , Noteholder,
address:⑥

the principal amount of $ ⑦ _____ , with interest at the annual rate of ⑧ _____ percent, on any unpaid balance.

This note may be prepaid in whole or in part at any time without penalty. This note is not assumable without the written consent of the Noteholder. The Borrower waives demand, presentment for payment, protest, and notice. In the event of such default of over ⑨ _____ days in making payment, the Borrower will be also be responsible for any costs of collection on this note, including court costs and attorney fees.

⑩ _____
Signature of Borrower

⑪ _____
Printed Name of Borrower

RELEASE OF PROMISSORY NOTE

In consideration of full payment of the promissory note dated ①_____ , 20 __ , in the face amount of $ ②_____ ,
③_____ , Noteholder,
address: ④

releases and discharges
⑤_____ , Borrower(s),
address: ⑥

from any claims or obligations on account of this note.

The party signing this release intends that it bind and benefit both itself and any successors.

Dated: ⑦_____ , 20 _____

⑧_____
Signature of Noteholder

⑨_____
Printed Name of Noteholder

DEMAND AND NOTICE OF DEFAULT ON INSTALLMENT PROMISSORY NOTE

Date: ①_____ , 20 _____

To: ②_____

RE: Default on Installment Promissory Note

Dear ③_____ :

Regarding the promissory note dated ④_____ , 20 _____ , in the original amount of $ ⑤_____ , of which you are the maker, you have defaulted on the installment payment due on ⑥_____ , 20 _____ , in the amount of $ ⑦_____ .

Demand is made upon you for payment of this past-due installment payment. If payment is not received by us within ten (10) days from the date of this notice, we will proceed to enforce our rights under the promissory note for collection of the entire balance.

Very truly,

⑧_____
Signature of Noteholder

⑨_____
Printed Name of Noteholder

235

Instructions for Business Operations Forms

In addition to selecting the type of structure that the business will take, the other important factor in the initial start-up of a business is where the basic assets of the business will come from. From the point of view of someone who is starting a business, the equipment and supplies needed to begin a business are often purchased from an on-going concern. A purchase of business assets for the purpose of beginning an enterprise will generally take two forms: the purchase of an entire business or the purchase of specific assets and equipment only. There are two legal agreements included in this chapter for these situations. Their use is outlined below. The sale of a complete and ongoing business is one of the most complex business transactions that a small businessperson will encounter. It may incorporate many other the legal documents. The following documents are included in this chapter for use in purchasing, selling, or forming a business:

Agreement for Sale of Business: This form should be used when one party is purchasing an entire business from another party. The form, as shown in this book, is set up for use in the sale of a sole proprietorship to an individual. This structure can be easily adapted to fit other particular situations if necessary. For example, if the business being sold is a partnership and the buyer is a corporation, a few simple substitutions will be necessary to change the document to the appropriate form. Simply substitute the name and address of the partnership for the seller's name wherever indicated and substitute the name and address of the corporate buyer where necessary. If changes are made in the type of entity doing the buying or selling on this form, the appropriate notarization and signature line from Chapter 4 must be used also. *Note:* The notarization on this form is only necessary if the sale of the business includes the sale of real estate. A notarization will be needed in order to record this document with the appropriate county office. The following information will have to be used to fill in this form:

1. Date of agreement
2. Name of seller
3. Address of seller with name of city and state
4. Name of buyer
5. Address of buyer with name of city and state
6. Type of business
7. Name of business
8. Address of business with name of city and state
9. Address of business premises with name of city and state
10. Amount of full purchase
11. Amount for premises
12. Amount for equipment/furniture

⑬ Amount for goodwill
⑭ Amount for stock-in-trade/inventory
⑮ Amount for notes/accounts receivable
⑯ Amount for any outstanding contracts
⑰ Breakdown of purchase price : amount of earnest money
⑱ Amount of cash down payment
⑲ Amount of promissory note
⑳ Amount of total price
㉑ Amount of promissory note
㉒ Interest rate of promissory note
㉓ Number of years to pay on note
㉔ Amount of payment per month of note
㉕ Amount of earnest money
㉖ Date of closing
㉗ Time of closing
㉘ Address of closing with name of city and state
㉙ List all other documents provided to buyer
㉚ State where sale takes place
㉛ Date of balance sheet
㉜ Radius from business that seller cannot compete
㉝ Number of years that seller cannot compete
㉞ Amount of insurance
㉟ Any additional terms
㊱ State where business is sold
㊲ Date of signatures
㊳ Signature of seller
㊴ Printed name of seller
㊵ Name of Business (Doing Business As)
㊶ Type of business
㊷ State where business will operate
㊸ Signature of buyer
㊹ Printed name of buyer
㊺ Notary will complete this section

Agreement for Sale of Business Assets: This form should be used when one party is purchasing only certain business assets from another party. As in the previous form, this form, as it is shown in this book, is set up for use in the sale of sole proprietorship assets to an individual. *Note*: Notarization is not provided for this form. Notarization of this form is only necessary if the sale of the business assets includes the sale of real estate. In that case, a notarization will be needed in order to record this document with the appropriate county real estate records office.

Sole Proprietorship: Small Business Start-Up Kit

The following information will have to be used to fill in this form:

1. Date of agreement
2. Name of seller
3. Address of seller with name of city and state
4. Name of buyer
5. Address of buyer with name of city and state
6. Type of business
7. Name of business
8. Adress of business with name of city and state
9. Amount of full purchase
10. Breakdown of purchase price : amount of earnest money
11. Amount of cash down payment
12. Amount of promissory note
13. Amount of total price
14. Amount of promissory note
15. Interest rate of promissory note
16. Number of years to pay on note
17. Amount of payment per month of note
18. Amount of earnest money
19. Date of closing
20. Time of closing
21. Address of closing with name of city and state
22. List all other documents provided to buyer
23. Other adjustments to purchase price
24. Amount of insurance
25. Any additional terms
26. State where business assets are sold
27. Date of signatures
28. Signature of seller
29. Printed name of seller
30. Name of Business (Doing Business As)
31. Type of business
32. State where business will operate
33. Signature of buyer
34. Printed name of buyer

Note that you may also need additional documents in conjunction with the basic Agreement for Sale of Business Assets form.

AGREEMENT FOR SALE OF BUSINESS

This agreement is made on ① _____ , 20 _____ , between ② _____ , seller, of ③ _____ , City of _____ , State of _____ , and ④ _____ _____ , buyer, of ⑤ _____ , City of _____ , State of _____ .

The seller now owns and conducts a ⑥ _____ business, under the name of ⑦ _____ _____ , located at ⑧ _____ , City of _____ , State of _____ .

For valuable consideration, the seller agrees to sell and the buyer agrees to buy this business for the following price and on the following terms:

1. The seller will sell to the buyer, free from all liabilities, claims, and indebtedness, the seller's business, including the premises located at ⑨ _____ , City of _____ , State of _____ , and all other assets of the business as listed on Exhibit A, which is attached and is a part of this agreement.

2. The buyer agrees to pay the seller the sum of $ ⑩ _____ , which the seller agrees to accept as full payment. The purchase price will be allocated to the assets of the business as follows:

   a. The premises $ ⑪ _____
   b. Equipment/furniture $ ⑫ _____
   c. Goodwill $ ⑬ _____
   d. Stock-in-trade/inventory $ ⑭ _____
   e. Notes/accounts receivable $ ⑮ _____
   f. Outstanding contracts $ ⑯ _____

3. The purchase price will be paid as follows:

   Earnest money $ ⑰ _____
   Cash down payment $ ⑱ _____
   Promissory note payable $ ⑲ _____

   TOTAL Price $ ⑳ _____

   The $ ㉑ _____ Promissory Note will bear interest at ㉒ _____ % (_____ percent) per year, payable monthly for ㉓ _____ years at $ ㉔ _____ per month with the first payment due one (1) month after the date of closing. The Promissory Note will be secured by a U.C.C. Financing Statement and a Security Agreement in the usual commercial form. The Promissory Note will be prepayable without limitation or penalty.

4. The seller acknowledges receiving the earnest money deposit of $ ㉕ _____ from the buyer. If this sale is not completed for any valid reason, this money will be returned to the buyer without penalty or interest.

5. This agreement will close on ㉖ _____ , 20 _____ , at ㉗ _____ o'clock ___ . m., at ㉘ _____ , City of _____ , State of _____ .

   At that time, and upon payment by the buyer of the portion of the purchase price then due, the seller will deliver to buyer the following documents:

   a. A Bill of Sale for all personal property (equipment, inventory, parts, supplies, and any other personal property)
   b. A Warranty Deed for any real estate
   c. All accounting books and records
   d. All customer and supplier lists
   e. A valid assignment of any lease
   f. All other documents of transfer as listed below: ㉙

   At closing, adjustments to the purchase price will be made for the following items:

   a. Changes in inventory since this agreement was made
   b. Insurance premiums

c. Payroll and payroll taxes
d. Rental payments
e. Utilities
f. Property taxes
g. The following other items:

6. The seller represents and warrants that it is duly qualified under the laws of the State of ㉚_____ to carry on the business being sold, and has complied with and is not in violation of any laws or regulations affecting the seller's business, including any laws governing bulk sales or transfers.

7. Attached as part of this agreement as Exhibit B is a Balance Sheet of the seller as of ㉛_____ , 20 _____ , which has been prepared according to generally accepted accounting principles. The seller warrants that this Balance Sheet fairly represents the financial position of the seller as of that date and sets out any contractual obligations of the seller. If this sale includes the sale of inventory of the business, the seller has provided the buyer with a completed Bulk Transfer Affidavit containing a complete list of all creditors of the seller, together with the amount claimed to be due to each creditor.

8. Seller represents that it has good and marketable title to all of the assets shown on Exhibit A, and that those assets are free and clear of any restrictions on transfer and all claims, taxes, indebtedness, or liabilities except those specified on the Exhibit B Balance Sheet. The seller also warrants that all equipment will be delivered in working order on the date of closing.

9. Seller agrees not to participate in any way, either directly or indirectly, in a business similar to that being sold to the buyer, within a radius of ㉜_____ miles from this business, for a period of ㉝_____ years from the date of closing.

10. Between the date of this agreement and the date of closing of the sale, the seller agrees to carry on the business in the usual manner and agrees not to enter into any unusual contract or other agreement affecting the operation of the business without the consent of the buyer.

11. The buyer represents that it is financially capable of completing the purchase of this business and fully understands its obligations under this agreement.

12. Buyer agrees to carry hazard and liability insurance on the assets of the business in the amount of $ ㉞_____ and to provide the seller with proof of this coverage until the Promissory Note is paid in full. However, the risk of any loss or damage to any assets being sold remain with the seller until the date of closing.

13. Any additional terms: ㉟

14. No modification of this agreement will be effective unless it is in writing and is signed by both the buyer and seller. This agreement binds and benefits both the buyer and seller and any successors. Time is of the essence of this agreement. This document, including any attachments, is the entire agreement between the buyer and seller. This agreement is governed by the laws of the State of ㊱_____ .

Dated: ㊲_____ , 20 _____

㊳_____
Signature of Seller

㊴_____
Printed Name of Seller

DBA
㊵_____
Name of Business

A(n) ㊶_____ (type of business)

State of Operation ㊷_____

㊸ _____
Signature of Buyer

㊹ _____
Printed Name of Buyer

㊺
State of _____
County of _____

On _____ , 20 _____ , _____ personally came before me and, being duly sworn, did state that he or she is the person who owns the business described in the above document and that he or she signed the above document in my presence on behalf of the business and on his or her own behalf.

_____
Signature of Notary Public

Notary Public, In and for the County of _____
State of _____

My commission expires: _____ , 20 _____   Notary Seal

㊺
State of _____
County of _____

On _____ , 20 _____ , _____ personally came before me and, being duly sworn, did state that he or she is the person described in the above document as the buyer and that he or she signed the above document in my presence.

_____
Signature of Notary Public

Notary Public, In and for the County of _____
State of _____

My commission expires: _____ , 20 _____   Notary Seal

AGREEMENT FOR SALE OF BUSINESS ASSETS

This agreement is made on ①_____ , 20 _____ , between ②_____ , seller, of③
_____ , City of _____ , State of _____ , and④
_____ , buyer, of ⑤_____ , City of _____ , State of _____ .

The seller now owns and conducts a ⑥_____ business, under the name of ⑦_____ , located
at ⑧_____ , City of _____ , State of _____ .

For valuable consideration, the seller agrees to sell and the buyer agrees to buy certain assets of this business for the following price and on the following terms:

1. The seller will sell to the buyer certain assets of the business as listed on Exhibit A, which is attached and is a part of this agreement. The assets will be transferred free from all liabilities, claims, and indebtedness, unless listed on Exhibit A.

2. The buyer agrees to pay the seller the sum of $ ⑨_____ , which the seller agrees to accept as full payment.

3. The purchase price will be paid as follows:

   Earnest money $ ⑩_____
   Cash down payment $ ⑪_____
   Promissory note payable $ ⑫_____

   TOTAL Price $ ⑬_____

   The $ ⑭_____ Promissory Note will bear interest at ⑮_____ % (_____ percent) per year, payable monthly for ⑯_____ years at $ ⑰_____ per month with the first payment due one (1) month after the date of closing. The Promissory Note will be secured by a UCC Financing Statement and a Security Agreement in the usual commercial form. The Promissory Note will be prepayable without limitation or penalty.

4. The seller acknowledges receiving the earnest money deposit of $ ⑱_____ from the buyer. If this sale is not completed for any valid reason, this money will be returned to the buyer without penalty or interest.

5. This agreement will close on ⑲_____ , 20 _____ , at ⑳_____ o'clock ___ . m., at ㉑_____ , City of _____ , State of _____ .

   At that time, and upon payment by buyer of the portion of the purchase price then due, the seller will deliver to buyer the following documents:

   a. A Bill of Sale for all personal property (equipment, inventory, parts, supplies, and any other personal property)
   b. All other documents of transfer as listed below:㉒

   At closing, adjustments to the purchase price will be made for changes in inventory since this agreement was made, and for the following other items: ㉓

6. The seller represents and warrants that it is in full compliance with and is not in violation of any laws or regulations affecting the seller's business, including any laws governing bulk sales or transfers.

7. Seller represents that it has good and marketable title to all of the assets shown on Exhibit A, and that those assets are free and clear of any restrictions on transfer, claims, taxes, indebtedness, or liabilities except those specified on the Exhibit A. If this sale includes the sale of inventory of the business, the seller has provided the buyer with a completed Bulk Transfer Affidavit containing a complete list of all creditors of the seller, together with the amount claimed to be due to each creditor. Seller also warrants that all equipment will be delivered in working order on the date of closing.

8. Between the date of this agreement and the date of closing of the sale, the seller agrees to carry on the business in the usual manner and agrees not to enter into any unusual contract or other agreement affecting the business assets being sold without the consent of the buyer.

9. The buyer represents that it is financially capable of completing the purchase of these business assets and fully understands its obligations under this agreement.

10. Buyer agrees to carry hazard and liability insurance on the assets of the business in the amount of $ ㉔_____ and to provide the seller with proof of this coverage until the Promissory Note is paid in full. However, the risk of any loss or damage to any assets being sold remain with the seller until the date of closing.

11. Any additional terms:㉕

12. No modification of this agreement will be effective unless it is in writing and is signed by both the buyer and seller. This agreement binds and benefits both the buyer and seller and any successors. Time is of the essence of this agreement. This document, including any attachments, is the entire agreement between the buyer and seller. This agreement is governed by the laws of the State of ㉖_____ .

Dated: ㉗_____ , 20 _____

㉘_____
Signature of Seller

㉙_____
Printed Name of Seller

DBA
㉚_____
Name of Business

A(n) ㉛_____ (type of business)

State of Operation ㉜_____

㉝_____
Signature of Buyer

㉞_____
Printed Name of Buyer

Instructions for General Contract

The foundation of most agreements is a contract. A *contract* is merely an agreement by which two or more parties each promise to do something. This simple definition of a contract can encompass incredibly complex agreements. The objective of a good contract is to clearly set out the terms of the agreement. Once the parties have reached an oral understanding of what their agreement should be, the terms of the deal should be put in writing. The written contract should be clearly written and easily understood by both parties to the agreement. It should be written in precise and unambiguous terms. The most common causes for litigation over contracts are arguments over the meaning of the language used. Remember that both sides of the agreement should be able to understand and agree to the language being used. A contract has to have certain prerequisites to be enforceable in court. These requirements are relatively simple and most will be present in any standard agreement. However, you should understand what the various legal requirements are before you prepare your own contracts. To be enforceable, a contract must have *consideration*. In the context of contract law, this simply means that both parties to the contract must have promised to do something or forego taking some type of action. If one of the parties has not promised to do anything or forego any action, he or she will not be able to legally force the other party to comply with the terms of the contract. There has to be some form of mutual promise for a contract to be valid. Another requirement is that the parties to the contract be clearly identified and the terms of the contract also be clearly spelled out. The terms and description need not be complicated, but they must be spelled out in enough detail to enable the parties to the contract (and any subsequent court) to clearly determine what exactly the parties were referring to when they made the contract.

General Contract: This basic document can be adapted for use in many situations. The terms of the contract that the parties agree to should be carefully spelled out and inserted where indicated. The other information that is required are the names and addresses of the parties to the contract and the date the contract is to take effect. This basic contract form is set up to accommodate an agreement between two individuals. If a business is party to the contract, please identify the name and type of business entity (for example: Jackson Car Stereo, a New York sole proprietorship, etc.) in the first section of the contract. In order to complete the General Contract form, fill in the following information:

① Date of contract
② Name of first party to the contract [If a business is party to the contract, please identify the name and type of business entity (for example: Jackson Car Stereo, a New York sole proprietorship, etc.)]
③ Address of first party

④ City of first party
⑤ State of first party
⑥ Name of second party
⑦ Address of second party
⑧ City of second party
⑨ State of second party
⑩ Exact terms of the contract to which Party One agrees
⑪ Exact terms of the contract to which Party Two agrees
⑫ Any additional terms
⑬ State whose laws will govern this contract (Generally, where the contract actions will take place)
⑭ Date of contract
⑮ Signature of Party One
⑯ Printed name of Party One
⑰ Signature of Party Two
⑱ Printed name of Party Two

Modification of Contract: Use this form to modify any other terms of a contract (other than the expiration date). The modification can be used to change any portion of the contract. Simply note what changes are being made in the appropriate place on this form. If a portion of the contract is being deleted, make note of the deletion. If certain language is being substituted, state the substitution clearly. If additional language is being added, make this clear. For example, you may wish to use language as follows:

- "Paragraph _____ is deleted from this contract."
- "The following new paragraph is added to this contract:"

A copy of the original contract should be attached to this form. In order to complete this form, fill in the following information:

① Date of modification contract
② Name of first party to the contract [If a business is party to the contract, please identify the _____ name and type of business entity]
③ Address of first party
④ Name of second party
⑤ Address of second party
⑥ Describe the original contract
⑦ Describe what modifications are being made to the original contract
⑧ Signature of Party One
⑨ Printed Name of Party One
⑩ Signature of Party Two
⑪ Printed Name of Party Two

GENERAL CONTRACT

This Contract is made on ① , between ② , Party One, of ③ , City of ④ , State of ⑤ , and ⑥ , Party Two, of ⑦ , City of ⑧ , State of ⑨ .

For valuable consideration, the parties agree to the following:

Party One agrees to: ⑩

Party Two agrees to: ⑪

Any additional terms: ⑫

No modification of this Contract will be effective unless it is in writing and is signed by both parties. This Contract binds and benefits both parties and any successors or assigns. Time is of the essence of this Contract. This document, including any attachments, is the entire agreement between the parties. This Contract is governed by the laws of the State of ⑬ .

Dated: ⑭

⑮
Signature of Party One

⑯
Printed Name of Party One

⑰
Signature of Party Two

⑱
Printed Name of Party Two

MODIFICATION OF CONTRACT

This Modification of Contract is made on ① , between ② , whose address is ③ , and ④ , whose address is ⑤ .

For valuable consideration, the parties agree as follows:

1. The following described contract is attached to this Modification and is made a part of this Modification: ⑥

2. The parties agree to modify this contract as follows: ⑦

3. All other terms and conditions of the original contract remain in effect without modification. This Modification binds and benefits both parties and any successors. This document, including the attached contract, is the entire agreement between the parties.

The parties have signed this Modification on the date specified at the beginning of this Modification of Contract.

⑧
Signature
⑨
Printed Name

⑩
Signature
⑪
Printed Name

Appendix of State Business Registration Laws

On the following pages are found state listings containing relevant information regarding the registration of business names. You are advised to check your state's listing carefully to determine the particular requirements in your jurisdiction. Following is an explanation of the components of each listing:

State website: This listing provide the location of the official state website on the internet. The addresses were current at the time of this books publication; however, like most websites, the page addresses are subject to change.

State revenue or taxation website: Most states require that you register with their departments of revenue or taxation prior to doing business in the state. If online registration or standard forms are available, the websites or forms are provided. However, the requirements and details of taxation registration are complex and may not be fully covered in this Appendix. Please check directly with your state's online taxation and/or revenue services for details.

Main state business website: Address for main state business website portal.

State law reference for name registration: This listing provides the statutory reference for name registration for each state.

Registration of business and/or business name requirements: Here is noted whether there are general business registration requirements that apply to a sole proprietorship and, additionally, whether there are state business name requirements. Also noted are whether the state's name registration requirements are mandatory or voluntary and whether registration of business names is as trade names or as fictitious names.

Online form and website: This listing shows title and the location of official state online forms if they are available. Generally, this is the state Secretary of State's office website in a state.

Forms provided on CD: This listing notes the title of the state registration and/or taxation registration forms or instructions that are provided on the enclosed CD.

Registration fee: This is the amount it costs to file your name registration.

Term of registration: This listing specifies the length of time that the registration of the business name will be valid.

Name requirements: Under this listing are any state requirements regarding the choice of a business name.

Name registration application requirements: The application generally must include the name of the owner(s), business address of the owner(s), a description of the type of business intended, and the fictitious or trade name to be used.

Publication requirements: A few states require that a notice of the intention to conduct business under an assumed or fictitious name be published in a newspaper.

Office for name registration: Here is listed the name and address or reference to the particular state or county office that handles business name registration.

Alabama

State website: www.alabama.gov
State revenue or taxation website: www.ador.state.al.us/
Main state business website: www.alabama.gov/portal/secondary.jsp?page=Business
State law reference for name registration: Code of Alabama, Title 8, Sections 8-12-7+.
Registration of business and/or business name requirements: Sole proprietors who engage in a wide range of businesses must register and obtain a license to operate (referred to as a 'privilege license') from the Department of Revenue. The list of businesses requiring licensing is extensive and is found in Code of Alabama, Title 40, Section 12-40 to 12-200. Name registration is optional. Alabama does not have a fictitious name statute, but has a trade name statute. A trade name is essentially a business name other than the owner's name. The applicant must register with the Secretary of State. (Section 8-12-7). Businesses must also register with for taxation purposes at: www.ador.state.al.us/salestax/register.html.
Online form: Application to Register Trademark, Service Mark or Trade Name;
www.sos.state.al.us/downloads/dl2.aspx?div1=Trademarks&types=Form
Forms provided on CD: Application to Register Trademark, Service Mark or Trade Name
Registration fee: $30.00 for Trade name registration; various fees for business privilege licenses
Term of registration: None stated in statute.
Name requirements: The statute is exhaustive, stating that the trade name can not be immoral, deceptive, or scandalous. Please refer directly to the statute. (Section 8-12-7).
Name registration application requirements: The application must include the name of the owner(s), business address of the owner(s), a description of the type of business the person is or intends to conduct, the date when the name was first used, a statement that the owner(s) is the only person with the right to use that name, three copies or specimens of the mark. The application must be signed and verified. (Section 8-12-8).
Publication requirements: None stated.
Office for name registration:
Alabama Secretary of State
PO Box 5616
Montgomery AL 36103-5616

Alaska

State website: www.state.ak.us
State revenue or taxation website: www.tax.alaska.gov/
Main state business website: alaska.gov/businessHome.html
State law reference for name registration: Alaska Statutes, Sections 10.35.010+.
Registration of business and/or business name requirements: All sole proprietorships must file an Alaska Business License Application. Name Registration is voluntary. Any person may register a business name by filing an application with the Commissioner of Corporations. Registration gives the person the exclusive right to use the name. (Sections 10.35.040-10.35.070). Businesses may have to register for taxation purposes at the website noted under **State State revenue and taxation website Website**.
Online form: Alaska Business License Application;
www.commerce.state.ak.us/occ/home_bus_licensing.htm
Forms provided on CD: Alaska Business License Application, Business Name Registration Application
Registration fee: $50.00 for Business License; $25.00 for Business Name Registration.
Term of registration: Annual for business license. Five years for business name. (Section 10.35.070).
Name requirements: The intended name must not be the same as or deceptively similar to a corporation or other reserved or registered name and must not give the impression that the business is incorporated. (Section 10.35.040).

Name registration application requirements: The business name application must be signed by the business owner(s) and contain the owner's name and address, the name and addresses of the business, the name and address of each person having an interest in the business, a statement that the owner(s) is doing business, and a brief statement of the nature of the business. (Section 10.35.050).

Publication requirements: None stated.

Office for name registration:
Alaska Department of Commerce and Economic Development
PO Box 110800
Juneau, AK 99811-0800

Arizona

State website: www.azleg.gov/
State revenue or taxation website: https://www.aztaxes.gov/
Main state business website: www.azcommerce.com/BusAsst/SmallBiz/
State law reference for name registration: Arizona Revised Statutes, Sections 44-1460+.
Registration of business and/or business name requirements: Name registration is voluntary. Any person, partnership, corporation, firm, association, society, foundation, federation, or organization doing business in Arizona may register the name of the business. (Section 44-1460). In Arizona, not all businesses are required to have a license and some businesses are required to have more than one license. There is not a "generic" state business license. See Arizona Guide to Business Taxes for more information.

Online form: Application for Registration of Trade Name;
www.azsos.gov/business_services/Forms/Tradename/apptn.pdf
Forms provided on CD: Application for Registration of Trade Name; Arizona Guide to Business Taxes
Registration fee: $10.00
Term of registration: Five years. (Section 44-1460.02).
Name requirements: The name to be registered must be distinguishable from other business names and not misleading to the public. (Section 44-1460.1(b)).
Name registration application requirements: The application must state the name and address of the applicant, the name to be registered, the nature of the business, and the length of time the name has been used. The applicant must sign the application. The Secretary of State will issue a Certificate of Registration upon compliance with the requirements. (Sections 44-1460-1460.1).
Publication requirements: None stated.
Office for name registration:
Arizona Secretary of State
1700 West Washington, 7th floor
Phoenix AZ 85007

Arkansas

State website: www.arkleg.state.ar.us
State revenue or taxation website: www.dfa.arkansas.gov
Main state business website: portal.arkansas.gov/business/Pages/default.aspx
State law reference for name registration: Arkansas Code of 1987 Annotated, Sections 4-70-203+.
Registration of business and/or business name requirements: "Doing business as" name registration is mandatory. The applicant must register in the office of the County Clerk in the county in which the person conducts or intends to conduct business. (Section 4-70-203). In addition, there may be privilege

license registration necessary for various types of businesses. Check with the County Clerk or local authorities. In addition, see Arkansas Business Taxation Guide for information on business taxation.

Online form: not available online

Forms provided on CD: Arkansas Business Taxation Guide (Starting a New Business in Arkansas), Note: May use "Statement of Intention to Conduct Business Under an Assumed or Fictitious Name" provided on CD under Chapter 10.

Registration fee: not available, varies by county

Term of registration: Perpetual until withdrawn. (Section 4-70-204).

Name requirements: None stated in statute.

Name registration application requirements: The certificate shall set forth the name under which the applicant intends to conduct business, and the full name and post office address of each person conducting the business. (Section 4-70-203).

Publication requirements: None stated.

Office for name registration: The applicant must register with the County Clerk in the counties in which the applicant will conduct business.

California

State website: www.state.ca.us

State revenue or taxation website: www.taxes.ca.gov/

Main state business website: www.business.ca.gov/Home.aspx

State law reference for name registration: California Codes Annotated, Business and Professional Code, Sections 17900+.

Registration of business and/or business name requirements: Fictitiuos Name registration is mandatory. The applicant must register with the City and/or County Clerk in the county where the person conducts or intends to conduct business. (Sections 17910, 17915). In addition, businesses within the incorporated area of a particular city should contact the business licensing section of that city government for specific rules and regulations and licensing requirements. In addition, most retailers, even occasional sellers of tangible goods, should register to collect sales or use tax.

Online form: Fictitious Name Registration Form; located in Business and Professional Code, Sections 17913; www.leginfo.ca.gov/cgi-bin/displaycode?section=bpc&group=17001-18000&file=17900-17930

Forms provided on CD: California Fictitious Business Name Statement; and California Fictitious Business Name Statement (LA County)

Registration fee: not available, varies with City or County.

Term of registration: Five years. (Section 17913).

Name requirements: None stated in statute.

Name registration application requirements: The applicant must file a statement within forty days after the person begins to conduct business. The statement shall contain the fictitious business name, the street address of the place of business, the name and address of the individual filing the statement, and the nature of the business (for example: sole proprietorship or partnership). (Section 17913).

Publication requirements: Within thirty days of filing the statement, the applicant must publish the name in the newspaper of general circulation in the county in which the applicant's principal place of business is located. (Section 17917).

Office for name registration: The applicant must register with the City and/or County Clerk of the county in which the registrant has his principal place of business. (Section 17915).

Colorado

State website: www.leg.state.co.us
State revenue or taxation website: www.colorado.gov/revenue/tax
Main state business website: www.colorado.gov/cs/Satellite/CO-Portal/CXP/Page/1165693060177/1165693060239
State law reference for name registration: Colorado Revised Statutes Annotated, Sections 7-71-101+.
Registration of business and/or business name requirements: Colorado does not have a statute for registration of assumed names for sole proprietors, However, tradenames for other business organization forms are registerable. The applicant must register with the Secretary of State and record a statement of trade name with the clerk in any county in which real estate is held. (Section 7-71-101). In addition, Colorado has a Business Registration Application for registration with the State Department of Revenue.
Online form: Trade Name Registration: www.sos.state.co.us/biz/TradeNameIndTransaction.do;jsessionid=0000gRTd_S_9Zc7OqHja0noZcOB:11nm17ad1?firstTime=true
Forms provided on CD: Business Registration Application (Trade name registration in provided online only)
Registration fee: Trade Name fee: $8.00; business taxation registration fees vary.
Term of registration: None stated in statute.
Name requirements: The name cannot be the same as or deceptively similar to any other registered name, or the name of a dissolved corporation within 120 days of dissolution. (Section 7-71-101).
Name registration application requirements: The certificate must state the name of the entity, the location of the principal office, any other name the business is transacted under, and the type of business transacted. (Section 7-7-101).
Publication requirements: None stated.
Office for name registration:
Colorado Secretary of State
1700 Broadway Ste 200
Denver, CO 80290

Connecticut

State website: www.cga.ct.gov
State revenue or taxation website: www.ct.gov/drs
Main state business website: www.ct.gov/ctportal/taxonomy/taxonomy.asp?DLN=27187&ctportalNav=|27187|
State law reference for name registration: Connecticut General Statutes Annotated, Sections 35-1+.
Registration of business and/or business name requirements: Name registration is mandatory. The applicant must register with the Town Clerk where the business is or where the person intends to conduct business. (Section 35-1). Note: you are also required to register with the Department of Revenue Services (DRS) before you may conduct business in Connecticut.
Online form: On-Line Business Taxes Registration Application
www.ct.gov/drs/cwp/view.asp?a=1433&q=265880
Forms provided on CD: Taxation registration is only provided online. Note: May use "Statement of Intention to Conduct Business Under an Assumed or Fictitiuos Name" provided on CD under Chapter 10.
Registration fee: not available, varies by locality and/or type of business
Term of registration: None stated in statute.

Name requirements: None stated in statute.
Name registration application requirements: The certificate must include the name of the business, and the full name, and the post-office address of the individuals transacting the business. (Section 35-1).
Publication requirements: None stated.
Office for name registration: The applicant must register with the Town Clerk in the town where the applicant intends to conduct business. (Section 35-1).

Delaware

State website: www.delaware.gov
State revenue or taxation website: revenue.delaware.gov/
Main state business website: dedo.delaware.gov/
State law reference for name registration: Delaware Code Annotated, Title 6, Chapter 31, Sections 3101+.
Registration of business and/or business name requirements: Name registration is mandatory. The applicant must register with the office of the Prothonotary in the county where the person is transacting business. (Section 3101). Businesses must also file a 'Combined Registration Application' with the Delaware Department of Revenue prior to starting business. See also the Delaware Small Business Guide on the enclosed CD.
Online form: Combined Application Registration
revenue.delaware.gov/services/Business_Tax/Step3.shtml
Forms provided on CD: Combined Application Registration, Delaware Small Business Guide, Note: May use "Statement of Intention to Conduct Business Under an Assumed or Fictitiuos Name" provided on CD under Chapter 10.
Registration fee: not available, varies by type of business
Term of registration: None stated in statute.
Name requirements: None stated in statute.
Name registration application requirements: The certificate shall contain the trade name, the Christian name and the surname of the persons transacting business, the date when the business was organized. The person signing shall attach an affidavit affirming that everything included is true. (Section 3101).
Publication requirements: None stated.
Office for name registration: The applicant must register with the office of the Prothonotary in the county where the applicant is transacting business. (Section 3101).

District of Columbia (Washington D.C.)

State website: dccouncil.washington.dc.us
State revenue or taxation website: https://www.taxpayerservicecenter.com/fr500/
Main state business website: brc.dc.gov/index.asp
State law reference for name registration: District of Columbia Code 1981, Title 47, Sections 47-2855.2+.
Registration of business and/or business name requirements: Name registration is mandatory. The applicant must register with the Department of Consumer and Regulatory affairs. (Section 47-2855.2). In addition, businesses must file a Basic Business License Application in most cases. Businesses must also file a Combined Business Tax Registration online at the web address noted above under **State revenue and taxation website**.
Online form: dcra.dc.gov/dcra
Forms provided on CD: Basic Business License Application; Trade Name Registration; (Combined

Business Tax Registration is provided online)
Registration fee: $50.00
Term of registration: None stated in statute.
Name requirements: None stated in statute.
Name registration application requirements: The certificate shall contain the name of the business, the name of the owner(s), and the address of the person conducting business. (Section 47-2855.2).
Publication requirements: None stated.
Office for name registration:
Department of Consumer and Regulatory Affairs -
Trade Name Registration
941 N. Capitol St. NE, Rm 7200
Washington DC, 20002

Florida

State website: www.leg.state.fl.us
State revenue or taxation website: dor.myflorida.com/dor/businesses/newbusiness_startup.html
Main state business website: www.myflorida.com/taxonomy/business/
State law reference for name registration: Florida Statutes, Chapter 865. Sections 865.09+.
Registration of business and/or business name requirements: Name registration is mandatory. The applicant may register online or by paper form with the Department of State. (Section 865.09). In addition, certain types of businesses may require business licensing. Please see online license registration with the Department of Business and Professional Regulation at: https://www.myfloridalicense.com/newapplicationinstruct.asp. Also, new business should register with the Department of Revenue using the website address noted above under **State revenue and taxation website** or using the Application to Collect Taxes that is on the CD.
Online form: Fictitious Name Application
https://efile.sunbiz.org/ficregintro.html
Forms provided on CD: Fictitious Name Application, Application to Collect Taxes
Registration fee: $50.00
Term of registration: Five years. (Section 865.09).
Name requirements: The name may not contain the words *incorporated* or *corporation* in the name. (Section 865.09).
Name registration application requirements: Before conducting the business, the person must file a sworn statement. The sworn statement must contain the name to be registered, the mailing address of the business, the name and address of the owner(s), and certification that the fictitious name has been published in a newspaper in the county where the principal place of business is located. (Section 865.09).
Publication requirements: The applicant must certify that the fictitious name has been published in a newspaper in the county in which the applicant's principal place of business is located. (Section 865.09).
Office for name registration:
Fictitious Name Registration
P O Box 1300
Tallahassee, FL 32302-1300

Georgia

State website: www.legis.state.ga.us
State revenue or taxation website: www.gataxinfo.org/
Main state business website: www.georgia.gov/00/channel_title/0,2094,4802_4971,00.html
State law reference for name registration: Official Code of Georgia Annotated, Title 10, Chapter 1, Sections 10-1-490+.
Registration of business and/or business name requirements: Name registration is mandatory. The applicant must register with the Clerk of the superior court in the county in which the person conducts the business. (Section 10-1-490). Businesses should also register with the Department of Revenue at the website noted above under **State revenue and taxation website**. Other business registrations may be necessary. Please consult the Georgia First Stop Business Guide.
Online form: not available online
Forms provided on CD: Georgia First Stop Business Guide, Georgia Trade Name Registration.
Registration fee: $15.00
Term of registration: None stated in statute.
Name requirements: None stated in statute.
Name registration application requirements: The applicant must file a statement within thirty days before the person intends to begin conducting the business. The statement is to include the name of the owner(s), the address of the owner(s), the nature of the business (for example: sole proprietorship or partnership), and the business name used. (Section 10-1-490).
Publication requirements: The name shall be published once a week for two weeks in paper in which the sheriff's advertisements are printed. (Section 10-1-490).
Office for name registration: The applicant must register with the Clerk of the Superior Court in the county in which the applicant conducts business. (Section 10-1-490).

Hawaii

State website: www.capitol.hawaii.gov
State revenue or taxation website: www.state.hi.us/tax/
Main state business website: www.ehawaii.gov/dakine/search.html?tag=business
State law reference for name registration: Hawaii Revised Statutes Annotated, Title 482, Sections 482-2+.
Registration of business and/or business name requirements: Registration is optional. Hawaii does not have a fictitious name statute, but has a trade name statute. A trade name is essentially a business name other than the owner's name. The applicant must register with the Director of Commerce and Consumer Affairs. (Section 482-2). Hawaii also provides a single website (Business Express) for general business registration where one simple online registration covers all the forms with all the state agencies and partners at: https://hbe.ehawaii.gov/BizEx. Note: This one-stop online registration includes Trade Name registration and Taxation registration.
Online form: Application for Registration of Trade Name
www.hawaii.gov/dcca/areas/breg/registration/trade/forms
Forms provided on CD: Application for Registration of Trade Name, Hawaii Basic Business Application for Taxation.
Registration fee: $25.00
Term of registration: None stated in statute.
Name requirements: None stated in statute.
Name registration application requirements: The application shall state that the person is the proprietor, or the assign of the proprietor, and shall state the nature of the business. (Section 482-2).
Publication requirements: None stated.
Office for name registration:

Hawaii Department of Commerce and
Consumer Affairs
P O Box 40
Honolulu, HI 96810

Idaho

State website: www.state.id.us
State revenue or taxation website: tax.idaho.gov/p-businesses.cfm
Main state business website: business.idaho.gov/
State law reference for name registration: Idaho Code, Title 53, Sections 53-503+.
Registration of business and/or business name requirements: Name registration is mandatory. The applicant must register with the Secretary of State. (Section 53-504). Idaho has a one-stop online business registration website at: www.idahobizhelp.org/cf/form1.cfm. Idaho also has a one-stop online business registration website for registration with the Department of Labor, State Tax Commission and Industrial Commission, located at: https://labor.idaho.gov/applications/ibrs/ibr.aspx. Certain types of businesses may be required to register with other state and local agencies as well. You may wish to visit www.idahobizhelp.org for additional information.
Online form: Certificate of Assumed Business Name,
www.idsos.state.id.us/corp/ABNform.htm
Forms provided on CD: Certificate of Assumed Business Name
Registration fee: $25.00
Term of registration: Five years. (Section 53-506).
Name requirements: None stated in statute.
Name registration application requirements: The applicant must file a certificate before the person intends to conduct business. The certificate must include the assumed business name, the true name of the owner(s), the address of the owner(s), and the general type of business conducted. (Section 53-505).
Publication requirements: None stated.
Office for name registration:
Idaho Secretary of State
P O Box 83720
Boise, ID 83720-0080

Illinois

State website: www.ilga.gov
State revenue or taxation website: www.revenue.state.il.us/Businesses/register.htm
Main state business website: business.illinois.gov/
State law reference for name registration: Illinois Compiled Statutes, Chapter 805, Sections 405+.
Registration of business and/or business name requirements: Name registration is mandatory. The applicant must register in the office of the County Clerk of the county in which the person conducts or intends to conduct business. (Section 805 ILCS 405/1). Businesses must also register for business taxation.
Online form: Illinois Business Application-Taxation;www.revenue.state.il.us/Businesses/register.htm
Forms provided on CD: Illinois Business Application-Taxation, Note: May use "Statement of Intention to Conduct Business Under an Assumed or Fictitiuos Name" provided on CD under Chapter 10.
Registration fee: not available
Term of registration: None stated in statute.
Name requirements: None stated in statute.

Name registration application requirements: The registration is to include the name of the business, the real name of the owner(s), the post office address of the owner(s), and the post office address of every business location. (Section 805 ILCS 405/1).

Publication requirements: The owner(s) is required to file proof of publication for three consecutive weeks in the newspaper of general circulation in the county in which the applicant conducts the business. (Section 805 ILCS 405/1).

Office for name registration: The applicant must register in the office of the County Clerk of the county in which the person conducts or intends to conduct business. (Section 805 ILCS 405/1).

Indiana

State website: www.state.in.us

State revenue or taxation website: www.in.gov/dor/3744.htm

Main state business website: in.gov/ai/business/

State law reference for name registration: Indiana Code, Chapter 23, Sections 23-15-1-1+.

Registration of business and/or business name requirements: Name registration is mandatory. The applicant must register with the office of the Recorder in the county in which business is conducted. (Section 23-15-1-1). Businesses must also register for business taxation. Indiana also has a new online business registration website located at: http://www.in.gov/ai/appfiles/sos-registration/landing.html

Online form: Business Tax Application
https://secure.in.gov/apps/dor/bt1/

Forms provided on CD: Indiana Business Tax Application Checklist, Certificate of Assumed Business Name.

Registration fee: not available, varies by location

Term of registration: None stated in statute.

Name requirements: None stated in statute.

Name registration application requirements: The certificate must state the name of the business, the full name of the owner(s), and the address of the owner(s). (Section 23-15-1-1).

Publication requirements: None stated.

Office for name registration: The applicant must register with the office of the Recorder in the county where the applicant conducts business. (Section 23-15-1-1).

Iowa

State website: www.legis.state.ia.us

State revenue or taxation website: www.iowa.gov/tax/business/business.html

Main state business website: www.iowa.gov/Business_and_Economic_Development

State law reference for name registration: Iowa Annotated Code, Sections 547.1+.

Registration of business and/or business name requirements: Name registration is mandatory. The applicant must register with the county Recorder in the county in which the person intends to conduct business. (Section 547.1). Businesses must also register with the Department of Revenue.

Online form: Business Tax Registration; https://www.idr.iowa.gov/CBA/start.asp

Forms provided on CD: Business Tax Registration, Iowa Trade Name Report (Note: This form must be printed on legal sized paper to comply with recording requirements)

Registration fee: not available

Term of registration: None stated in statute.

Name requirements: None stated in statute.

Name registration application requirements: The applicant must file a statement before the person intends to conduct business. The statement must include the name of the owner(s), the post office address of the owner(s), the residence address of the owner(s), and the address where the person intends to conduct business. (Section 547.1).

Publication requirements: None stated.

Office for name registration: The applicant must register with the county Recorder in the county in which the applicant intends to conduct business. (Section 547.1).

Kansas

State website: www.kansas.gov/index.php

State revenue or taxation website: www.ksrevenue.org/

Main state business website: www.kansas.gov/business/

State law reference for name registration: Kansas Revised Statutes, Sections 81-205+.

Registration of business and/or business name requirements: Name registration is optional. Kansas does not have a fictitious name statute, but has a trade mark statute. There is no method in Kansas to register d/b/a's, assumed, fictitious or trade names. A business may use an assumed name in Kansas, but there is no way to register it as such. However, many business names will qualify for registration as a "service mark". The applicant may register with the Secretary of State. Businesses must also file a Business Tax Application either online or by mail.

Online form: Kansas Business Trademark Registration

www.kssos.org/forms/business_services/TM.pdf

Kansas Business Tax Application

https://www.accesskansas.org/businesscenter/index.html?appid=1&submit=register

Forms provided on CD: Business Trademark/Service Mark Registration; Kansas Business Guide-Steps to Success; Kansas Business Tax Application

Registration fee: $40.00

Term of registration: Ten years. (Section 81-215).

Name requirements: None stated in statute.

Name registration application requirements: The signed and verified registration must include the name of the owner(s), the business address of the owner(s), a description of the type of business, three copies or specimens of the trade name, and a statement that the owner(s) is the exclusive user of the name. (Section 81-213).

Publication requirements: None stated.

Office for name registration:

Office of the Secretary of State

First Floor, Memorial Hall

120 S.W. 10th Ave.

Topeka, KS 66612-1594

Kentucky

State website: www.lrc.state.ky.us

State revenue or taxation website: revenue.ky.gov/business/register.htm

Main state business website: kentucky.gov/business/Pages/default.aspx

State law reference for name registration: Kentucky Revised Statutes Annotated, Chapter 365, Sections 365.015+.

Registration of business and/or business name requirements: Name registration is mandatory. The applicant must file the certificate with the County Clerk where the person resides. (Section 365.015). Businesses must also file a Business Tax Application. In addition, Kentucky doesn't have a statewide business license that applies to all businesses, but many types of businesses are required to have a special license or permit to legally operate their business. Please see the website: www.thinkkentucky.com/BIC/license.aspx

Online form: Kentucky Business Tax Application

revenue.ky.gov/business/register.htm
Certificate of Assumed Name
www.sos.ky.gov/business/filings/forms/
Forms provided on CD: Kentucky Business Tax Application; Certificate of Assumed Name
Registration fee: not available
Term of registration: Five years. (Section 365.015).
Name requirements: None stated in statute.
Name registration application requirements: The applicant must file a certificate before the person intends to conduct business. The certificate must state the assumed name of the business, the name of the owner(s), and the address of the owner(s). (Section 365.015).
Publication requirements: None stated.
Office for name registration: The applicant must file the certificate with the County Clerk where the person resides. (Section 365.015).

Louisiana

State website: www.legis.state.la.us
State revenue or taxation website: revenue.louisiana.gov/SECTIONS/business/intro.aspx
Main state business website: www.louisiana.gov/Business/
State law reference for name registration: Louisiana Statutes Annotated, Sections 51:281+.
Registration of business and/or business name requirements: Name registration is mandatory. The applicant must register with the Clerk of the court in the parish or parishes in which the person intends to or conducts the business. (Section 51:281). Businesses must also register with the Department of Revenue (see website above under **State revenue and taxation website** or use Application for Revenue Account Number provided on CD.
Online form: Application to Register Tradename; www.sos.louisiana.gov/tabid/814/Default.aspx
Application for Revenue Account Number; revenue.louisiana.gov/SECTIONS/business/intro.aspx
New Business Checklist; www.sos.louisiana.gov/portals/0/newbusinesschecklist.pdf
Forms provided on CD: Application to Register Tradename; Application for Revenue Account Number; New Business Checklist (can submit online)
Registration fee: $50.00 for name registration.
Term of registration: None stated in statute.
Name requirements: The name can be in any language, but must be in English on the certificate. The name shall not suggest that the business is a government agency. The name also shall not contain the name of a public facility. In addition, the name must not falsely suggest that the business is incorporated. (Sections 51:281, 281.2).
Name registration application requirements: The applicant must file a certificate before the person intends to conduct business. The certificate must set forth the name of the business, the real full name of the owner(s), and the post office address of the owner(s). (Section 51:281).
Publication requirements: None stated.
Office for name registration: The applicant must register with the Clerk of the Court in the parish or parishes in which the person intends to or conducts the business and with the Secretary of States office. (Section 51:281).
Sec. of State Commercial Division
P O Box 94125
Baton Rouge, LA 70804-9125

Maine

State website: janus.state.me.us/legis/
State revenue or taxation website: www.maine.gov/online/suwtaxreg/
Main state business website: www.maine.gov/portal/business/
State law reference for name registration: Maine Revised Statutes Annotated, Sections 31-2+.
Registration of business and/or business name requirements: Name registration is mandatory. The applicant must register with the office of the Clerk in the city or town where the person intends to conduct business. (Section 31-2). Businesses must also register with the Maine Revenue Service at the website noted above under **State revenue and taxation website**.
Online form: Maine Business Taxation Registration Online; www.maine.gov/online/suwtaxreg/
Forms provided on CD: Maine Business Resource Guide, Note: May use "Statement of Intention to Conduct Business Under an Assumed or Fictitiuos Name" provided on CD under Chapter 10.
Registration fee: not available
Term of registration: None stated in statute.
Name requirements: The name must not contain the words or abbreviations of: *corporation*, *incorporated*, or *limited*. (Section 31-6).
Name registration application requirements: The applicant must file a certificate before the person intends to conduct business. The signed certificate shall state the name of the owner, the residential address of the owner, the name of the business, the style or designation under which the business is to be conducted, and that the owner is a sole proprietor. (Section 31-2).
Publication requirements: None stated.
Office for name registration: The applicant must register with the office of the Clerk in the city or town where the applicant intends to conduct business. (Section 31-2).

Maryland

State website: mlis.state.md.us/index.html
State revenue or taxation website: https://interactive.marylandtaxes.com/webapps/comptrollercra/entrance.asp
Main state business website: www.maryland.gov/working/pages/morelinks.aspx?Keyword=Business
State law reference for name registration: Annotated Code of Maryland, Business Regulation, Sections 1-406+.
Registration of business and/or business name requirements: Name registration is mandatory. The applicant must also register for business taxation with the Comptroller of Maryland (see website noted above under revenue or taxation for access to 'combined registration application'). (Section 1-406). There is also an online business license application system found at: www.blis.state.md.us/, which should be used in addition to the combined registration application.
Online form: Trade Name Application; www.dat.state.md.us/sdatweb/nameappl.pdf
Forms provided on CD: Trade Name Application
Registration fee: $25.00
Term of registration: Five years. (Section 1-406).
Name requirements: None stated in statute.
Name registration application requirements: The certificate must be in writing, affirmed under oath, and it must state the true name of the owner(s), the address of the owner(s), the character of the business, the street address of the business, and the name the business is going to be conducted under. (Section 1-406).
Publication requirements: None stated.
Office for name registration:

Maryland State Department of Assessments and Taxation
301 West Preston Street
Baltimore, MD 21201-2305

Massachusetts

State website: www.mass.gov
State revenue or taxation website: https://wfb.dor.state.ma.us/webfile/business/Public/Webforms/Login/Login.aspx
Main state business website: www.mass.gov/?pageID=mg2constituent&L=2&L0=Home&L1=Business&sid=massgov2
State law reference for name registration: Annotated Laws of Massachusetts, Sections 110:5+.
Registration of business and/or business name requirements: Name registration is mandatory. The applicant must register with the office of the Clerk in every city where the business has an office. (Section 110:5). In addition, the business must register with the Department of Revenue, which has an online registration system at the website noted above under revenue or taxation. Certain businesses and occupations require licenses to operate. A listing of those businesses is located at: www.mass.gov/?pageID=ocatopic&L=3&L0=Home&L1=Licensee&L2=License+Types%2c+Forms+%26+Requirements&sid=Eoca
Online form: not available online;
Forms provided on CD: Massachusetts "Doing Business As" Certificate
Registration fee: not available
Term of registration: Four years. (Section 110:5).
Name requirements: None stated in statute.
Name registration application requirements: The certificate must include the full name of the owner(s), the residence address of the owner(s), the street address of the business, and the name of the business. (Section 110:5).
Publication requirements: None stated.
Office for name registration: The applicant must register with the office of the Clerk in every city where the business has an office. (Section 110:5).

Michigan

State website: www.legislature.mi.gov
State revenue or taxation website: michigan.gov/taxes/0,1607,7-238-46621---,00.html
Main state business website: www.michigan.gov/som/0,1607,7-192-29943---,00.html
State law reference for name registration: Michigan Compiled Laws Annotated, Sections 445.1+.
Registration of business and/or business name requirements: Name registration is mandatory. The applicant must register with the office of the Clerk in the county or counties where the business is or where the applicant intends to conduct business. (Section 445.1). Michigan has a one-stop business registration system on its website at: www.michigan.gov/business. Businesses must also register for business taxation.
Online form: not available online
Forms provided on CD: Michigan Assumed Name Certificate
Registration fee: not available
Term of registration: Five years.
Name requirements: The statute does not set guidelines. However, the County Clerk can reject an assumed name that is likely to mislead the public or a name that is similar to another business name. (Section 445.2).
Name registration application requirements: The applicant must file a certificate before the person

intends to conduct business. The certificate shall state the name of the business, the real full name of the owner(s), and the address of the owner(s). (Section 445.1).

Publication requirements: None stated.

Office for name registration: The applicant must register with the office of the Clerk in the county or counties where the business is or where the applicant intends to conduct business. (Section 445.1).

Minnesota

State website: www.leg.state.mn.us

State revenue or taxation website: www.taxes.state.mn.us/business_taxpayers/index.shtml

Main state business website: www.state.mn.us/portal/mn/jsp/hybrid.do?ct=30&home=30&id=-8491&agency=NorthStar

State law reference for name registration: Minnesota Statutes Annotated, Section 333.01+.

Registration of business and/or business name requirements: Name registration is mandatory. The applicant must register with the Secretary of State. (Section 333.01). Businesses must also register for business taxation at the website noted above under **State revenue or taxation website**.

Online form: Certificate of Assumed Name

www.sos.state.mn.us/business/forms.html

Forms provided on CD: Certificate of Assumed Name

Registration fee: $25.00

Term of registration: Ten years. (Section 333.055).

Name requirements: The name shall not include any of these words or their abbreviations: *corporation, incorporated, limited, chartered, professional, cooperative, association, limited partnership, limited liability company, professional limited liability company, limited liability partnership,* or *professional limited liability partnership.* (Section 333.01).

Name registration application requirements: The certificate must state the name of the business, the address of the business, the true name of the owner(s), and the address of the owner(s). (Section 333.01).

Publication requirements: The applicant must publish the certificate for two consecutive issues in a qualified newspaper where the principal place of business is located. (Section 333.01).

Office for name registration:

Minnesota Secretary of State

Business Services Division

180 State Office Building, 100 Rev. Dr. Martin Luther King Jr. Blvd

St. Paul, MN 55155-1299

Mississippi

State website: www.mscode.com

State revenue or taxation website: www.mstc.state.ms.us/taxareas/sales/main.html

Main state business website: www.ms.gov/ms_sub_template.jsp?Category_ID=3

State law reference for name registration: Mississippi Code Annotated, Sections 75-25-3+.

Registration of business and/or business name requirements: Mississippi does not have a fictitious name or trade name statute, but the name of a business may be registerable as a service mark or trademark. The State of Mississippi does not currently require a business to register an assumed business name. (Sections 75-25-3, 75-25-5). Mississippi also provides for registration for sales and use taxes for sole proprietorships. See website above noted under **State revenue and taxation website** and/or see Mississippi Tax Registration form provided on CD. In addition, an owner of a new business must get a city or county license from the city or county tax collector if the business is located within a city's corporate limits or within a county. but outside a city's corporate limits.

Online form: not available online
Forms provided on CD: Mississippi Tax Registration Form
Registration fee: not available
Term of registration: None stated in statute.
Name requirements: The statute is exhaustive, stating that the trade name cannot be immoral, deceptive, or scandalous. Please refer directly to the statute. (Section 75-25-3).
Name registration application requirements: The signed and verified application must include the name of the owner(s), business address of the owner(s), a description of the type of business the person intends to conduct, the date when the name was first used, and a statement that the owner(s) is the only person with the right to use that name. The applicant must provide three examples of the name in use. (Section 75-25-5).
Publication requirements: None stated.
Office for name registration: Mississippi Secretary of State
P O Box 136
Jackson, MS 39205-0136

Missouri

State website: www.mo.gov/
State revenue or taxation website: https://dors.mo.gov/tax/coreg/index.jsp
Main state business website: www.business.mo.gov/
State law reference for name registration: Missouri Statutes, Sections 417.200+.
Registration of business and/or business name requirements: Name registration is mandatory. The applicant must register with the Secretary of State. (Section 417.200). There is an online Fictitious Name registration site noted below under Online forms, or you may use the form provided on the CD. Missouri also has an online business registration site located at: www.business.mo.gov/. Finally, Missouri has an online registration site for business tax registration located at the address noted above under **State revenue and taxation website** or you may use the form provided on the CD.
Online form: https://www.sos.mo.gov/BusinessEntity/BusinessEntitiesOnline/Fictitious
Forms provided on CD: Missouri Business Registration Checklist, Missouri Tax Registration Application, Missouri Fictitious Name Registration
Registration fee: $7.00
Term of registration: 5 years.
Name requirements: None stated in statute.
Name registration application requirements: The applicant must file a statement within five days after the person begins to conduct business. The statement must contain the fictitious business name, the name of the owner(s), and the residence address of the owner(s). (Section 417.210).
Publication requirements: None stated.
Office for name registration: Missouri Secretary of State
P O Box 2050
Jefferson City, MO 65102

Montana

State website: leg.mt.gov/css/default.asp
State revenue or taxation website: revenue.mt.gov/forbusinesses/taxes_licenses_fees_permits/default.mcpx
Main state business website: mt.gov/business.asp
State law reference for name registration: Montana Code Annotated, Sections 30-13-201+.
Registration of business and/or business name requirements: Name registration is mandatory. The

applicant must register with the Secretary of State. (Section 30-13-203). Montana also maintains a one-stop online business licensing website at: business.mt.gov/BusinessAssistance/licensing.asp.
Online form: Application for Registration of Assumed Business Name
www.sos.state.mt.us/BSB/business_Forms.asp
Forms provided on CD: Registration of Assumed Business Name
Registration fee: $20.00
Term of registration: Five years. (Section 30-13-206).
Name requirements: None stated in statute.
Name registration application requirements: The form must contain the name of the owner(s), the street address of the owner(s), the proposed business name, the date of first use of the name, a description of the business, and the name of the county or counties where the business is being conducted. (Section 30-13-203).
Publication requirements: None stated.
Office for name registration: Secretary of State
P O Box 202801
Helena, MT 59620-2801

Nebraska

State website: nebraskalegislature.gov/
State revenue or taxation website: www.revenue.ne.gov/tax/current/salestax_forms.html
Main state business website: www.nebraska.gov/dynamicindex.html#
State law reference for name registration: Revised Statutes of Nebraska, Sections 87-209+.
Registration of business and/or business name requirements: Name registration is mandatory. Nebraska does not have a fictitious name statute, but has a trade name statute. A trade name is essentially a business name other than the owner(s)'s name. The applicant must register with the Secretary of State. (Section 87-219). Nebraska also requires most businesses to register for taxes at the website noted above under **State revenue and taxation website** or using the form provided on the CD. Nebraska also has a one-stop business registration website located at: https://www.nebraska.gov/osbr/index.cgi
Online form: www.sos.state.ne.us/business/corp_serv/pdf/210_219.pdf
Forms provided on CD: Nebraska Tax Application, Application for Registration of Trade Name
Registration fee: $100.00
Term of registration: Ten years. (Section 87-211).
Name requirements: The statute is exhaustive, stating that the trade name cannot be immoral, deceptive, or scandalous. Please refer directly to the statute. (Section 87-209).
Name registration application requirements: The registrant must provide the name of the business owner(s), the street address of the business owner(s), the trade name, the general nature of the business, the length of time the business has been operating, and the notarized signature of the owner(s). (Section 87-210).
Publication requirements: Registration of a trade name shall be published by the applicant once in a newspaper of general circulation published in the city or village where the business is to be located, or, if there is no newspaper in the city or village, in some newspaper of general circulation in the county. Proof of such publication shall be filed in the office of the Secretary of State and with the county clerk of the county where the principal office is located, within thirty days from the date of registration with the Secretary of State. If proof of publication is not filed with the Secretary of State and the county clerk within the thirty days, the registration may be canceled.
Office for name registration: Secretary of State
P O Box 94608
Lincoln, NE 68509

Nevada

State website: www.leg.state.nv.us
State revenue or taxation website: tax.state.nv.us
Main state business website: www.nv.gov/NV_default4.aspx?id=182
State law reference for name registration: Nevada Revised Statutes, Sections 600.310+.
Registration of business and/or business name requirements: Name registration is optional. Nevada does not have a fictitious name statute, but has a trade name statute. A trade name is essentially a business name other than the owner(s)'s name. The applicant must register with the Secretary of State. (Section 600.340). Nevada also has a one-stop business registration form that is included on the CD. This provides for registration with the Department of Revenue for sole proprietorships. See also the website noted under **State revenue and taxation website** above.
Online form: Trade Name Registration; nvsos.gov/index.aspx?page=57
Forms provided on CD: Trade Name Registration, Nevada Business Registration form
Registration fee: $100.00
Term of registration: Five years. (Section 600.360).
Name requirements: The statute is exhaustive, stating that the trade name cannot be immoral, deceptive, or scandalous. Please refer directly to the statute. (Section 600.330).
Name registration application requirements: The application for registration must set forth that the person is applying for trade name, a description of the name. It must include the name of the owner(s), the business address of the owner(s), the type of business being conducted, the date when the name was first used, a statement that the owner(s) is the only person with the right to use that name. The application must be signed and verified, and contain three copies of the trade name. (Section 600.340).
Publication requirements: None stated.
Office for name registration:
Nevada Secretary of State
555 E. Washington Ave. #4000
Las Vegas, NV 89101

New Hampshire

State website: www.nh.gov
State revenue or taxation website: www.nh.gov/revenue
Main state business website: www.nh.gov/business/
State law reference for name registration: New Hampshire Revised Statutes Annotated, Sections 349:1+.
Registration of business and/or business name requirements: Name registration is mandatory. The applicant must register with the Secretary of State. (Sections 349:1, 349:5). Business tax registration is also mandatory for sole proprietorships and the registration form is provided on the CD. See also the website noted above under **State revenue and taxation website**. A license is required in New Hampshire for restaurants, grocery stores, bakeries, hotels, lodging establishments and motor vehicle rental establishments to collect and remit taxes on meals, rooms, and motor vehicle rental services. (Section 78-A:4) For a complete list of regulated activities and licensed professionals, contact the New Hampshire Department of Justice, 33 Capitol Street. Concord, NH 03301 - (603) 271-3658.
Online form: Application for Registration of Trade Name; www.sos.nh.gov/corporate/tradenameforms.html
Forms provided on CD: Application for Registration of Trade Name, Business Tax Registration
Registration fee: $50.00
Term of registration: Five years. (Section 349:6).
Name requirements: The name cannot be deceptively similar to any instrumentality of the United States or New Hampshire government, or any recognized political party. (Section 349:1).

Name registration application requirements: The signed certificate must state the principal place of the business, a brief description of the business, the name of the owner(s), the address of the owner(s), the date when the business was established, and the date when the business will end if anticipated. (Section 349:5).

Publication requirements: None stated.

Office for name registration:
New Hampshire Secretary of State
107 North Main Street
Concord, NH 03301-4989

New Jersey

State website: www.njleg.state.nj.us
State revenue or taxation website: https://www.state.nj.us/cgi-bin/treasury/revenue/dcr/reg/sos_dcrnew01_page1.cgi
Main state business website: www.nj.gov/njbusiness/
State law reference for name registration: New Jersey Statutes, Sections 56:1-2+.
Registration of business and/or business name requirements: Name registration is mandatory (as a service mark). The applicant must register with the Clerk of the county or counties where the business is or the person intends to conduct business. In addition, the applicant must register with the Secretary of State. (Section 56:1-2). New Jersey also requires registration for taxation for all sole proprietorships. Registration is provided online at the website noted under **State revenue and taxation website** above.
Online form: New Jersey Trademark Registration; www.state.nj.us/treasury/revenue/pdforms/tmsm01.pdf
Forms provided on CD: New Jersey Trademark/Service Mark Registration
Registration fee: $50.00
Term of registration: None stated in statute.
Name requirements: None stated in statute.
Name registration application requirements: The certificate must contain the name of the business, the true name of the owner(s), the post-office address of the owner(s). The certificate must be sworn to by the owner(s). In addition, if the person filing for the certificate is not a resident, then the owner(s) must give a power of attorney to the County Clerk for service of process. (Section 56:1-2).
Publication requirements: None stated.
Office for name registration: The applicant must register with the Clerk of the county or counties where the business is or the applicant intends to conduct business. In addition, the applicant must register with the Secretary of State. (Section 56:1-2).
New Jersey Secretary of State
125 West State Street
Trenton, NJ 08608-1101

New Mexico

State website: legis.state.nm.us/lcs/
State revenue or taxation website: www.tax.state.nm.us/BizPge.htm
Main state business website: www.newmexico.gov/business.php
State law reference for name registration: New Mexico Statutes Annotated, Sections 57-3B-1+.
Registration of business and/or business name requirements: The State of New Mexico does not require that a business register its use of a trade name (sometimes referred to as a fictitious name, doing business as or d.b.a.). Registration is optional. New Mexico's statute is for trade names which are names used to identify a person's business. The applicant must register with the Secretary of State.

(Section 57-3B-5). Sole proprietorships must also apply for a New Mexico Business Tax ID and register to pay state taxes. See Application for Business Tax ID on the CD and the website noted above under revenue or taxation.

Online form: Application for Registration of Trademark; www.sos.state.nm.us/sos-Trademarks.html
Forms provided on CD: Application for Registration of Trademark, Application for Business Tax ID
Registration fee: $25.00
Term of registration: Ten years. (Section 57-3B-8).
Name requirements: None stated in statute.
Name registration application requirements: The application must include the type of business, a sworn statement that the owner(s) is claiming the exclusive right to use. The owner(s) shall sign the certificate. (Section 57-3B-5).
Publication requirements: None stated.
Office for name registration:
Office of the Secretary of State
Operations Division
325 Don Gaspar, Suite 300
Santa Fe, NM 87503

New York

State website: assembly.state.ny.us
State revenue or taxation website: www.tax.state.ny.us/sbc/starting_business.htm
Main state business website: www.nysegov.com/citGuide.cfm?superCat=28
State law reference for name registration: New York General Business Law, Article 9B, Sections 130+.
Registration of business and/or business name requirements: Name registration is mandatory. The applicant must register with the Clerk of the county or counties where the business is or the applicant intends to conduct business. (Section 130). Businesses must also apply for New York State taxation and may do so online at:
www.tax.state.ny.us/online/bus.htm. For additional information regarding taxes, see website above noted under **State revenue and taxation website**
Online form: Certificate of Assumed Name; www.dos.state.ny.us/corp/pdfs/dos1338.pdf
Forms provided on CD: Certificate of Assumed Name
Registration fee: $25.00, plus any additional county fees
Term of registration: None stated in statute.
Name requirements: The name cannot appear to be the full name, the initials, or a word that appears to be a real name. The exception to that law is if the owners are the successors of the person for which the business was originally named. (Section 130).
Name registration application requirements: The certificate must include the name of the business, the address of the business, the full name of the person conducting the business, the residence address of the person conducting the business, and the age of the owner(s), if under eighteen. (Section 130).
Publication requirements: None stated.
Office for name registration: The applicant must register with the Clerk of the county or counties where the business is or the applicant intends to conduct business (Section 130).and with the:
NYS Department of State
Division of Corporations, State Records
41 State Street,
Albany, NY 12231-0001.

North Carolina

State website: www.ncga.state.nc.us
State revenue or taxation website: www.dornc.com/business/index.html
Main state business website: www.ncgov.com/2,2,North_Carolina_A_better_place_to_do_business,North_Carolina_A_better_place_to_do_business.html
State law reference for name registration: General Statutes of North Carolina, Sections 66-68+.
Registration of business and/or business name requirements: Name registration is mandatory. The applicant must register with the office of the Register of Deeds in the county or counties where the person intends to conduct business. (Section 66-68). Businesses must also register for withholding and/or sales taxation, depending on the type of business that will be operated. See above website under **State revenue and taxation website**.
Online form: Assumed Name Certificate;
www.nccommerce.com/en/BusinessServices/StartYourBusiness/Forms/
Forms provided on CD: Assumed Name Certificate
Registration fee: not available
Term of registration: None stated in statute.
Name requirements: None stated in statute.
Name registration application requirements: The applicant must file a certificate before transacting the business. The Certificate must state the name of the business, the name of the owner(s), the address of the owner(s), and the applicant must sign the certificate. (Section 66-68).
Publication requirements: None stated.
Office for name registration: The applicant must register with the office of the Register of Deeds in the county or counties where the person intends to conduct business. (Section 66-68).

North Dakota

State website: www.nd.gov
State revenue or taxation website: www.nd.gov/tax/salesanduse/
Main state business website: www.nd.gov/category.htm?id=69
State law reference for name registration: North Dakota Century Code, Sections 47-25-01+.
Registration of business and/or business name requirements: Name registration is mandatory. North Dakota's statute is for trade names which is a name other than the owner(s)'s name used to identify a person's business. The applicant must register with the Secretary of State. (Section 47-25-02). In addition, numerous specific types of businesses require business licenses in North Dakota. A list of such businesses is found at: www.nd.gov/category.htm?id=140. In addition, retail businesses must register for state sales and use taxation. See website above under **State revenue and taxation website**.
Online form: Trade Name Registration; www.state.nd.us/eforms/Doc/sfn13401.pdf
Forms provided on CD: Trade Name Registration
Registration fee: $25.00
Term of registration: Five years. (Section 47-25-04).
Name requirements: A trade name can not be deceptively similar to the name of any other registered business name in the state. (Section 47-25-03).
Name registration application requirements: The applicant must file a statement before the person intends to conduct business. The statement must state the name of the business, the name of the owner(s), the address of the owner(s), the address of the principal place of business, and the nature of the business. (Section 47-25-02).
Publication requirements: None stated.
Office for name registration: North Dakota Secretary of State
600 East Boulevard Avenue, Dept 108
Bismarck, ND 58505-0500

Ohio

State website: www.ohio.gov
State revenue or taxation website: www.tax.ohio.gov/online_services/business_online_services.stm
Main state business website: business.ohio.gov/
State law reference for name registration: Ohio Revised Code, Sections 1329.01+.
Registration of business and/or business name requirements: Name registration is optional. Ohio's statute is for trade names. Generally, a trade name is a name used to identify a person's business, and to which the owner(s) asserts the exclusive right to use. The applicant must register with the Secretary of State. (Section 1329.01). The state also provides one-stop business registration at: www.development.ohio.gov/1ststop/onestop/index.cfm.
Online form: Ohio Name Registration;
www.sos.state.oh.us/SOS/businessServices/Filing%20Forms%20%20Fee%20Schedule/534A.aspx
Forms provided on CD: Ohio Name Registration (for "Fictitious Name")
Registration fee: $50.00
Term of registration: Five years. (Section 1329.04).
Name requirements: The name cannot imply that the business is connected with a government entity if not so connected, the name can not imply that the business is incorporated if not incorporated, and the name shall not be indistinguishable from any other previously registered business name. (Section 1329.02).
Name registration application requirements: The application must state the name of the owner(s), the business address of the owner(s), the trade name to be registered, the general nature of the business, and the length of time the name has been in use. (Section 1329.01).
Publication requirements: None stated.
Office for name registration:
Ohio Secretary of State
P O Box 670
Columbus, OH 43216

Oklahoma

State website: www.ok.gov
State revenue or taxation website: www.tax.ok.gov/bustax.html
Main state business website: www.ok.gov/section.php?sec_id=4
State law reference for name registration: Oklahoma Statutes, Sections 18-1140+.
Registration of business and/or business name requirements: Name registration is mandatory. The applicant must register with the Secretary of State. (Section 18-1140). Applicant may use Trade Name Report included on CD or use online registration at: https://www.sos.ok.gov/corp/tradeName.aspx?Ety=3. Sole proprietorships must also register for state taxation and may **not** do so online but must use the Oklahoma Business Registration Packet forms that are included on the CD.
Online form: Trade Name Report; https://www.sos.state.ok.us/forms/FM0021.PDF
Forms provided on CD: Trade Name Report, Oklahoma Business Registration Packet
Registration fee: $25.00
Term of registration: None stated in statute.
Name requirements: The name must be distinguishable from the registered name of other business entities, and foreign business entities qualified to do business in Oklahoma, or if either of the above existed within the last three years the name is also barred. The name must also be distinguishable from names reserved with the Secretary of State. These restrictions are avoidable with the written consent of a registered business entity, or if the applicant establishes prior right to a registered name. (Sections 18-1140, 1141).

Name registration application requirements: The report must include the trade name, the type of business, and the address where the business will be conducted. (Section 18-1140).
Publication requirements: None stated.
Office for name registration:
Oklahoma Secretary of State
2300 North Lincoln Blvd. #101
Oklahoma City, OK 73105-4897

Oregon

State website: www.leg.state.or.us
State revenue or taxation website: www.oregon.gov/DOR/BUS/faq-withhold.shtml
Main state business website: www.oregon.gov/menu_files/business_kut.shtml
State law reference for name registration: Oregon Revised Statutes, Sections 648.005+.
Registration of business and/or business name requirements: Name registration is mandatory. The applicant must register with the Secretary of State. (Section 648.010). There is now an online business registration site located at: https://secure.sos.state.or.us/ABNWeb/. Businesses also need to register for taxation and may do so online at the website noted above under **State revenue and taxation website** or using the Combined Tax Registration form provided on the CD.
Online form: Assumed Business Name; www.filinginoregon.com/forms/abn.htm
Forms provided on CD: Assumed Business Name, Combined Tax Registration Form
Registration fee: $50.00
Term of registration: Two years. (Section 648.017).
Name requirements: The name must be distinguishable from any other registered name. (Section 648.051).
Name registration application requirements: The applicant must file an application before the person intends to conduct business. The application must include the name of the business, the real name of the owner(s), the street address of the owner(s), the address of the principal place of business, the mailing address of the authorized agent for transactions with the Secretary of State, and the applicant's primary business activity. (Section 648.010).
Publication requirements: None stated.
Office for name registration:
Oregon Secretary of State
255 Capitol Street NE, Ste 151
Salem, OR 97310-1327

Pennsylvania

State website: www.state.pa.us
State revenue or taxation website: www.doreservices.state.pa.us/BusinessTax/default.htm
Main state business website: pa.gov/portal/server.pt?open=512&objID=3017&&level=1&css=L1&mode=2&in_hi_userid=2&cached=true
State law reference for name registration: Pennsylvania Consolidated Statutes, Sections 54:301+.
Registration of business and/or business name requirements: Registration is mandatory. The applicant must register with the Department of State. (Section 54:311). Pennsylvania has a one-stop business tax registration website online at: www.pa100.state.pa.us. Businesses may also use the Pennsylvania Business Tax Registration form included on the CD.
Online form: Application for Reservation of Fictitious Name;
www.dos.state.pa.us/portal/server.pt/community/corporations/12457/forms/571880
Forms provided on CD: Application for Reservation of Fictitious Name, Pennsylvania Business Tax

Registration
Registration fee: $70.00
Term of registration: Ten years. (Section 54:321).
Name requirements: The statute is exhaustive, the name cannot imply that the business is incorporated or that the business is a professional organization. Please refer directly to the statute. (Section 54: 311).
Name registration application requirements: The application must include the business name, the nature of the business, the street address of the principal place of business, the name of the owner(s), and the street address of the owner(s). (Section 54:311).
Publication requirements: The applicant must publish the fictitious name in the county in which the applicant conducts or intends to conduct business. The notice must contain the fictitious name, street address of the principal place of business, name of the owner(s), statement that an application for fictitious name is or was filed. (Section 54:311).
Office for name registration:
Pennsylvania Department of State
P O Box 8722
Harrisburg, PA 17105-8722

Rhode Island

State website: www.state.ri.us
State revenue or taxation website: https://www.ri.gov/taxation/BAR/
Main state business website: www.ri.gov/business/
State law reference for name registration: General Laws of Rhode Island, Sections 6-1-1+.
Registration of business and/or business name requirements: Name registration is mandatory. The applicant must register with the Clerk in the town or city where the person conducts business. (Section 6-1-1). Registration for business taxation is available online at the website noted above under **State revenue and taxation website**. Businesses may also use the form on the CD.
Online form: None available for name registration
Forms provided on CD: Rhode Island Business Taxation Application, Rhode Island Cerficicate of Assumed Name
Registration fee: not available
Term of registration: None stated in statute.
Name requirements: None stated in statute.
Name registration application requirements: The certificate must state the name of the business, the full name of the owner(s), and the post office address of the owner(s). The certificate must be sworn to by the owner(s). (Section 6-1-1).
Publication requirements: None stated.
Office for name registration: The applicant must register with the Clerk in the town or city where the person conducts conduct business. (Section 6-1-1).

South Carolina

State website: sc.gov/Pages/default.aspx
State revenue or taxation website: www.sctax.org/default.htm
Main state business website: https://www.scbos.sc.gov/
State law reference for name registration: Code of Laws of South Carolina, Sections 39-13-10+.
Registration of business and/or business name requirements: Sole proprietorships operating under an fictitious or assumed name are not generally required to register with a government agency. The Secretary of State's Office does not register DBA or trade names, but does register trademarks or service

marks. Businesses must also register for business taxation. There is a one-stop website for business registration at: https://www.scbos.sc.gov/Start_Your_Business/Registering_for_the_First_Time.aspx
Online form: not available online
Forms provided on CD: South Carolina Business Taxation Application, South Carolina Checklist for Sole Proprietorship; South Carolina Trademark Registration
Registration fee: Not available.
Term of registration: Five years.
Name requirements: The name cannot be deceptively similar to any other previously registered name.
Name registration application requirements: None
Publication requirements: None stated.
Office for name registration:
South Carolina Secretary of State
Attn: Trademarks Division
Post Office Box 11350
Columbia, SC 29211.

South Dakota

State website: www.state.sd.us
State revenue or taxation website: https://apps.sd.gov/applications/rv23cedar/main/main.aspx
Main state business website: www.sdreadytowork.com/
State law reference for name registration: South Dakota Compiled Laws, Sections 37-11-1+.
Registration of business and/or business name requirements: Name registration is mandatory. You are required to file a fictitious name statement if you operate a business as a proprietorship and do not include the last name of each owner in the business name. The applicant must register electronically with the Office of the Secretary of State (at the website noted below under online form) or with the office of the Register of Deeds in each county where the person intends to conduct business. (Section 37-11-1). Business sales and contractors tax application should be done online at the website noted above under **State revenue and taxation website**.
Online form: Fictitious Name Registration;
https://www.state.sd.us/Applications/st08bnrs/secure/ASPX/BNRS_Process.aspx
Forms provided on CD: Name registration is provided online only for Secretary of State registration. Note: May use "Statement of Intention to Conduct Business Under an Assumed or Fictitiuos Name" provided on CD under Chapter 10 for registration in individual counties in South Dakota.
Registration fee: $10.00
Term of registration: Five years. (Section 37-11-1).
Name requirements: None stated in statute.
Name registration application requirements: The applicant must file a statement before the person intends to conduct business. The statement must contain the name of the owner(s), the post office address of the owner(s), the residence address of the owner(s), and the address where the principal place of business is located. (37-11-1).
Publication requirements: The applicant is not required to publish the fictitious name. However, the Register of Deeds does have the fictitious name published. (Section 37-11-1).
Office for name registration: The applicant must register with the office of the Register of Deeds in each county where the person intends to conduct business or electronically on the Secretary of State web site. www.sdsos.gov/(Section 37-11-1).

Tennessee

State website: www.tennessee.gov/
State revenue or taxation website: www.tennesseeanytime.org/bizreg/
Main state business website: www.tennesseeanytime.org/business/index.html
State law reference for name registration: Tennessee Code Annotated. Sections 47-25-501+.
Registration of business and/or business name requirements: Name registration is optional. Tennessee does not have a fictitious name statute, but allows an individual to register a business name under the trademark statute. The applicant must register with the Secretary of State. (Section 47-25-503). Businesses should also register for business taxation at the website noted above under **State revenue and taxation website**.
Online form: Application for Registration of Trademark: www.state.tn.us/sos/forms/ss-4264.pdf
Forms provided on CD: Application for Registration of Trademark
Registration fee: $20.00
Term of registration: Ten years. (Section 47-25-505).
Name requirements: The statute is exhaustive, stating that the trade name cannot be immoral, deceptive, or scandalous. Please refer directly to the statute. (Section 47-25-502).
Name registration application requirements: The signed and verified application must include the name of the owner(s), the business address of the owner(s), the type of business transacted, the date when the name was first used, a statement that the owner(s) has the exclusive right to use the name, and three copies or specimens of the name. (Section 47-25-503).
Publication requirements: None stated.
Office for name registration:
Tennessee Department of State
312 8th Ave. North
6th Floor, Snodgrass Tower
Nashville, TN 37243

Texas

State website: www.state.tx.us
State revenue or taxation website: www.cpa.state.tx.us/taxpermit/
Main state business website: www.texas.gov/en/discover/Pages/topic.aspx?topicid=/business
State law reference for name registration: Vernon's Texas Business and Commerce Code, Sections 36.02+.
Registration of business and/or business name requirements: Name registration is mandatory. The applicant must register with the County Clerk in each county where the person intends to conduct business. (Section 36.10). Businesses should register online for sales and use taxation at the website noted above under **State revenue and taxation website**.
Online form: None provided.
Forms provided on CD: Texas Assumed Name Certificate
Registration fee: Check with County Clerk
Term of registration: Ten years. (Section 36.13).
Name requirements: None stated in statute.
Name registration application requirements: The sworn certificate must include the business name, the full name of the owner(s), and the residence address of the owner(s). (Section 36.10).
Publication requirements: None stated.
Office for name registration: The business must register with the county clerk in the county in which the person intends to conduct business.

Utah

State website: www.utah.gov
State revenue or taxation website: https://secure.utah.gov/osbr-user/user/welcome.html
Main state business website: business.utah.gov/
State law reference for name registration: Utah Code Annotated, Sections 42-2-5+.
Registration of business and/or business name requirements: Name registration is mandatory. The applicant must register with the Division of Corporations and Commercial Code. Registration may be done online under the website noted below under Online Forms or may be done using the form provided on the CD. (Section 42-2-5). Utah also maintains a one-stop online business registration website at the location noted above under **State revenue and taxation website**.
Online form: corporations.utah.gov/osbr_phase_2.html
Forms provided on CD: Utah Name Registration, Utah Name Registration Instructions
Registration fee: $22.00
Term of registration: None stated in statute.
Name requirements: Basically, the name cannot imply a type of business organization that the business is not, or be the name of any already registered trade name. The statute is exhaustive. Please refer directly to the statute. (Section 42-2-6.6).
Name registration application requirements: The certificate must state the name of the business, the full true name of the owner(s), the street address of the owner(s), and the location of the principal place of business. It must be filed within 30 days after beginning to conduct business. (Section 42-2-5).
Publication requirements: None stated.
Office for name registration:
Utah Department of Commerce
Division of Corporations and Commercial Code
160 East 300 South, 1st Floor Box 146705
Salt Lake City, Utah 84145-6705

Vermont

State website: www.leg.state.vt.us
State revenue or taxation website: www.state.vt.us/tax/business.shtml
Main state business website: www.vermont.gov/portal/business/
State law reference for name registration: Vermont Statutes Annotated, Sections 11:1621+.
Registration of business and/or business name requirements: Name registration is mandatory. The applicant must register with the Secretary of State using the online form noted below. (Section 11: 1621). Businesses must also register for business taxation.
Online form: www.sec.state.vt.us/corps/forms/tradeapp.htm
Forms provided on CD: Application for Business Tax Account, Vermont Trade Name Registration (Note: this form is an HTML form and you must have an internet connection to use this form)
Registration fee: not available
Term of registration: None stated in statute.
Name requirements: The name cannot be deceptively similar to any other previously registered name. (Section 11:1621).
Name registration application requirements: The applicant must file a sworn statement within ten days after the person begins to conduct business. The sworn statement must include the name of the business, the name of the town where the business is located, a description of the type of business, the name of the owner(s), and the address of the owner(s). (Section 11:1621).
Publication requirements: None stated.
Office for name registration: Vermont Secretary of State
26 Terrace Street
Montpelier, VT 05602-2972

Virginia

State website: www.virginia.gov
State revenue or taxation website: www.tax.virginia.gov/site.cfm?alias=BusinessHome
Main state business website: www.virginia.gov/cmsportal3/business_4096/
State law reference for name registration: Code of Virginia, Sections 59.1-69+.
Registration of business and/or business name requirements: Name registration is mandatory. The applicant must register with the Clerk of the Court for deeds in the county or city where the person intends to conduct business. (Section 59.1-69). Businesses should also register for business taxation noted above under **State revenue and taxation website**. Virginia also maintains an online one-stop business registration website noted below under Online Forms.
Online form: https://apps.cao.virginia.gov/IDC/index.html
Forms provided on CD: Virginia Business Taxation Registration, Virginia Assumed Name Certificate
Registration fee: $50.00
Term of registration: None stated in statute.
Name requirements: None stated in statute.
Name registration application requirements: The signed and acknowledged certificate must state the name of the business, the name of the owner(s), the post office address of the owner(s), and the residence address of the owner(s). (Section 59.1-69).
Publication requirements: None stated.
Office for name registration: The applicant must register with the Clerk of the Court for deeds in the county or city where the person intends to conduct business. (Section 59.1-69).

Washington

State website: www.leg.wa.gov/legislature/
State revenue or taxation website: dor.wa.gov/content/doingbusiness/registermybusiness/
Main state business website: access.wa.gov/business/start.aspx
State law reference for name registration: Revised Code of Washington, Sections 19.80.010+.
Registration of business and/or business name requirements: Name registration is mandatory. The applicant must register with the Department of Licensing. This may be done using the Master Business Application online or provided on the CD. (Section 19.80.010). Businesses must also generally register with the state for business taxation purposes at the website noted above under **State revenue and taxation website**.
Online form: Master Business Application
www.dol.wa.gov/forms/700028fillable.pdf
Forms provided on CD: Master Business Application
Registration fee: $5.00
Term of registration: None stated in statute, but the Department of Licensing may have rules. (Section 19.80.040).
Name requirements: None stated in statute, but the Department of Licensing may have rules. (Section 19.80.040).
Name registration application requirements: The registration must state the true full name of the owner(s), and the post office address of the owner(s). (Section 19.80.010).
Publication requirements: None stated.
Office for name registration:
Department of Licensing
Master License Service,
PO Box 9034,
Olympia, WA 98507-9034

West Virginia

State website: www.legis.state.wv.us
State revenue or taxation website: www.wva.state.wv.us/wvtax/businessTaxFormsAndRegistration.aspx
Main state business website: www.business4wv.com/b4wvpublic/
State law reference for name registration: West Virginia Code, Sections 47-8-2+.
Registration of business and/or business name requirements: Name registration is mandatory. The applicant must register with the Clerk of the County Commission in the county where the person intends to have the principal place of business. (Section 47-8-2). Businesses must also register for business taxation.
Online form: Application for Tradename:
www.sos.wv.gov/business-licensing/Pages/FormIndexforBusinessFilings.aspx
Forms provided on CD: Application for Trade Name
Registration fee: $25.00
Term of registration: None stated in statute.
Name requirements: None stated in statute.
Name registration application requirements: The duly acknowledged certificate must state the name of the business, the true full name of the owner(s), the residence address of the owner(s), and the post office address of the owner(s). (Section 47-8-2).
Publication requirements: None stated.
Office for name registration: The applicant must register with the Clerk of the County Commission in the county where the person intends to have the principal place of business. and may register with the Secretary of State. (Section 47-8-2).
Secretary of State
Corporations Division
1900 Kanawha Blvd. E
Bldg. 1, Suite 157-K
Charleston WV 25305

Wisconsin

State website: www.legis.state.wi.us
State revenue or taxation website: www.revenue.wi.gov/faqs/my_tax_account/index.html
Main state business website: www.wisconsin.gov/state/core/business.html
State law reference for name registration: Wisconsin Statutes Annotated, Sections 132.001+.
Registration of business and/or business name requirements: Registration is mandatory if doing business under and assumed or fictitious name. Sole proprietors that wish to conduct business under a name other than the real name of the person(s) must file a Registration of Firm Names (also known as "doing business as" application) with the county Register of Deeds (Section 132.01). Businesses should also register for business taxation at the website noted above under **State revenue and taxation website** or using the Wisconsin Business Taxation Application supplied on the CD.
Online form: Application for Registration of Firm Name
www.wisconsin.gov/state/byb/name.html
Forms provided on CD: Application for Registration of Firm Name; Wisconsin Business Taxation Application
Registration fee: $15.00
Term of registration: Twenty years. (Section 132.01).
Name requirements: The trade name may not consist of any flag, coat of arms, or insignia of the United States, a foreign nation, other state of the Union, or any municipality. (Section 132.01).
Name registration application requirements: The sworn statement must include the name(s) of the

applicant, type of business conducted, and the residence or business address of the applicant. The applicant must claim the sole right to use of the trade name. (Section 132.01).

Publication requirements: None stated.

Office for name registration: Sole proprietors that wish to conduct business under a name other than the real name of the person(s) must file a Registration of Firm Names (also known as "doing business as" application) with the county Register of Deeds (Section 132.01).

Wyoming

State website: legisweb.state.wy.us

State revenue or taxation website: revenue.state.wy.us/PortalVBVS/DesktopDefault.aspx

Main state business website: www.wyoming.gov/business.aspx

State law reference for name registration: Wyoming Statutes, Sections 40-2-102.

Registration of business and/or business name requirements: Name registration is optional. The applicant must register with the Secretary of State. (Section 40-2-104).

Online form: Application For Registration Of Trade Name:

Forms provided on CD: Application For Registration Of Trade Name

soswy.state.wy.us/Forms/FormsFiling.aspx?startwith=Business

Registration fee: $100.00

Term of registration: Ten years. (Section 40-2-105).

Name requirements: Basically, the name can not imply a type of business organization that the business is not or be the name of any already registered trade name. The statute is exhaustive. Please refer directly to the statute. (Section 42-2-6.6).

Name registration application requirements: The application, in duplicate, must contain the name of the owner(s), the business address of the owner(s), the name of the business, the general nature of the business The signature of the owner(s) must be notarized. (Section 40-2-104).

Publication requirements: None stated.

Office for name registration:

Wyoming Secretary of State
200 West 24th Street
Cheyenne, WY 82001-0020

Glossary

Account: A separate record of an asset, liability, income, or expense of a business.

Accounting: The process for recording, summarizing, and interpreting business financial records.

Accounting method: The method of recording income and expenses for a business; can be either accrual method or cash method.

Accounting period: A specific time period covered by the financial statements of a business.

Accounting system: The specific system of record-keeping used to set up the accounting records of a business. See also *single-entry accounting* or *double-entry accounting.*

Accounts payable: Money owed by a business to another for goods or services purchased on credit. Money that the business intends to pay to another.

Accounts receivable: Money owed to the business by another for goods or services sold on credit. Money that the business expects to receive.

Accrual method: Accounting method in which all income and expenses are counted when earned or incurred regardless of when the actual cash is received or paid.

Accrued expenses: Expenses that have been incurred but have not yet been paid.

Accrued income: Income that has been earned but has not yet been received.

ACRS: Accelerated Cost Recovery System. Generally, a method of depreciation used for assets purchased between 1980 and 1987.

Agent: A person who is authorized to act on behalf of another. A corporation acts only through its agents, whether they are directors, employees, or officers.

Aging: The method used to determine how long accounts receivable have been owed to a business.

Amend: To alter or change.

Articles of Incorporation: The charter of the corporation, the public filing with a state that requests that the corporation be allowed to exist. Along with the Corporate Bylaws, they provide details of the organization and structure of the business. They must be consistent with the laws of the state of incorporation.

Assets: Everything a business owns, including amounts of money that are owed to the business.

Assumed name: A name, other than the corporation's legal name as shown on the Articles of Incorporation, under which a corporation will conduct business. Most states require registration of the fictitious name if a company desires to conduct business under an assumed name. The corporation's legal name is not an assumed name.

Balance sheet: The business financial statement that depicts the financial status of the business on a specific date by summarizing the assets and liabilities of the business.

Balance sheet accounts: Asset and liability accounts used to prepare business balance sheets.

Balance sheet equation: Assets = Liabilities + Equity, or Equity = Assets − Liabilities.

Board of directors: The group with control of the general supervision of the corporation. They are elected by the shareholders and the directors, in turn, appoint the officers of the corporation.

Bookkeeping: The actual process of recording the figures in accounting records. Business corporation laws: For each individual state, these provide the legal framework for the operation of corporations. The Articles of Incorporation and the Bylaws of a corporation must adhere to the specifics of state law.

Business liabilities: Business debts. Also the value of the owner's equity in his or her business.

Bylaws: The internal rules that govern the management of the corporation. They contain the procedures for holding meetings, appointments, elections and other management matters. If these conflict with the Articles of Incorporation, the provision in the Articles will be controlling.

C-corporation: A business entity owned by shareholders that is not an S-corporation. Subject to double taxation, unlike S-corporations.

Calendar year: Year consisting of 12 consecutive months ending on December 31st.

Capital: Initially, the actual money or property that shareholders transfer to the corporation to allow it to operate. Once in operation, capital also consists of accumulated profits. The net worth of the corporation, the owner's equity in a business, and/or the ownership value of the business.

Capital expense: An expense for the purchase of a fixed asset; an asset with a useful life of over one year. Generally, must be depreciated rather than deducted as a business expense.

Cash: All currency, coins, and checks that a business has on hand or in a bank account.

Cash method: Accounting method in which income and expenses are not counted until the actual cash is received or paid.

Cash out: Cash paid out for business purposes, such as a refund.

Certificate of Incorporation: See Articles of Incorporation. Note, however, that some states will issue a Certificate of Incorporation after the filing of the Articles of Incorporation.

Chart of Accounts: A listing of the types and numbers of the various accounts that a business uses for its accounting records.

Check register: A running record of checks written, deposits made, and other transactions for a bank account.

Common stock: The standard stock of a corporation that includes the right to vote the shares and the right to proportionate dividends. See also *preferred stock.*

Consent Resolution: Any resolution signed by all of the directors or shareholders of a corporation authorizing an action, without the necessity of a meeting.

Corporation: A business entity owned by shareholders; can be a C-corporation or an S-corporation.

Cost basis: Total cost to a business of a fixed asset.

Cost of goods sold: The amount that a business has paid for the inventory that it has sold during a specific period. Calculated by adding beginning inventory and additions to inventory and then deducting the ending inventory value.

Credit: In double-entry accounting, an increase in liability or income accounts or a decrease in asset or expense accounts.

Current assets: Cash and any other assets that can be converted to cash or consumed by the business within one year.

Current debt: Debt that will normally be paid within one year.

Current liabilities: Debts of a business that must be paid within one year.

Current ratio: A method of determining the liquidity of a business. Calculated by dividing current assets by current liabilities.

Debit: In double-entry accounting, a decrease in liability or income accounts or an increase in asset or expense accounts.

Debt: The amount that a business owes to another. Also known as "liability."

Debt ratio: A method of determining the indebtedness of a business. Calculated by dividing total liabilities by total assets.

Depreciation: Cost of fixed asset deductible proportionately over time.

Dissolution: Methods by which a corporation concludes its business and liquidates. Dissolutions may be involuntary because of bankruptcy or credit problems or voluntary on the initiation of the directors or shareholders of a corporation.

Dividend: A distribution of money or property paid by the corporation to a shareholder based on the amount of shares held. A proportionate share of the net profits of a business that the board of directors has determined should be paid out to shareholders, rather than held as retained earnings. Dividends must be paid out of the corporation's net earnings and profits. The board of directors has the authority to declare or withhold dividends based on sound business discretion.

Domestic corporation: A corporation is a domestic corporation in the state in which it is incorporated. See also *foreign corporation.*

Double-entry accounting: An accounting system under which each transaction is recorded twice: as a credit and as a debit. A very difficult system of accounting to learn and understand.

Equity: Any debt that a business owes. It is owner's equity if owed to the business owners and liabilities if owed to others.

Expenses: The costs to a business of producing its income. Any money that it has paid or will pay out during a certain period.

FEIN: Federal Identification Number, used for tax purposes.

FICA: Federal Insurance Contributions Act. Taxes withheld from employees and paid by employers for Social Security and Medicare.

Fictitious name: See *assumed name*.

FIFO: First-in, first-out method of accounting for inventory. The inventory value is based on the cost of the latest items purchased.

Financial statements: Reports that summarize the finances of a business; generally a profit and loss statement and a balance sheet.

Fiscal year: A 12-month accounting period used by a business.

Fiscal-year reporting: For income tax purposes, reporting business taxes for any 12-month period that does not end on December 31 of each year.

Fixed assets: Assets of a business that will not be sold or consumed within one year. Generally, fixed assets (other than land) must be depreciated.

FUTA: Federal Unemployment Tax Act. Federal business unemployment taxes.

Gross pay: The total amount of an employee's compensation before the deduction of any taxes or benefits.

Gross profit: Gross sales minus the cost of goods sold.

Gross sales: The total amount received for goods and services during an accounting period.

Gross wages: The total amount of an employee's compensation before the deduction of any taxes or benefits.

Income: Any money that a business has received or will receive during a certain period.

Income statement: Financial statement that shows the income and expenses for a business. Also referred to as an "operating statement" or "profit and loss statement."

Incorporator: The person who signs the Articles of Incorporation. Usually a person, but some states allow a corporation or partnership to be an incorporator.

Indemnify: To reimburse or compensate. Directors and officers of corporations are often reimbursed or indemnified for all the expenses they may have incurred in incorporating.

Initial capital: The money or property that an owner or owners contribute to starting a business.

Intangible personal property: Generally, property not attached to land that you cannot hold or touch (for example: copyrights, business goodwill, etc.).

Inventory: Goods that are held by a business for sale to customers.

Invoice: A bill for the sale of goods or services that is sent to the buyer.

Ledgers: The accounting books for a business. Generally, refers to the entire set of accounts for a business.

Liabilities: The debts of a business.

LIFO: Last-in, first-out method of valuing inventory. Total value is based on the cost of the earliest items purchased.

Liquidity: The ability of a company to convert its assets to cash and meet its obligations with that cash.

Long-term assets: The assets of a business that will be held for over one year. Those assets of a business that are subject to depreciation (except for land).

Long-term debts: Debts that will not be paid off in one year.

Long-term liabilities: The debts of a business that will not be due for over one year.

Long-term loans payable: Money due on a loan more than one year in the future.

Long-term notes payable: Money due more than one year in the future.

MACRS: Modified accelerated cost recovery system. A method of depreciation for use with assets purchased after January 1, 1987.

Managers: In a limited liability company, those persons selected by the members of the company to handle the management functions of the company. Managers of limited liability companies may or may not be members/owners of the company. Managers are roughly analogous to the officers of a corporation.

Members: In a limited liability company, those persons who have ownership interests (equivalent to shareholders in a corporation). Most states allow single-member limited liability companies.

Minutes: A written record of the activities of a meeting.

Net income: The amount of money that a business has after deducting the cost of goods sold and the cost of all expenses. Also referred to as "net profit."

Net loss: The amount by which a business has expenses and costs of goods sold greater than income.

Net pay: The amount of compensation that an employee actually will be paid after the deductions for taxes and benefits.

Net profit: The amount by which a business has income greater than expenses and cost of goods sold. Also referred to as "net income."

Net sales: The value of sales after deducting the cost of goods sold from gross sales.

Net wages: The amount of compensation that an employee will actually be paid after the deductions for taxes and benefits.

Net worth: The value of the owner's share in a business. The value of a business determined by deducting the debts of a business from the assets of a business. Also referred to as "owner's equity."

Nontaxable income: Income that is not subject to any state or local sales tax.

Not-for-profit corporation: A corporation formed under state law that exists for a socially worthwhile purpose. Profits are not distributed but retained and used for corporate purposes. May be tax-exempt. Also referred to as "nonprofit."

Officers: Manage the daily operations of a corporation. Generally consists of a president, vice president, secretary, and treasurer. Appointed by the board of directors.

Operating margin: Net sales divided by gross sales. The actual profit on goods sold, before deductions for expenses.

Operating statement: Financial statement that shows the income and expenses for a business. Also referred to as "income statement" or "profit and loss statement."

Owner's equity: The value of an owner's share in a business. Also referred to as "capital."

Partnership: An unincorporated business entity that is owed by two or more persons.

Payee: Person or business to whom a payment is made.

Payor: Person or business that makes a payment.

Personal property: All business property other than land and the buildings that are attached to the land.

Petty cash: Cash that a business has on hand for payment of minor expenses when use of a business check is not convenient. Not to be used for handling sales revenue.

Petty cash fund: A cash fund. Considered part of cash on hand.

Petty cash register: The sheet for recording petty cash transactions.

Physical inventory: The actual process of counting and valuing the inventory on hand at the end of an accounting period.

Piercing the corporate veil: A legal decision that allows a court to ignore the corporate entity and reach the assets of the shareholders, directors, or officers.

Plant assets: Long-term assets of a business. Those business assets that are subject to depreciation (other than land).

Posting: In double-entry accounting, the process of transferring data from journals to ledgers.

Pre-paid expenses: Expenses that are paid for before they are used (for example: insurance, rent, etc.).

Profit and loss statement: Financial statement that shows the income and expenses for a business. Also referred to as an "income statement" or "operating statement."

Quorum: The required number of persons necessary to officially conduct business at a meeting. Generally, a majority of the shareholders or directors constitutes a quorum.

Real property: Land and any buildings or improvements that are attached to the land.

Reconciliation: The process of bringing a bank statement into agreement with the business check register.

Recovery period: Specific time period for dividing up the cost into proportionate amounts.

Registered agent: The person designated in the Articles of Incorporation who will be available to receive service of process (summons, subpoena, etc.) on behalf of the corporation. A corporation must always have a registered agent.

Registered office: The actual physical location of the registered agent. Need not be the actual principal place of business of the corporation.

Resolution: A formal decision that has been adopted by either the shareholders or the board of directors of a corporation.

Retail price: The price for which a product is sold to the public.

Revenue: Income that a business brings in from the sale of goods or services or from investments.

S-corporation: A type of business corporation in which all of the expenses and profits are passed through to its shareholders to be accounted for at tax time individually in the manner of partnerships. A specific IRS designation that allows a corporation to be taxed similarly to a partnership, yet retain limited liability for its shareholders.

Salary: Fixed weekly, monthly, or annual compensation for an employee.

Sales: Money brought into a business from the sale of goods or services.

Sales income: Revenue derived from selling a product of some type.

Salvage value: The value of an asset after it has been fully depreciated.

Service income: Income derived from performing a service for someone.

Service of process: To accept subpoenas or summonses for a corporation.

Shareholder's equity: In a corporation, the owner's equity of a business divided by the number of outstanding shares.

Shareholders: Owners of issued stock of a corporation and, therefore, owners of an interest in the corporation. They elect the board of directors and vote on major corporate issues.

Short-term loans payable: Money due on a loan within one year.

Short-term notes payable: Money due within one year.

Single-entry accounting: A business recordkeeping system that generally tracks only income and expense accounts. Used generally by small businesses, it is much easier to use and understand than double-entry accounting.

Sole proprietorship: An unincorporated business entity in which one person owns the entire company.

Stock transfer book: The ledger book (or sheets) in which the registered owners of shares in the corporation are recorded.

Straight-line depreciation: Spreads the deductible amount equally over the recovery period.

Supplies: Materials used in conducting the day-to-day affairs of a business (as opposed to raw materials used in manufacturing).

Tangible personal property: Property not attached to land that you can hold and touch (for example:machinery, furniture, equipment).

Taxes payable: Total of all taxes due but not yet paid.

Trial balance: In double-entry accounting, a listing of all the balances in the general ledger in order to show that debits and credits balance.

Wages: Hourly compensation paid to employees, as opposed to salary.

Wages payable: Total of all wages and salaries due to employees but not yet paid out.

Wholesale price: The cost to a business of goods purchased for later sale to the public.

Working capital: The money available for immediate business operations. Current assets minus current liabilities.

Index

Accounting
- methods 102
- periods 103
- simplified system 105
- software 104
- systems 103

Accounts payable record 137

Annual
- expense summary 148
- income summary 160
- payroll summary 184
- tax schedules 188

Appendix of state business information 248

Asset and liability accounts 113

Assumed name
- statement of intention to conduct business under 87

Balance sheet chart of accounts 114

Balance sheet 64, 98

Business
- accounts 108
- financial plan 56
- financial recordkeeping 97
- financial worksheet 57
- marketing plan 50
- marketing worksheet 51
- payroll 174
- plan 33
    - compiling your 48
    - preparing your 43
    - worksheet 35
- start-up checklist 31

Contractor/subcontractor agreement 90

Contracts 244

Corporation 21

Cost of goods sold report 128

Credit memo 172

Credit sales aging report 165

Current assets 117

Current balance sheet 66

Deductible expenses/depreciable property 133

Employee
- payroll record 180
- documents 88

Estimated profit and loss statement 62

Executive summary 45
- preparing your 44

Expense
- accounts 111
- chart of accounts 112

Fictitious name
- statement of intention to conduct business under 87

Financial
- plan 56
- recordkeeping 97
    - checklist 106
- worksheet 57

Fixed assets 130

Fixed asset account record 134

Formation of a sole proprietorship 68

Forms-on-CD instructions 11

General employment contract 88

Income accounts 109

Income chart of accounts 110

Independent contractor agreement 89

Inventory 120
- periodic record 124
- perpetual record 126
- physical report 122

Invoice 167

Limited liability company 26
Long-term debt record 139

Monthly
    -cash report summary 154
    -credit sales records 163
    -expense summary 146
    -income summary 158
    -tax schedules 188

Name registration 85

Operating a sole proprietorship 67

Partnership 18
Past due statement 169
Payroll
    -checklist 177
    -depository record 182
    -setting up 175
Periodic inventory record 124
Perpetual inventory record 126
Physical inventory report 122
Pre-start-up
    -activities 75
    -checklist 80
    -worksheet 78
Profit and loss statement 60, 101
Promissory notes 233

Quarterly
    -payroll timesheet 178
    -tax schedules 188

Receipts 218
Recordkeeping
    -review 104
    -terminology 98
Registration of sole proprietorship
    name 85
Releases 213
Rental/sale of personal property 222

S-corporation 25
Sale of business 236
Sample
    -chart of accounts 115
    -irs tax forms 189
    -sole proprietorship plan 86
Simplified accounting system 105
Sole proprietorship
    -annual tax schedules 188
    -books and records 70
    -liability 69
    -monthly tax schedules 188
    -name registration 85
    -paperwork 71
       - checklist 74
    -plan 81
       -worksheet 82
    -property 68
    -quarterly tax schedules 188
    -startup checklist 32
    -tax forms checklist 187
Startup checklist 32
Statement of intention to conduct
    business under an assumed or
    fictitious name 87
Statement 169

Taxation of sole proprietorships 186
Tax forms checklist 187
Technical support 16

Tracking
    -income 148,156
    -credit sales 162
    -cash 151
    -debts 136
    -expenses 141
Travel, auto, meals, and entertainment
expenses 141

Weekly
    -cash report 151
    -credit sales records 162
    -expense record 143
    -income records 156

Nova Publishing Company
Small Business and Consumer Legal Books and Software

Legal Toolkit Series

Business Start-Up Toolkit	ISBN 13: 978-1-892949-43-1	Book w/CD	$39.95
Estate Planning Toolkit	ISBN 13: 978-1-892949-44-8	Book w/CD	$39.95
Legal Forms Toolkit	ISBN 13: 978-1-892949-48-6	Book w/CD	$39.95
No-Fault Divorce Toolkit	ISBN 13: 978-1-892949-35-6	Book w/CD	$39.95
Personal Bankruptcy Toolkit	ISBN 13: 978-1-892949-42-4	Book w/CD	$29.95
Will and Living Will Toolkit	ISBN 13: 978-1-892949-47-9	Book w/CD	$29.95

Law Made Simple Series

Personal Legal Forms Simplified (3rd Edition)	ISBN 0-935755-97-7	Book w/CD	$28.95
Powers of Attorney Simplified (2nd Edition)	ISBN 13: 978-1-892949-56-1	Book w/CD	$29.95

Small Business Made Simple Series

Limited Liability Company: Start-up Kit (4th Edition)	ISBN 13: 978-1-892949-54-7	Book w/CD	$29.95
Real Estate Forms Simplified (2nd Edition)	ISBN 13: 978-1-892949-49-3	Book w/CD	$29.95
S-Corporation: Small Business Start-up Kit (4th Edition)	ISBN 13: 978-1-892949-53-0	Book w/CD	$29.95
Small Business Accounting Simplified (5th Edition)	ISBN 13: 978-1-892949-50-9	Book w/CD	$29.95
Small Business Bookkeeping System Simplified	ISBN 0-935755-74-8	Book only	$14.95
Small Business Legal Forms Simplified (4th Edition)	ISBN 0-935755-98-5	Book w/CD	$29.95
Small Business Payroll System Simplified	ISBN 0-935755-55-1	Book only	$14.95
Sole Proprietorship: Start-up Kit (3rd Edition)	ISBN 13: 978-1-892949-59-2	Book w/CD	$29.95

Legal Self-Help Series

…orce Yourself: The National Divorce Kit (6th Edition)	ISBN 1-892949-12-1	Book w/CD	$39.95
…are Your Own Will: The National Will Kit (6th Edition)	ISBN 1-892949-15-6	Book w/CD	$29.95

…ional Legal Kits

…d Divorce Kit (3rd Edition)	ISBN 13: 978-1-892949-39-4	Book w/CD	$19.95
…Family Legal Forms Kit (2nd Edition)	ISBN 13: 978-1-892949-41-7	Book w/CD	$19.95
…ncorporation Kit	ISBN 1-892949-33-4	Book w/CD	$19.95
…imited Liability Company Kit	ISBN 1-892949-32-6	Book w/CD	$19.95
…ing Will Kit (2nd Edition)	ISBN 13: 978-1-892949-45-5	Book w/CD	$19.95
…orporation Kit	ISBN 1-892949-31-8	Book w/CD	$19.95
…Kit (3rd Edition)	ISBN 1-892949-38-5	Book w/CD	$19.95

Ordering Information

…200

Phone orders with Visa/MC: (800) 462-6420
Fax orders with Visa/MC: (800) 338-4550
Internet: www.novapublishing.com
Free shipping on all internet orders (within in the U.S.)